0 4 JUIN 1998

IN THE EYE OF THE STORM

IN
THE EYE
OF THE STORM

A HISTORY OF CANADIAN PEACEKEEPING

Fred Gaffen

DENEAU & WAYNE

Deneau & Wayne Publishers Ltd.
760 Bathurst Street
Toronto, Ontario
M5S 2R6

© 1987
Printed in Canada

This book has been published with the assistance of the Canada Council and
Ontario Arts Council under their block grant programs.

CANADIAN CATALOGUING IN PUBLICATION DATA

Gaffen, Fred
In the eye of the storm: a history of Canadian peacekeeping
ISBN 0-88879-158-5 (bound) ISBN 0-88879-160-7 (pbk.)

1. Canada – Armed Forces – Middle East. 2. Canada – Armed Forces – South Asia.
3. Canada – Armed Forces – Africa. 4. United Nations – Armed Forces – Middle
East. 5. United Nations – Armed Forces – South Asia. 6. United Nations – Armed
Forces – Africa. I. Title.

JX1981.P7G33 1987   341.5'8   C87-094300-6

To Canada's Peacekeepers

CONTENTS

PREFACE 11

ACKNOWLEDGMENTS 16

A RETROSPECT 17

PART I — THE MIDDLE EAST

1. United Nations Truce Supervision
   Organization 21
2. United Nations Emergency Force I 39
3. The Withdrawal of Canada and UNEF I
   from Egypt 65
4. United Nations Yemen Observation Mission 75
5. United Nations Peacekeeping Force in Cyprus 85
6. United Nations Emergency Force II 113
7. United Nations Disengagement Observer Force 137
8. Lebanon 146
9. Multinational Force and Observers 158

PART II — SOUTH ASIA

10. India and Pakistan 165
11. Indochina 179
12. West New Guinea 209

PART III — AFRICA

    13. The Congo 217
    14. Nigeria 240
    15. Other African Countries 242

PART IV — LATIN AMERICA

    16. Dominican Republic 247

CONCLUSION 251

APPENDIX A 257

APPENDIX B 260

APPENDIX C 262

APPENDIX D 272

ABBREVIATIONS 276

NOTES 279

BIBLIOGRAPHY 288

INDEX 297

MAPS

UN Truce Supervision Organization 31

UN Emergency Force I, 1956-1967 53

Yemen, 1963-1964 79

Cyprus (pre-1974, post-1974) 99

UN Emergency Force II, 1973-1979 125

UN Disengagement Observer Force, 1974- 141

Lebanon, 1958 149

Lebanon, 1978 155

Multinational Force and Observers, 1986- 159

India and Pakistan, 1949- 171

Indochina, 1954-1973 193

West New Guinea, 1962-1963 211

Congo, 1960-1964 229

PREFACE

PICTURE A SMALL OBSERVATION POST with the letters "UN" written on the outside. Inside on a quiet moonlit night on Cyprus is a young Canadian, Private J.B. Tweedie, 2nd Battalion, The Royal Canadian Regiment. He is monumentally bored. For him and most of the other Canadians that was the worst part of peacekeeping duty. In a letter to me, Private Tweedie confessed, "I don't talk too much about my stint in Cyprus [October 1983 to April 1984] unless I am with fellow servicemen as I find that civilians simply cannot comprehend the situation." The aim of this publication is to provide a book about Canadian peacekeeping operations that will help enlighten the civilian as well as the military reader.

Previous books published about peacekeeping written by non-Canadians mention the contributions of Canadian forces only in passing. Although accounts have been written about the contribution of Canadians towards peacekeeping, this book is the first which presents a comprehensive up-to-date account from a Canadian military standpoint. While the taxpayers of this country have contributed financially, members of the armed forces have given their time and effort and often sacrificed family life. Some have been killed or badly injured.

If you believe that the question of war and peace is the most important issue facing the world today, this book will be of special interest to you. But what you may ask, can the military trained primarily for war possibly teach anyone about peace? It is however from those versed in military conflict that a realistic approach of how to try to limit fighting or to stop it once it has started can be garnered. In the Congo, Cyprus, Kashmir and elsewhere, Canada's peacekeepers have used their powers of persuasion as well as bluff to help prevent further fighting or even its escalation. Peacekeeping has also proven to be a face-saving device for all parties involved in conflict. The presence of a peacekeeping force has proven helpful to the superpowers. This book does not claim to be the final word on this topic or period of history. It is hoped, however, that it may encourage others to follow.

"War makes rattling good history but peace is poor reading." This quote from the verse of Thomas Hardy might well apply to Canadian military history. A look at library shelves or at the number of books written by this country's military historians clearly reveals that the emphasis has been on war. This should not be surprising. War is a form of crisis that brings out the best and worst of human qualities. It makes for readable history. The excitement and drama of battle is vastly more interesting than peacetime routine.

> Peace is the dream of the wise;
> War is the history of man.

This was written by Comte Louis Phillipe de Ségur (1753-1830), who was an officer and writer, as well as a diplomat. That quote is at the entrance of the Canadian War Museum in Ottawa and I see it each day as I enter and leave work. War has permeated this country's history whether under the fleur-de-lis, the Union Jack, the Red Ensign or the Maple Leaf. Since the Second World War, however, Canada's military forces have served under another flag, the blue and white ensign of the United Nations, adding a different dimension to this country's military history.

Canada has supported most United Nations and some non-UN peacekeeping operations with both men and money. Indeed peacekeeping has become so much a part of our foreign policy that successive governments, be they Liberal or Conservative, have endorsed and committed Canada to additional peacekeeping ventures.

Peacekeeping has been defined by the International Peace Academy in New York as, "the prevention, containment, moderation and termination of hostilities between or within states, through the medium of a peaceful third party intervention organized and directed internationally using multinational forces of soldiers, police and civilians to restore and maintain peace." Peacekeeping activities have ranged from observation and reporting only, to investigation, supervision and control, to the interposition of armed military units between the parties. The purpose of international peacekeeping in a dispute is not only to prevent further conflict, but also to create conditions that will allow the settling of the dispute. There ought to be a closer link established between peacekeeping and peacemaking. Canada's direct involvement in peacekeeping, as so defined, began under the auspices of the United Nations. This study will trace this country's involvement with those operations that were strictly peacekeeping. The Korean War is not included because it was a full-scale war that went far beyond peacekeeping as it is popularly understood. I have also avoided delving into the causes of conflicts that necessitated a peacekeeping force.

Professor Albert Legault of the department of political science, Laval University, has estimated the financial outlay by

Canada to international peacekeeping (excluding Korea) from 1949 to 1980 at 226 million dollars, less than one-half of one percent of the total budget of the Department of National Defence over that period. In terms of relative resource allocation for peacekeeping, the Middle East accounted for over 90 percent of our human and financial resources. It was followed by Asia with about 5 percent and Africa around 4 percent. It is not inappropriate, therefore, that in terms of space within this book the Middle East portion occupies the largest section, followed by Asia and then Africa.

Canadians are a peace-loving people who have been forced to take up arms in defence of their independence, way of life and ideals. We have fought not only external threats but internal uprisings to preserve this country. Canadian involvement in two world wars and in Korea has demonstrated, too, that events overseas pose a threat to our well-being. As the globe has grown smaller, Canadians' wish for a peaceful world has resulted in our commitment to help maintain the peace in lands far from our shores. As with any new endeavour, there have been obstacles to overcome and lessons to learn. Although this country cannot on its own make universal peace, it can try to do something and that is better than nothing.

A good number of the major Canadian participants in peacekeeping operations have since died. Thus I thought it essential that experiences and reminiscences of surviving participants be collected and preserved at this time. I believed it worthwhile to piece together a glimpse of what has happened. As a result of that exercise, I have come away encouraged rather than filled with despair about the future. This country's peacekeeping endeavours have been positive not negative as some would have us believe. Canadians should draw strength from our accomplishments in this field so that we may face the future with greater confidence for new challenges that will undoubtedly arise.

Canadians have done more than their share over the last thirty years as peacekeepers. The countries that have benefitted most from peacekeeping ought to be the ones to contribute first to new ventures. Canadians should be willing to help with expertise and experience but should be circumspect about committing their forces to new peacekeeping assignments.

ACKNOWLEDGMENTS

I AM GRATEFUL TO THE FOLLOWING individuals and institutions: George Bell of the Canadian Institute of Strategic Studies; Philip Robert and Victor Suthren of the Canadian War Museum; Bruce Beatty of the Chancellery of Canadian Orders and Decorations, Government House; Vicent Bezeau of the Directorate of Ceremonial, National Defence Headquarters; Dacre Cole of the Department of External Affairs; Owen Cooke, David Kealy and Paul Marshall of the Directorate of History; H. Hagner of the United Nations Archives; Joan Broughton of the United Nations Association in Canada; and Marie Duhamel of the University of Ottawa Library. The noted historian, the Honourable George F.G. Stanley, read the manuscript and offered his comments. My appreciation to William Constable who prepared the maps. I am indebted to Frank McGuire for editorial assistance. My wife, Susan, allowed me the use of weekends to work on this book. Thanks also to Sandra Tooze, my editor, for her superb and meticulous work.

A RETROSPECT

THE SYSTEM OF SECURITY established upon the formation of the United Nations in the summer of 1945 at San Francisco depended upon harmony and cooperation between the great powers. According to Article 47 of the UN Charter, the military staff committee, consisting of the chiefs of staff of the permanent members of the Security Council or their representatives was, "to advise and assist the council on all questions relating to the Security Council's military requirements for the maintenance of international peace and security, the employment and command of forces placed at its disposal . . . ." However, the wartime spirit of cooperation quickly disappeared and committee members were unable to agree on arrangements for a world peacekeeping force. The hope that the United Nations could help assure international peace and security dwindled as the United States and the Soviet Union became rivals in the postwar world.

Peacekeeping began with the formation of small groups of observers to monitor compliance with UN resolutions and was expanded to the formation of much larger forces. There have been, as well, non-UN sponsored peacekeeping or observer missions. In areas remote from the national borders of both superpowers and in areas where racial, religious and national tensions developed from the withdrawal of colonial authority, peacekeeping has proved to be a useful measure.

After the Second World War Canada occupied a unique position among the nations. Although it joined the North Atlantic Treaty Organization, this country's past evolution from a British colony to nationhood stood it in good stead with many newly emerging non-aligned Afro-Asian nations. Canada became steadily involved in peacekeeping activity. While our military planners have been constantly preparing for the use of the forces in the event of war, it was their peacekeeping role that distinguished them on the international stage. As such, whenever a force or observers are contemplated as a result of conflict anywhere in the world, Canada is usually considered as a potential contributor. This is a role in which we have now become well-known in all parts of the world.

PART
I

THE MIDDLE EAST

1

UNITED NATIONS TRUCE
SUPERVISION ORGANIZATION

Introduction

THE MIDDLE EAST IS A term that evolved during the Second World War to cover the area for which the British military command based in Egypt was responsible. It included Cyprus, Syria, Lebanon, Palestine (now Israel), Jordan, Egypt and Yemen. That region may be described as a land bridge between Europe, Asia and Africa. Strategically, it is one of the most important geographical areas in the world, joining, as it does, three continents and being integrally related to one of the world's major waterways, the Suez Canal. Since the dawn of history, its geostrategic uniqueness has been recognized by world powers. Its history of conflict and mixture of cultures, religions and political ideologies, have served to divide rather than unite the area. It is in this region that the United Nations became involved three years after its establishment and has so remained.

The eastern Mediterranean or Red Sea region conveys several images to Canadians: terrorism, religious fanaticism, oil wealth, poverty, endless barren desert and war. Our attention is, almost every day, directed towards the region by newspaper, television and radio news. Overexposure, however, tends to dull our sensitivities and today, it is only when something extraordinarily violent or shocking occurs in the Middle East, or world peace appears to be directly threatened, that we pay attention to what is going on there. How many of the younger generation of Canadians are aware today that during the mid-1950s world peace was, in fact, teetering in the balance as a result of events in that region and that Canada assumed an important role as a mediator?

The end of the First World War marked not only the defeat of Germany but its ally, the Ottoman Empire. Britain and France divided up the empire in the Middle East. The UN's predecessor, the League of Nations, approved the arrangement and designated the states under their control mandated territories. Both Britain and France were to prepare these lands to rule themselves. Arabs and Jews both vied for control of Palestine under British mandate.

Unable to solve the problems of Palestine, Britain had placed the issue of its future government with the United Nations. The UN recommended the partition of Palestine into an Israeli and an Arab section along defined boundaries. Upon Britain's surrender of its mandate there, Israel proclaimed its part independent on 14 May 1948. Soon after, the armed forces of its Arab neighbours crossed the newly defined border and fighting broke out. The Security Council asked Belgium, France and the United States to contribute military observers when the fighting temporarily stopped. A UN Truce Supervision Organization (UNTSO) was established in 1948 to observe and report upon any violations of the armistice. The efforts of the United Nations, however, were unable to bring real peace. The problem of the Palestinians continued to fester.

The United Nations Truce Supervision Organization (UNTSO) came into being as a result of a cease-fire obtained in 1948 between Israel and neighbouring Arab states and remains in operation today. Four Mixed Armistice Commissions (MACs) were established to supervise the execution of the separate agreements between Israel and Egypt, Jordan, Syria and Lebanon. UNTSO's authority, however, was limited to monitoring the cease-fire. As each agreement was reached, UN military observers moved into fixed posts along the Armistice Demarcation Line and also patrolled demilitarized zones between Israel and Egypt and Israel and Syria. UNTSO's role was limited due to its relatively small size.

Since 1973 the Soviet Union has actively participated in UNTSO including the provision of observers. UNTSO can only be terminated by the Security Council. It is unlikely that all the permanent members would agree to such a resolution, thus the power of the veto ensures the continued existence of UNTSO for the foreseeable future.

CANADIAN INVOLVEMENT

Canada's direct participation in UNTSO began in February 1954 when four Canadian army officers were seconded to duty there. Major-General E.L.M. Burns was named chief of staff in September 1954 and continued in that position until the creation of the United Nations Emergency Force. The usual term of duty as a military observer with UNTSO has been one year. In 1956 the number of Canadians of field rank (lieutenant-colonel or major) was nine, then fourteen in 1958, and a year later seventeen. The Canadian contribution rose to, and has continued to be, twenty officers since the 1960s. The number of UNTSO observers began at seventy, increased to about six hundred in 1948 and was three hundred in 1987.

Following the Israeli-United Arab Republic war of 1956, UNTSO observers arrived prior to and were replaced by UNEF. However, UNTSO was kept busy along the Syrian-Israeli and Jordanian-Israeli borders. Lieutenant-Colonel George A. Flint, a Canadian, headed the Mixed Armistice Commission of the latter and another Canadian, Lieutenant-Colonel Paul Bertrand the former. Flint and a fellow officer were seriously wounded on 24 July 1956 when one of their party set off an anti-personnel mine while investigating a house in a disputed area on Mount Scopus, Jerusalem, that had been occupied by Jordanian soldiers. All the injured made a good recovery.[1] Almost two years later, Colonel Flint was shot and killed while holding a white flag on 26 May 1958, on Mount Scopus along the Armistice Demarcation Line. He was attempting to stop the shooting between both sides and rescue some Israeli policemen who were on patrol in a disputed area. The white truce flag was recovered and returned to Flint's regiment, Princess Patricia's Canadian Light Infantry.[2]

HOSTILITIES RESUME

At the outbreak of war again on 5 June 1967 most UNTSO observation posts (OPs) were evacuated. Unknown to the Israelis, observation posts along the demarcation line between Israel and Syria remained manned until 6 June. They were not clearly identifiable at high speed from the air. As a result, OP Delta, at the north end of Lake Tiberias, was strafed by Israeli aircraft several times. Fortunately the observers — a Swede, an Italian and a Canadian — were unhurt and safely evacuated that afternoon to Damascus.[3] Once the fighting ended UNTSO contributed to securing the cease-fire, especially on the Jordanian and Syrian fronts.

Following the Middle East War of 1967, UNTSO was given responsibility for monitoring the cease-fire along the Suez Canal and Golan Heights. Larger UN contingents were sent soon after. Their presence did not prevent commando raids or heavy shelling particularly in 1969-1970. Although there was a lull in fighting it was only temporary, for full-scale hostilities were renewed once more on 6 October 1973.

When fighting broke out in 1973 there were only UNTSO observers stationed on the west and east banks of the Suez Canal and on the Golan Heights. (The UN Emergency Force I had ceased to exist.) UNTSO posts on the west bank of the canal were passed by the Egyptian army while those on the east bank came under fire. On 12 October one Canadian officer, Major William Bailey, was on his way to the lavatory when a bomb struck blowing him against the door and onto the toilet seat. When he returned to his former room, he found it in shambles and the book he had been reading in shreds. Two other UNTSO observers nearby, a French and an Italian officer, had been less fortunate — they were killed by the Egyptians on the first day of the fighting.[4]

CANADIAN EXPERIENCES

Lieutenant-Colonel Georges Boulanger of St-Côme, Quebec, served first on the Israel-Syria Mixed Armistice Commission and later with the Israel-Lebanon Mixed Armistice Commission. His tour of duty was from 28 July 1972 to 28 July 1973, during which time he spent 203 days and nights on observation post duty, seventy-two days as the duty or immediate standby officer at headquarters, with seventy-two days off and eighteen days leave. Time spent at an observer post were four days and nights at a time with an observer of a different nationality. Both men thus had to adapt to someone with different manners and customs. The number of cease-fire violations, firing incidents and investigations varied with the state of tension or hostilities at the time.

Major W.R. MacNeil, a Canadian artillery officer, served with UNTSO, first in the Sinai from May to December 1973, then in Lebanon. The two observers who had just relieved him and his partner were the ones who were killed. He recounts what it was like to be in Israel at the time:

My family had arrived in August and were living on Mount of Olives in Jerusalem. On Saturday 6 October, the Canadians, who had also been assigned to the canal, were at my house for a Bar B-Q: Majors Bill Bailey, Irv Kerr and Barry Helman. Although Yom Kippur was the holiest day of the year for the Israelis, it was business as usual for the Arabs and Christians. My daughter Kimberly and I had bought some charcoal before noon.

At 2:00 p.m., I turned on the radio to catch the latest news. Shortly into the broadcast, the announcer excitedly related that aircraft were attacking and bombing the refinery at Ashqelon, alluded to air battles and then quickly went off the air. Between long periods of sombre music, news bulletins reported Syrian troops attacking all along the Golan Heights and Egyptian troops crossing the Suez Canal. Initially there was a brief period of dead silence among us then chatter about what we all suspected was about to happen had happened.

Almost immediately air raid sirens were screaming. Contrails of high flying jet aircraft high over the Jordan Valley and the Golan were visible. The penalty that the Israelis had to pay for not pre-empting

26

the Egyptian and Syrian attacks with air power was severe but it would not have been possible to receive massive American aid had Israel initiated hostilities. In retrospect there was a role reversal between 1967 and 1973. In 1967 President Nasser caused the war and the Israelis started it, while in 1973 the Israelis by refusing to return occupied territories, caused the war, while Egypt and Syria actually started it.

The next day mobilization was in full swing, the radio blurting numerous warnings with sketchy reports about the fighting. The news was not good but official Israeli radio was reporting everything was under control and that the military was defeating the attackers. This subtle propaganda flew in the face of Jordanian TV re-broadcasting Syrian and Egyptian news which was clearly visible over most of Israel showing Israeli aircraft being shot down by missiles over the Golan and scenes of hundreds of Egyptian soldiers crossing the canal. In one case, within hours of being captured, I watched the commander of the Israeli 190th Armoured Brigade being interviewed on Egyptian television. Lieutenant-Colonel Asaf Yagouri had just lost his whole armoured brigade to Egyptian infantry using wire guided missiles. He was in a state of shock and no one can imagine what effect this had on the national psyche of the State of Israel . . . .

Those who normally staffed the Sinai desk in UNTSO headquarters, Jerusalem, were stranded outside of Israel when the war started. In their absence I was detailed to work there. Working conditions were awful and an antique high frequency radio made things worse. I had no duty relief and was putting in sixteen-hour days. Most of the work was writing daily summaries and then having them transmitted to New York.

On 13 October the UN El Qantara Control Centre at Rabah was bombed by Egyptian aircraft. It was decided that the chief administrative officer, the chief communications officer and the chief transportation officer should go down to the Sinai for an inspection to decide whether to keep the operation open or to close it down. I went along as the military representative.

On 14 October as we were processing through the northern Sinai there was very noticeable heavy aircraft activity. When we arrived at

Rabah, there were vehicles burning. Some Arab workers had sustained injuries as well as a couple of members of the field kitchen staff. The only vehicles damaged were the kitchen and the officers' mess. The attacking aircraft were Mirages with Egyptian markings but it was no secret they were Libyan. This also helps explain why the same UN installation was bombed by Mirages two consecutive days in a row. Canadian Majors Bill Bailey and Irv Kerr were on duty in Rabah at the time. Israeli troops were on the road nearby when the UN installation was hit. They couldn't believe their eyes. The Israelis, having themselves been bombed earlier, sent medics to render first aid without even being asked . . . .

I was agape at the seemingly non-stop artillery barrage being fired by the Egyptians. It lasted for hours. Super-imposed were Israeli aircraft attacks. I watched one Mirage and one Phantom line up at very high altitude and fly right along the canal. The Mirage was for fighter protection and, of course, the Phantom for electronic jamming. The next thing in sequence from north to south was missile fire following the aircraft through the sky. I counted 32 SAM-2 missiles fired on one pass. No hits! As the SAM batteries were firing, other Israeli aircraft at medium altitude were releasing 'smart' bombs to destroy the missile radar in the Egyptian Second Army sector. Unbelievably at low level were Skyhawks boring into the cauldron taking out anti-aircraft gun and missile emplacements. Other aircraft including rescue or medical evacuation helicopters were awaiting their turn to perform. I reported back what I observed . . . .

The war soon turned against the Syrians. The last major event on the Golan Heights was the recapture of a secret Israeli installation on Mount Hermon—the eyes and ears of the Golan plateau . . . .

The first cease-fire on 22 October was doomed from the start as Security Council Resolution 338 did not call for UNTSO supervision. It broke down on its own momentum due to lack of discipline by senior ranking officers and Israeli politicians.

With the Egyptians barely holding at Ismailia, the Israelis advanced from Deversoir on the west bank of the Suez Canal to the city of Suez and the port of Adabiya by 24 October. With rapid armoured movement and aircraft support they quickly overran the soft underbelly of the Egyptian army without any hard fighting.

On Tuesday 23 October, Resolution 339 of the Security Council mandated immediate dispatch of United Nations observers to supervise the cease-fire using UN personnel then in the Middle East. The new cease-fire was scheduled for 0700 hours 24 October.

The wheels for a successful cease-fire were in motion. Our first patrol, call sign 21, was to reach Suez city late on 24 October, to be relieved by patrol call sign 22 on 25 October and then by patrol 23 on 27 October. The first patrol was to make contact, the second patrol was to spend two nights in Suez while the third patrol was to find the furthest locations of the Israeli units. I found myself with patrol call sign 23 assigned to a four-day patrol in the Israeli pocket. Unexpectedly, the patrol lasted nine days . . . . My partner and I picked up an Israeli liaison officer and proceeded towards El Tasa. I was surprised to discover how badly the Israeli military treated the UN. But I learned that there are good and bad in every society.

When we were about ten miles from El Tasa we passed an Israeli military convoy of mixed vehicles a mile long. The only thing different from any other convoy was that it was stopped and consisted of burned out wrecks practically bumper to bumper. A couple of miles later we passed a repeat of the first except this was about one-half mile long. I was shocked to think that the Israelis had gotten themselves trapped and wiped out so effortlessly by the Egyptians. I couldn't stop to investigate as Suez city was another two to three hours drive. As we passed El Tasa there were knocked out Egyptian tracked vehicles so they had gotten that far in this sector. We then turned southwest passing the area of 'Chinese Farm' (Galan) and much wreckage.

We reached the canal where I did my first duty. There were many Israeli tanks and anti-aircraft guns and whatever located there. As I got closer I could see half of them were knocked out. In one spot six tanks were burned out so close to each other that one could jump back and forth . . . .

We crossed the canal on a floating bridge that was badly listing due to over-use, lack of maintenance and shell-fire. Getting off the bridge we entered a new world of agricultural land. Tall date palms, sugar cane and varieties of grass were abundant. Every 100 metres for at least one mile were knocked-out Israeli tanks. After we got free of the green belt, we were back into desert . . . .

At Suez city there was absolute pandemonium. Confusion abounded around Israeli Defence Forces' command headquarters. Orders were given then countermanded then rescinded. Everybody in their army from the top brass to the lowest rank had an opportunity to be seen as well as heard. Major Bill Bailey and his partner handed over the reins, wished us luck and happily sped away towards the west . . . .

My partner and I ventured out of town about five miles and inspected some abandoned positions along the canal. As I was driving parallel on a trail through the heavily-vegetated jungle-like area, we were stopped at gun point by an Egyptian soldier. So much for the Israelis having the Egyptian Third Army surrounded. They had bypassed this area and the Egyptians were in strength. We then crossed a steel bridge over the Sweet Water Canal and met with the Egyptians . . . . The Israelis claimed the Egyptians had moved into this area after the Israelis had cleared it. Clearly this was a ruse as the Egyptians could not possibly have prepared fortifications in a couple of hours.

What I believe to be the first peace talks of the Yom Kippur War then took place. Can you imagine a small group of Israelis and Egyptians who were about to kill each other having a meeting? An Israeli officer offered an Egyptian a cigarette. He noticed the man was trembling badly. How can you kill somebody who you have just met and offered a cigarette?

An Israeli officer came out from hiding with his weapon in hand and spoke to us saying, "You had better leave. We are attacking this position in ten minutes." He was either a Canadian or an American Jew because he did not have an English accent. We replied: "There is a cease-fire and there is to be no more fighting." Soon another Israeli force moved in from the side we had entered and we were stuck in the middle. The Egyptian soldiers were in a frenzy being pushed on two sides by the Israeli army. To distract their attention, I broke open a carton of cigarettes and gave them out. It was just enough to stop them from getting nervous and pulling a trigger.

We were given until 1700 hours to get out by the Israeli Defence Forces. My partner and I moved our vehicle onto the bridge to prevent the Israelis crossing over the Sweet Water Canal. At ten minutes

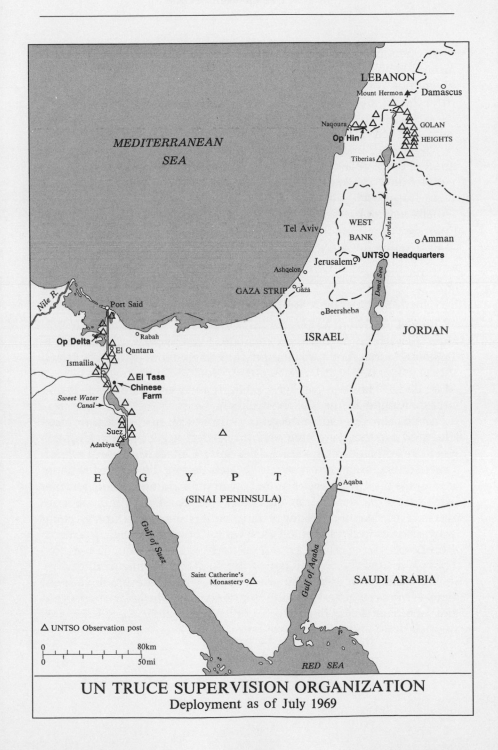

UN TRUCE SUPERVISION ORGANIZATION
Deployment as of July 1969

before the attack, we both took off our flak jackets and helmets, threw them out onto the bridge, sat on the hood of our vehicle and began smoking cigarettes.

Around 17:30 a cigar-smoking, short, squat, grey-haired Israeli colonel arrived and then angrily left in a cloud of cigar smoke. It was getting dark. The Israeli combat team commander then told us to stay. "After all," he said, "this is my fourth war and I see no need to die this late in the war especially now that you have made this cease-fire stick . . . ." The Israeli forces soon withdrew and we were the last out.[5]

When war broke out in 1973, Captain H.S. Bloom of the Princess Patricia's Canadian Light Infantry was manning an observation post just south of the Damascus-Qneitra highway along with a Dane, Captain P. Jacobsen. In a report to the Canadian military attaché to Israel, Colonel H.C.F. Elliot, Bloom described his experience:

Hostilities broke out at approximately 1300 hours local time on 6 October. At that time I was on duty at Observation Post 6 which lies approximately 700 yards south of the Qneitra-Damascus road . . . . At about 1230 hours 7 October, Syrian infantry entered the site itself. I was standing in the shelter walkway when a Syrian soldier approached, saw me and proceeded to fire. As he turned to open fire, I jumped around the corner and proceeded to yell at him that we were United Nations personnel. This had no effect on him as he fired a second long burst at my helmet, which I was showing and waving at him. He hit the helmet knocking it out of my hands. He then came half-way down the walkway and fired a long burst of a light machine-gun into the sleeping/working area of the shelter. At this time Captain Jacobsen was fired upon in the west walkway. Fortunately, all rounds missed.

Captain Jacobsen walked out of the shelter first, followed by myself, both with our hands up, wearing our flak jackets and UN helmets. He was struck with a rifle butt three times in quick succession and then rushed at with a fixed bayonet. Fortunately, the soldier was stopped but then came at me thrusting at my leg. I managed to jump aside and only felt the point of the bayonet prick my right leg. We were ordered onto our knees with our hands up while they searched us for weapons. I spoke in French to them again explaining that we were United Nations personnel and neutral. One man, a corporal, seemed to understand and our treatment became better.

We were marched out of the compound site and commenced walking in a south-east direction with many stops to seek cover while tank, artillery or machine gun fire came down near us . . . . We were finally evacuated with 3 wounded Syrians to Damascus about 1630 hours.

We reached Damascus at about 1830 hours after stopping at a forward military headquarters and intelligence headquarters. My impression at that time was and still is that we were believed to be downed Israeli pilots or agents/spies. The showing of UN identity papers had little or no effect on the Syrians. In Damascus we were taken to a military security/intelligence headquarters and asked some general type of questions. Our treatment was good and at about 2000 hours we were released.[6]

Major MacNeil of Halifax recounts a memorable incident that occurred on the Israeli-Lebanese border:

On 30 May 1974, Major B. Rasmussen from Denmark and myself had just spent our third day of Observation Post duty at OP HIN. The OP is located one kilometre from Israel. The 31st of May was to be a day of major importance as the disengagement treaty between Israel and Syria was to be ratified in Geneva. The Palestine Liberation Organization were objecting strongly as they wanted the struggle against Israel to continue and vowed to fight on by themselves . . . .

At 23:30 that night an old sheep dog I had befriended started to growl and crawled out from under our caravan. His barking became a steady howl when I heard the sickening thud of a solid object striking tissue. There was a feeble yelp then silence. I told my partner I was going outside to see what was happening. I then crawled to the far corner of our compound.

Approximately thirty feet away was a Fedayeen [freedom fighter] who fired a burst of small arms fire directly at me. I instinctively fell flat to the ground and crawled backwards. Before I reached the caravan there was the crackling of small arms [Israeli] fire coming from the south end of our compound aimed at the insurgents running towards me. Reaching the caravan I dove through the open door onto the floor and tried to take cover under the lower bunk. No such luck! It was occupied by Major Rasmussen . . . . I next called Beirut on the radio for help: "Beirut, Beirut, Beirut. OP HIN. This f------ OP is under attack!" Heavy firing then broke out reaching a crescendo when there were a series of explosions. Between lapses in the shooting I could hear men speaking Arabic and they were very close by. I could also make out the voices of Israeli soldiers shouting back and forth.

Our radio finally came on. We were told that the Lebanese Army had been altered and that help was on the way . . . . Approximately one-half hour before first light on 31 May the Lebanese army reported they were ready to enter the OP compound. I suspected there was profound reluctance to come to terms with the insurgents as the Lebanese army delayed their arrival . . . . Major Rasmussen and I were two very happy men as we lived to see the light of the new day.

Captain Pericles Metaxis of Edmonton served one year with UNTSO beginning in July 1984 and was stationed in Beirut from October until the end of June 1985. Excerpts from his diary give some indication of what it was like there:

11 January (Friday)

Heavy artillery duel between Progressive Socialist Party militiamen and the Lebanese Armed Forces. One airburst and two groundbursts missed our Observation Post by 100 metres . . . . Situation here now calm with the exception of the bombing of a bank.

14 January (Monday)

Extensive fighting and shelling between Druze and Christian militias in the Shouf Mountains dominating Beirut. Two members of the United Nations while on vehicle patrol near the Bourj el-Barajneh refugee camp for Palestinians were murdered. They were shot at point blank by AK 47 automatic rifles by three partisans of the extremist "Party of God" or Hozbollah.

15 January (Tuesday)

Situation in the city quiet with the exception of sporadic heavy machine-gun and small arms fire. Reference yesterday's murder of the two French observers, the pro-Iranian Islamic Jihad for the liberation of Palestine (the operational arm of the Hozbollah) has claimed responsibility. (France was a major supplier of arms to Iraq, a haven for anti-Khomeini Iranians, and had called for the withdrawal of all non-Lebanese forces from Lebanon.)

16 January (Wednesday)

We are restricted temporarily in patrolling near the Bourj el-Barajneh camp due to the UN assassinations. The night life in West Beirut is practically non-existent. Fear has started to spread . . . .

19 January (Saturday)

Situation in Beirut quite tense today. Six car/house bombs exploded at different sectors of West Beirut. Four persons were killed and twelve injured. Extensive material damage.[7]

The UNTSO experience is somewhat different from other peacekeeping operations in the region for Canadians. They live among the people and are not isolated to the same extent as other Canadian peacekeeping troops whose environment was a UN military camp. At their own expense officers have brought their wives and even children to live in the region during their tour. But there is constant danger. In recent years, Captain R.G. Elms and his wife, Shirley, had a small shell go through their apartment in Beirut. Captain G.R. and Katie Bennett were less fortunate. Their apartment was taken over and wrecked by Druze militiamen.

In 1986 Bloom observed:

As a group, the Canadians generally did very well but rather than getting a pat on the back for having done a good job during some pretty difficult times, we ended up being chastised for having our families in the area with us which in the opinion of our leaders at National Defence Headquarters was detrimental to our carrying out our duties. At the same time, of course, Vietnam was in progress and the Cyprus war was going strong. We became the "forgotten theatre." A number of us came back extremely annoyed and in fact angry.

Canada continues to have military observers stationed with UNTSO in Cairo and the Sinai in Egypt (following the 1974 peace treaty) although the situation there remains quiet. They also serve in Jerusalem and Tiberias in Israel, Damascus in Syria, and Naqoura and Beirut in Lebanon. UNTSO's main contribution over the last decade or so has been to act as observers along the Israeli-Lebanese and Israeli-Syrian borders. The unarmed observers of UNTSO, in effect, serve as the eyes and ears of the United Nations Interim Force in Lebanon and the United Nations Disengagement Observer Force in the Golan Heights. They inform both groups of unauthorized crossings by guerrillas, local militias or regular forces.

Canadian peacekeepers have become extensions of their country's foreign policy. The eviction from Egypt in 1967 demonstrated the vulnerability of its peacekeeping troops. The government should keep in mind the safety of its military personnel serving as peacekeepers in different countries of the world in its foreign policy pronouncements and actions. Whether Canadian servicemen ought to continue, for example, serving with UNTSO in Lebanon, particularly Beirut, is debatable.

The Functioning of UNTSO

UNTSO's tasks continue to be to observe and report on breaches of the cease-fire and to help prevent incidents. It reports to the secretary-general on complaints submitted by the parties concerned. Canada provided over six hundred officer observers between 1954 and 1985. Having an indefinite mandate, UNTSO continues to require men. Their presence cannot hurt the situation and it may likely help.

Participation by officers from the the USSR on UNTSO began in 1973. Colonel Boulanger, while with UNDOF in 1975-1976, visited UNTSO at Damascus to find that the thirty Americans and thirty Russians were only working half a day a month as duty officers in the headquarters of the Mixed Armistice Commission. Since the Russians were not accepted by the Israelis nor the Americans by the Syrians, they could not be employed at observation posts. Thus they worked only a half-day each month and became the best dart players in the region.

Israel's invasion of Lebanon in June 1982 and its push to Beirut in pursuit of the Palestine Liberation Organization in August of that year prompted a need for an increase in the number of UN observers based in that city. The ten observers already there reported on events such as the arrival and departure of the non-UN multinational force representing the United States, France, Great Britain and Italy, and the occupation of West Beirut by Israeli forces. In view of the massacre of Palestinians in two West Beirut refugee camps in mid-September, the Security Council was able to increase the number of observers in Beirut to fifty. These observers were to monitor the situation there by means of observation posts and mobile patrols with the emphasis being on the Israelis and the Palestinians. Following the withdrawal of

Israeli forces from the Beirut area in September 1983, the size of the UN group was reduced. About twenty UNTSO observers, including several Canadians, continue to observe and report on the situation there.

The members of UNTSO, including the Canadians, are rotated during their year of duty to give them exposure to peaceful as well as dangerous areas. These unarmed officers face the constant possibility of death or kidnapping, particulary along the Israeli-Lebanese border. A UN jeep is a tempting prize to irregulars in the area. Along the Lebanese border, UNTSO members on jeep patrol must report back at fairly short intervals to ensure their safety.

One of the unofficial roles of UNTSO has been to serve as a reserve from which experienced observers can be drawn in case of an emergency in the region or elsewhere. Such was the case with the United Nations Observer Group in Lebanon, the force in the Congo, or with UNEF I, when UNTSO observers preceded their arrival in order to try to maintain calm and prevent a flare-up in the fighting. Canada still has some twenty officers serving throughout the region with UNTSO in 1987. Their work generally consists of outpost duty and mobile patrols.

At the time of the founding of the UN there was hope among some diplomats that soldiers from foreign countries who might join a UN force would put aside national allegiances giving their first loyalty instead to the UN. This has not happened and was perhaps an unrealistic expectation. Peacekeepers have continued to function as representatives of their own countries. If in the course of their duties they were required to serve in what was perceived to be their countries' national interest or security, they have done so.

2

UNITED NATIONS EMERGENCY FORCE I

DURING 1955-1956 THERE were continual flare-ups between Israel and its neighbours. Following Egypt's nationalization of the Suez Canal on 26 July 1956, the British and French governments were apprehensive about their freedom of movement through the canal. The canal was nationalized a week after the United States reneged on its previous agreement to finance the High Dam at Aswan on the Nile. Britain as well as the United States was also upset at Egypt's acceptance of Russian military aid. Some British politicians were concerned about the erosion of British influence in the region as a result of the rise of pan-Arab nationalism under the leadership of President Gamal Abdel Nasser of Egypt. France had built the Suez Canal and along with its French shareholders was embittered by its loss. Nasser's military and moral support of Arab nationalists fighting for independence in Algeria also provoked France.

HOSTILITIES

In the late afternoon of Monday, 29 October 1956, an Israeli parachute battalion landed near the Mitla Pass, the strategic key to the Sinai Peninsula. There were also armed thrusts by other Israeli forces into the Sinai. On 30 October, Britain and France, according to a previously orchestrated plan with Israel, presented an ultimatum to both Egypt and Israel demanding that fighting cease within twelve hours (by 6:30 a.m. Cairo time the same day, Tuesday, 30 October). They directed Israel to halt its forces some ten miles east of the Suez Canal and Egypt to withdraw its military forces to ten miles west of the canal.[1] Britain and France also stated that they intended to dispatch forces to the key positions of Port Said, Ismailia and Suez in the Canal Zone to protect their "vital interests."[2] President Nasser, not surprisingly, rejected the ultimatum and ordered mobilization.[3] British and French air attacks began on the evening of 31 October and their troops arrived on 5-6 November. Meanwhile, the Israeli military attack continued.

At an emergency meeting of the UN General Assembly in order to implement the cease-fire resolution of 2 November 1956, Lester B. Pearson, Canada's minister for external affairs, proposed the formation of an emergency United Nations force to secure and supervise the cessation of hostilities. His suggestion was rapidly approved during an all-night session on 3-4 November. This was the first peacekeeping force, as distinct from observer groups, established by the UN. Dag Hammarskjöld, the UN secretary-general, appointed Major-General Eedson Louis Millard Burns, a Canadian, then chief of staff of the United Nations Truce Supervision Organization, as head of the new UN force.[4] While serving in this capacity, Burns was promoted to the rank of lieutenant-general in November 1957. Burns, the most experienced UN military commander available, had previously led the 1st Canadian Corps in Italy in 1944 and worked as a senior public servant in Ottawa.

CEASE-FIRE

On 6 November the British and French governments, faced with hostile world opinion, including that of the governments of Canada and the United States, agreed to a cease-fire. Considerable debate was aroused in Canada by its failure to support Great Britain. Anglo-French forces halted their advance about a quarter of the way down the canal from Port Said, some two miles north of El Qantara.

The United Nations Emergency Force (UNEF I) became a legal entity at 7:00 p.m. on Wednesday, 7 November 1956. The General Assembly had approved its creation by fifty-seven votes to none, with nineteen abstentions. Control was placed in the hands of the secretary-general. The great powers were to be ineligible to participate in this operation. At its maximum strength in early 1957 this peacekeeping force consisted of almost six thousand officers and men drawn from ten countries: Brazil, Canada, Colombia, Denmark, Finland, India, Indonesia, Norway, Sweden and Yugoslavia.

The force sent by the UN to Palestine in 1948 differed outwardly from UNEF I. UNTSO was strictly an observer operation, while UNEF I served as a lightly armed barrier that all could see. While UNEF members carried weapons and could defend themselves, UN observers were unarmed. The 1948 group had the various nationalities intermixed.

41

UNEF troops consisted of separate national contingents that were kept intact.

STATUS OF THE FORCE AGREEMENT WITH EGYPT

After a good deal of negotiation, a comprehensive agreement was reached, in 1957, between the United Nations and Egypt covering the status of the peacekeeping force. Two key provisions concerned freedom of movement and criminal jurisdiction. Members of the force were granted permission to move freely in the performance of their duties. Each national contingent was to be subject to the exclusive jurisdiction of its national government in respect to any criminal offences its members might commit; thus Canada's troops were subject to Canadian criminal and military law. The agreement provided an important precedent for arrangements for later peacekeeping forces.

THE CANADIAN FORCES AND UNEF

Originally, it was decided that the 1st Battalion, Queen's Own Rifles of Canada, stationed at Calgary would form Canada's contribution. It was, accordingly, moved to Halifax for embarkation. These infantrymen were to be augmented by a headquarters and records section, ordnance, electrical and mechanical engineers, signallers, pay corps, provost, chaplains, public relations personnel as well as service corps, medical and dental detachments totalling almost three hundred.

While planning was underway, Egypt was objecting to the

acceptance of Canadian troops. The ostensible reason given by Egypt was that their British-style uniforms might easily be mistaken for those of the United Kingdom forces. Not only were the uniforms the same but they spoke the same language and even the name "Queen's Own Rifles" increased the likelihood of mistakes in identification. However, the real reasons for Egypt's reluctance to accept the Canadians were more profound. In the General Assembly it was remembered that Canada had abstained when the vote had been taken on the resolution calling for an immediate cease-fire.[5]

On 14 November 1956, Egypt granted permission for UNEF to enter its territory on condition that Egyptian sovereignty was fully respected.[6] Egypt was persuaded to accept Canadian participation. General Burns had even threatened the Egyptians with his resignation if they continued to object to Canadian personnel. Denmark also threatened to withdraw if Canada was excluded from UNEF. However, it would not be the Queen's Own Rifles that represented Canada.

Canada's initial involvement was limited to the shuttle of UN supplies and equipment from Italy to UNEF. As few countries had personnel with specialized logistical and administrative skills, Canada was asked to contribute a signals squadron, a field hospital, a transport company and an RCAF communications squadron. UNEF became not a combat-ready strike force as first envisaged by Burns[7] but a buffer force.

Between 12-21 November a group to support a Canadian infantry battalion in the Middle East was being concentrated at the Royal Canadian Ordnance Corps School at Longue Pointe, Montreal. Total strength was approximately three hundred. Of these, the first group of sixteen officers and 132 other ranks left Dorval Airport in three North Star passenger aircraft, the first departing on 22 November. The flight to Lajes in the Azores was tiring and the bucket seats not the most comfortable. From the Azores the aircraft stopped at Gibraltar and arrived at Naples in the early hours of 24 November.

The troops slept in late that day at the US naval barracks, the main meal being arranged for two o'clock. Between 3:00 and 5:00 a.m., two Swiss Air flights flew the main body from Capodichino Airport, Naples, to Abu Suweir, nine miles west of Ismailia on the Suez Canal. Sitting in comfortable, soft cushioned seats, the men marvelled as the sun came up and brought light to the Mediterranean far below, followed by their first view of the delta of Egypt, the winding Nile, and the wide expanse of desert sand — an impressive sight to all who arrived by air.

When the younger members of the forces landed, they were filled with idealism. Some gave the famous peace symbol of the 1960s with their fingers. From what they had heard or been told in Canada, many servicemen felt their mission was to be of tremendous importance to global peace; that each would be contributing their share to help save the world from catastrophe. Initial motivation and idealism, however, quickly wore thin.

For the early arrivals, their stay was unpleasant. The troops deplaned to Abu Suweir and were moved to old British barracks nearby. Most recently occupied by Egyptian personnel, the barracks were dirty and inadequate. The troops had brought most items but lacked cleaning equipment. As well, personnel were crowded six to eight in small rooms. The advance party began to prepare Abu Suweir for the arrival of the troops and stores.

As a result of recent fighting most of the buildings were in a poor state. The first task was to repair buildings and clean up from bomb damage. According to Canadian Major S.G. Tait:

When we arrived . . . not one window or door remained! Water and power facilities were long gone. . . . We had to repair buildings, build showers, level ground, install power . . . . [8]

The Canadian camp was guarded by Egyptian troops and initially UNEF personnel were not even permitted outside the barbed-wire camp unless accompanied by an Egyptian escort. As well, a blackout was applicable at ten o'clock and a curfew was in effect from 10:00 p.m. to 6:00 a.m. The camp was still under Egyptian command and partially in use by Egyptian troops. Egyptian guards at the main gate stopped everyone from going in or out without an Egyptian pass. Because of anxiety to prevent any "incidents" between the UN troops and the Egyptian populace, nobody got a pass for weeks after the arrival except for strictly business purposes. As one Canadian private remarked at the time, "I thought we was here to clear them Egyptians out of the canal zone . . . . Instead, damned if they aren't treating us like prisoners of war."[9]

Gradually, UNEF took control of their own security. Although the Canadians did not have the manpower, being the only administrative troops in UNEF capable of doing the job they assumed the duties of logistic support of the whole force.[10] Within ten days adequate stores began to arrive. While nations from other countries were initially more visible to the international press, it was the Canadian contingent working behind the scenes that provided the logistics enabling the force to function.

Like foreign tourists, the Canadians were warned about the local food and the water. Some at first disbelieved any such advice and instead put their faith in whisky. Lectures and notices warning that syphilis could be contacted from local prostitutes or hepatitis from a nearby tattoo artist only seemed to increase their business.

The movement of personnel and supplies continued until by 6 December there were almost three hundred Canadian Army personnel in Egypt, thus fulfilling the initial contribution requested by the UN. In response to General Burns' appeal for additional Canadian help, on 17 December three new units were authorized for Middle East duty: 56 Signal Squadron, 56 Transport Company and 56 Infantry Workshop. In addition requests for an air component for communication and observation and officers for Burns' staff were granted.

HMCS *MAGNIFICENT*

In late 1956, Canada's only aircraft carrier, HMCS *Magnificent* was called upon to transport this country's contribution for UNEF. A total of 405 all ranks — 140 Royal Canadian Signals, 140 Royal Canadian Electrical and Mechanical Engineers, ninety-one Royal Canadian Army Service Corps and thirty-four headquarters personnel — along with one hundred tons of stores, 230 vehicles, and four light aircraft — made the voyage. The ship left Halifax on 29 December at 10:00 p.m. passing under the Angus L. MacDonald Bridge.[11] After a few days of rough seas and unfamiliarity, the soldiers settled into shipboard life. Shared duties for tradesmen combined with a lively program of sports and recreation made the time pass quickly. There were no rest stops as the UNEF commander was anxious that the carrier arrive as soon as possible. An oiler and supply ship from the US Sixth Fleet transferred fuel, fresh water and provision to "Maggie" as she proceeded en route. In spite of a short, severe Mediterranean storm, she arrived at Port Said on 11 January 1957 to be immediately greeted by diplomats, officials and a swarm of local trades- men and peddlers.[12] Unloading began soon after and a week later "Maggie" left Port Said having helped significantly to fulfill Canada's obligations to the UN. The Canadian contin- gent with UNEF came to number some one thousand, or more than 20 percent of UNEF's average total strength of 4,700.

It is difficult to stress the importance of the arrival of HMCS *Magnificent* but one report described her appearance at Port Said as "tantamount to the lifting of siege."[13] Although it appeared the crew would not be allowed off the ship, Gen- eral Burns interceded with Egyptian authorities and, as a result, three groups of 120 from the ship were taken on organized sightseeing trips to Cairo and the pyramids. Lim- ited leave was also given in Port Said as the situation there had calmed down.

Two of the most important vehicles transported by *Mag- nificent* were a helicopter and a wrecker or towtruck. The helicopter was painted with the UN emblem and used to fly the UNEF commander around. It arrived, carrying General Burns, just after the Israeli evacuation at El Arish on 15 January and unleashed a wave of hysterical celebration amongst the Egyptians.[14] Its presence, although just for that week, helped to demonstrate very visibly that UNEF was taking charge. The services of the towtruck were also invalu- able. It was kept busy either trying to recover UNEF vehicles involved in accidents or those that had broken down or be- come stuck in the sand.

47

CANADIAN DEPLOYMENT

The Canadian contingent of UNEF was initially split among several locations. Most of the detachments, however, first remained at Abu Suweir. Engineers, signals, legal and headquarters detachments were also stationed at El Ballah, near the Suez Canal.[15] In March a Canadian armoured unit, 56 Reconnaissance Squadron, composed of 105 all ranks (from across Canada) was sent to Egypt by air to be followed shortly afterwards by their twenty-nine Ferret scout cars. An additional forty Canadian specialists in various fields were also flown to Egypt in March. In spite of UN requests for additional personnel, no further Canadian manpower was committed.

Probably the most outstanding Canadian commander of any of the peacekeeping forces was General Burns who commanded UNEF from its inception until 1959. He proved to be the right man in the right place. He knew he could depend on Canadian servicemen and placed them in key organizational and support roles. They did not let him down. From nothing they created a logistical and communications system for the force. Outwardly, Burns manifested a grim, colourless personality, singularly lacking in levity. This reinforced the impression of an intent individual determined to be scrupulously objective. In my limited contacts with him, I found the general to be affable, cooperative and did indeed have a sense of humour.

What was common to all the operations in which the Canadian forces were involved was their humanity. No matter in what country they served, the Canadian serviceman or servicewoman generally treated the inhabitants with respect and as human beings. The same cannot be said for all the other foreign soldiers in these operations. Troops from Latin

America, particularly, showed less respect for human rights or life. They preferred to shoot intruders rather than take them as prisoners.

All three branches of the Canadian forces had responded well in a new and fluid situation. On short notice the Canadian Army mustered a special force; the Royal Canadian Navy transformed its aircraft carrier into an effective transport and headquarters ship; and the Royal Canadian Air Force provided the necessary airlift facilities. As well, Canada's contribution to the Military Advisory Group at the UN had been extremely helpful. Fortunately, Canada had the men and transport equipment available to enable this country to play an important role in the organization and establishment of UNEF.

At first UNEF was interposed between the Anglo-French and Egyptian forces in the Suez Canal area and between the Israeli and Egyptian troops in the Sinai. Once the Anglo-French troops withdrew by the end of December 1956, UNEF took control of the Suez Canal to help ensure the clearance operation. As mentioned, the Canadians were generally stationed in Abu Suweir, about twelve miles west of Ismailia, from 25 November 1956 to 5 September 1957 and also at El Ballah, just west of the canal, where a UN communications centre was set up. They then moved to Rafah Camp.

At El Ballah the Canadian field engineers did just about every job imaginable. They drove the supply train from El Qantara to Port Said, laid out a landing strip, and operated the water supply at Port Said for a week following the Anglo-French evacuation. They also supervised the construction of accommodation for the men in the force.[16]

Heavy supplies for UNEF came to Port Said where Royal Canadian Army Service Corps personnel were assigned the task of supervising the offloading of all sorts of stores from cargo ships. After removal from a ship via a lighter, the stores were kept in warehouses and later forwarded. The Canadians' main tasks were the accounting of goods and supervision of operations.

As the Israelis gradually withdrew, first from the Sinai behind the 130-mile-long international boundary between Egypt and Israel, then from the Gaza Strip on 7 March 1957, UNEF was deployed. On the 8th, the Israelis left Sharm el Sheikh. As a result of the destruction of the Egyptian communications system by Israeli forces and the presence of minefields, largely Egyptian, the move into the Sinai was not easy.

The first death among the Canadians with UNEF occurred when Sapper R.H. Vezina on 9 March suffered a heart attack while going to the aid of an Egyptian wounded by a mine. He is buried at Muascar Commonwealth Cemetery near Ismailia.[17]

In mid-April 1957, after UNEF had taken over the Gaza Strip, the workshop for the Royal Canadian Army Service Corps and the Royal Canadian Electrical and Mechanical Engineers was moved to Rafah Camp, 160 miles east of Port Said. The camp was serviced by rail as well as by the main road from the Canal Zone through El Arish to Gaza. Rafah Camp was formerly a British army base that contained a Royal Army Ordnance Corps depot. It was necessary to reinstall power and water facilities looted by the locals and repair heavy damage inflicted by Israeli forces during the fighting. As a result of the variety of British and North American makes and models of vehicles, parts often had to be manufactured in the workshop rather than await spares. To add to the strain of getting established, surprises such as unexploded grenades and booby traps were found in the officers' living quarters.[18] Security, supply, and food improved with time as the Canadians became better organized.

In 1957 Egypt had permitted the reopening of the Suez Canal once Israeli forces had withdrawn from Gaza. An irksome problem came to be the transporting of supplies across the canal. The bridge at Ismailia was closed between 7:00 and 9:00 a.m. and 2:00 and 4:00 p.m. daily to allow ships to pass through. The ferry at El Qantara was slow and could only accommodate two vehicles at a time.[19]

Following the Israeli withdrawal, the Canadians moved into the Gaza Strip. Among the first UN troops there were members of 56 Transport Company on 7 March.[20] People celebrating in the streets of Gaza also made vehicle movement difficult for Canadian engineers who arrived the next day to set up the water supply and repair electrical fixtures.[21] The mood of the populace soon changed and UNEF turned over the administration of the Gaza Strip to the Egyptians that month.

Within the Strip the Canadians established a UN communications centre in the town of Gaza on 12 April 1957 and operated it for more than ten years, until 29 May 1967. The headquarters for the Canadian armoured reconnaissance squadron was at Rafah Camp, at the southern end of the Gaza Strip. This unit patrolled the area from 16 April 1957 to 15 February 1966 when they left. For much of that period the squadron generally patrolled the northern part of the border between Egypt and Israel. A Yugoslav reconnaissance battalion did likewise in the southern section. UNEF air reconnaissance by the Canadians was responsible for the Sinai coast from the northern end of the Gulf of Aquaba to the Strait of Tiran.

Canadian signallers were also scattered amongst the various national contingents. Signallers could be found at UNEF headquarters in Gaza, at the maintenance area at Rafah Camp, with the RCAF at El Arish or at Sharm el Sheikh. A rotation system gave most signallers a change of scenery.

The climate of the Sinai is dry and harsh. Only winter low-pressure systems over the Mediterranean or Red Sea bring rains, as well as floods, to the area. Low-pressure systems from the Sahara bring blinding sandstorms. This is the climate the Canadians faced.

The hottest spot on the UNEF tour, literally not figuratively, was Sharm el Sheikh. The Canadian signallers' main job was to transmit the observation reports of the reconnaissance unit located there. The only escape from the oppressive heat was a swim in shark-infested waters and relief from the boredom was eased by the arrivals of a supply aircraft from El Arish.[22] For excitement one Finnish soldier would attract a shark in the Red Sea and then swim for shore. His comrades on the cliffs, with rifles and automatic weapons, would shoot at the shark for target practice.[23] While the Finns suffered no casualties the same cannot be said for the sharks.

THE RCAF AND UNEF

In November 1956, 435 RCAF Air Transport Squadron was detailed to help in providing air transport for the UN peacekeeping force in Egypt. Assistance was given by 436 Squadron based at Downsview, Ontario. Support was also given by 426 Squadron from Dorval, Quebec. 114 Air Transport Unit was set up as the control organization at Capodichino Airport near Naples. Initially, it had twelve C-119 military-transport aircraft.

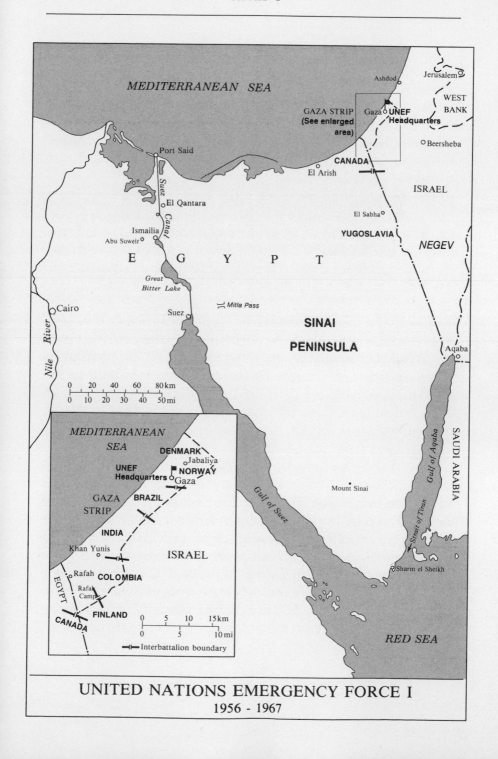

MEDITERRANEAN SEA

Ashdod

Jerusalem

WEST BANK

GAZA STRIP
(See enlarged area)

Gaza UNEF
Headquarters

Beersheba

Port Said

CANADA

El Arish

ISRAEL

El Qantara

El Sabha

YUGOSLAVIA

NEGEV

Ismailia
Abu Suweir

E   G   Y   P   T

Great
Bitter Lake

Mitla Pass

Cairo

SINAI

Suez

PENINSULA

Aqaba

Nile River

0   20   40   60   80 km
0   10   20   30   40   50 mi

Mount Sinai

Gulf of Aqaba

SAUDI ARABIA

Strait of Tiran

Gulf of Suez

MEDITERRANEAN
SEA

DENMARK
Jabaliya

UNEF
Headquarters

NORWAY
Gaza

GAZA
STRIP

BRAZIL

INDIA

Khan Yunis

ISRAEL

Rafah

COLOMBIA

Rafah
Camp

EGYPT

FINLAND

CANADA

0   5   10   15 km
0   5   10 mi

Interbattalion boundary

Sharm el Sheikh

RED SEA

UNITED NATIONS EMERGENCY FORCE I
1956 - 1967

The RCAF began the airlift of UNEF's men and supplies in late November and by January the work of 435 and 436 Squadrons had been completed.[24] However, RCAF flights continued from Canada. To support the ground forces there were two units — 114 first at Capodichino until 1 March 1958, and then 115 at El Arish until the final UNEF withdrawal.[25]

From the window of the North Star the terrain ahead appeared vastly different from anything I had ever seen. The brown and white desert sand stood out in marked contrast to the blue Mediterranean over which we had been flying for the past four hours. Near the Egyptian shoreline appeared a small town my fellow-passengers would come to know as El Arish, and a few miles inland was the airport which would be their working headquarters in the year ahead.[26]

Such was the first impression of Flying Officer J.G. Burge in 1960. From the El Arish Airport he was taken by jeep over seven miles of rough pavement to the RCAF's living quarters at the "Marina," so named because of its proximity to the sea. The El Arish Airport where he landed was located about thirty miles from the main Canadian Army camp at Rafah, sixty miles from UNEF headquarters at Gaza, and seven miles inland from the Mediterranean.

Should the newcomer arriving at the El Arish Airport between 1957 and 1967 have driven to Gaza, he would first have been impressed by the barrenness of the place. Taking the road built by the British from El Arish to Rafah, the visitor might have caught sight of gangs of ragged Egyptians slowly at work with crude shovels clearing drifting sand off the road. Moving north the sand gives way to a mixture of sand and clay which is sufficient to nurture scattered scrub and bushes. Here, one would have caught sight of flocks of sheep and goats together with a few browsing camels, tended perhaps by young Bedouin girls dressed in black who would have veiled their faces on the approach of a UN vehicle.

Driving north to Gaza the land becomes more and more fertile until at Gaza there are orange groves and flowers, the result of irrigation from underground cisterns. While accommodation for UN staff was scattered throughout the town, the Canadians there were first issued tents. The headquarters of UNEF was a modern single-storied block in the new part of town.

At the El Arish Airport were Canadian twin-engined Dakotas and single-engined Otters. The Dakotas or DC-3s were used for transportation flights in the region, mainly to Beirut and also to Sharm el Sheikh. On the flight to Beirut and back they would land on the hard sand runway at Gaza to pick up or deliver mail and personnel. The Otters' primary role was daily reconnaissance along the international frontier between Egypt and Israel and also along the Armistice Demarcation Line separating the Gaza Strip from Israel for about thirty-five miles. Members of the Canadian armoured squadron on patrol would call on 115 Air Transport Unit for air reconnaissance when required. The Otters were monoplanes designed for civil bush operations and not equipped for desert conditions. As a result a good deal of time was spent on their maintenance.

For the men of 115 Air Transport Unit each day followed much the same routine. The men rose at 7:30 a.m., dressed, washed, had their breakfast and then were ready for the seven mile drive to work. In the summer months they left one hour earlier because of the heat.

During the summer the temperature would rise to 120 degrees Fahrenheit. The summer heat became unbearable whenever the wind changed at El Arish and blew in from the desert. That sensation has been compared to walking past the open door of a blast furnace.[27] The Mediterranean, only about 150 yards from the men's quarters, offered some relief from the heat to bathers. In winter, high winds created a dangerous undertow. From November to February, it was often necessary to use small heaters to warm the sleeping quarters at night.[28] The rains fell in November and December and desert wadis (dry gullies) briefly became foaming torrents.

Among those Canadians who served at El Arish was Flying Officer C.G. Ferguson:

I was posted to 115 Air Transport Unit, El Arish, Egypt, from September 1963 to August 1964, piloting DHC-3 Otters, DHC-4 Caribous and a DC-3 Dakota. These were used in light transport [passengers and cargo], reconnaissance and medical evacuation roles. Flying in the Middle East theatre posed some small hazards — dust storms, extremely limited navigational aids, etc., but the only killer we experienced during my time there was vehicle related. On 2 November 1963 our commanding officer, Wing Commander E.D. Harper, was killed in a two-vehicle accident while driving his staff car from Rafah to El Arish. On 26 December Sergeant J.K. Hermann was killed in a single-vehicle jeep accident on the same stretch of road.[29]

The recreation program at El Arish and Rafah grew to include a variety of hobbies and sports. There were short-wave receivers which provided news from the outside. Sports news was especially welcome. Movies were shown. At lights out, the men retired to their living quarters.

Apart from the weather, the two most disagreeable things were land mines and local thieves who would steal anything. For example, at night they would sever telephone lines and steal the metal connectors. Clothes, even crucifixes, were stolen. A favourite trick was to string barbed or concertina wire across a road forcing the driver of a UN supply truck to get out. While the driver removed the obstacle, children would ransack the vehicle. Often a weapon was fired to frighten away pilferers. A popular gag in skits was to have someone dressed in Bedouin garb steal the scenery during the performance.

THE LOCALS

Along the international frontier, the Bedouins would transplant mines in the hope of incapacitating a patrol vehicle and then salvaging vehicle parts.[30] However, Canadian gifts such as surplus water and medical care made it in the Bedouin's self-interest to keep on good terms with the Canadians. Despite this, mines did remain an ever-present problem.

To the Canadians the Bedouins seemed like people from another world. Larry Worthington, wife of the late Major-General F.F. Worthington, the "father" of Canada's armoured corps, in her book *The Spur and the Sprocket*, recalled several officers of the Royal Canadian Dragoons being invited to dine with the sheik of a neighbouring tribe:

The guests arrived to find that the dinner consisted of nothing but a complete sheep wrapped in soggy sand-impregnated dough and quantities of strong tea and coffee to wash it down.

It being good Arab manners to refuse several times before yielding to a host's pressure the Canadians' protests got them nowhere. The sheik was impressed by their repeated refusals and insisted on practically hand-feeding them with tasty morsels from the inside of the sheep. . . . Canadian stomachs protested audibly with the prolonged belches that won the admiration of their host. To the Arab, this indicated appreciation and good manners.[31]

In an unpublished article, "The Strangest Police Force in

the World," Captain G.R. Tomalin, Canadian Provost Corps, a member of the UNEF police force wrote:

Despite the precautions of UNEF drivers, many goats, sheep and camels are struck and killed. UNEF makes reparations on a sliding scale. A goat, for example, is usually valued at ten Egyptian pounds, a sheep at fifteen pounds, and a camel at twenty or twenty-five. One wise shepherd complained that his goat was worth at least fifteen pounds since it was pregnant. This was allowed. Since that time, only pregnant animals have been involved in accidents . . . .

Black marketing is an ever-present problem and UNEF goods, including Canadian tax-free cigarettes, are to be seen publicly displayed on the streets of Gaza town. Recently the author attended the public court in Gaza town. While there a ragged Arab peddlar passed through the court selling a well-known brand of Canadian cigarettes. Complaints against black marketing seem to be confined to the Egyptian cigarette companies . . . . Egyptian officials consistently refused to prosecute the shopkeepers for selling UNEF goods and materials openly.

Members of UNEF are subject to the exclusive jurisdiction of the national state to which they belong in respect of any offence they commit while in Egypt . . . . The Military Police cells have been used only once in three years . . . .

From time to time the Military Police company is called upon to help with tasks such as tracking down hashish peddlers. Under Egyptian law the sentence for being in possession of, or even being involved in the hashish trade, is life imprisonment . . . .

At Christmas 1958 during the visit of the secretary-general, the author was assigned as a personal guard . . . . the visit through the refugee-clogged villages of over 216,000 displaced persons was an exciting and arduous task. The crowds of Arabs chanted slogans such as: "Give us back our land . . . . " One curly-headed youth who shouted "Down with Eisenhower" was whisked away by the secret police . . . . The omnipotent police are everywhere and . . . have a surfeit of power.[32]

Warrant Officer Lloyd McKenna of Charlottetown tells of

an incident where, in order to reach a lush pasture (usually on the Israeli side of the border), Bedouins had to cross a stretch of land containing a suspected minefield. Several women were sent across the field without incident. Then a herd of camels followed. Unfortunately, several camels triggered a few live anti-tank mines killing themselves in the process. Seeing this, the Bedouin men became so enraged that they proceeded to berate and beat their women for the loss of the camels.

UNEF veterans have numerous tales. One true story to be found in a unit's war diary concerns a medical assistant with the Royal Canadian Dragoons. Lance Corporal A.M. Hills tended several Bedouins and as a result word spread that there was a miraculous Canadian "doctor" who cured headaches with yellow pills, cramps with red pills, etc. Investigation revealed that the patients were hypochondriacs to whom Hills had doled out Smarties as placebos.[33] Serious authentic cases, however, were taken to the UNEF hospital.

With considerable spare time available it was not difficult to find fault with local conditions. The most persistent complaints, however, were directed against civilians sent over from UN headquarters in New York, such as the chief administrative officer, who controlled the purse strings as well as the system of procurement. As far as the locals, there were complaints by Canadians about the effectiveness of labourers who were inclined to idle. Another accusation was that some of the workers supplied by the Egyptians were also spies used to keep the governor of Rafah informed about UN activities.[34] Armed Egyptian soldiers at checkpoints, road permits and a host of Egyptian bureaucratic rules could make life frustrating. On the other hand, Israel was seen as the green grass on the other side of the fence. As travel there was rarely given except for medical emergencies, it became all the more attractive. "Stories of bronzed amazons dressed in brief shorts and open blouses working in the fields whetted the appetites of lonely troops in the desert."[35]

The following excerpts from notes made at Rafah Camp by Sergeant D.R. Mathews, who was with 56 Infantry Workshop from November 1963 to November 1964, provide typical observations of an average serviceman:

The locals are easily aroused and can form uncontrollable mobs in a very short time. A mob can form in an instant and a knife can flash just as quickly. We have been told unofficially that if while driving we accidentally kill one of these people to keep on going.

Polygamy is a way of life here. A civilian employee pointed out a fellow worker with several wives. He was of the type you would least expect — a little tiny shrimp of a man.

The food that we get through normal rations is not the best quality . . . . The meat is usually, but not always, tough. Fowl is particularly prone to this condition . . . . The local food for some reason also tends to be very tough . . . . The army, however, never runs out of marmalade and one wonders why.

Every evening in camp is a challenge to see what film is being shown and whether it is worth the effort to attend.

The final months have been relatively quiet . . . . [36]

CANADIAN MORALE

The highlight for those on peacekeeping duty were the periods of leave. The UN provided leave centres in Alexandria and Beirut, from May to October and in Cairo in the winter. Prior to 1964 there was also a UNEF leave centre on Cyprus. Some made the slow arduous trip to St. Catherine's Monastery at Mount Sinai.[37] Some of the aircrews, however, took their leave at the end of their tour in order to visit Europe.

60

Among the memorable times for personnel of UNEF were Dominion Day celebrations. On such occasions there were special menus, sometimes entertainers from Canada. The different units would take part in various sport, float and variety-entertainment competitions. There were speeches praising the men for their efforts in helping to maintain world peace. Also memorable were the medal parades with the presentation of the UNEF medal. Those who served a tour can recall Canadian entertainers, politicians or other notables who paid a visit.

For the average Canadian soldier with UNEF, the one-year tour of duty was often boring. Some made good use of their leisure time and found it preferable, for example, to isolated postings in the Canadian North. There were various classes and hobby clubs for those so inclined. Some kept busy writing letters to loved ones. Whether enjoyed or not, the tour proved to be a memorable experience for all.

As time passed, greater effort went into improving recreational facilities. But most efforts were not devoted to selfish pastimes. There were voluntary gifts of water, food, clothing and money for the Palestinian refugees and Bedouins in the area. A Christmas charity drive in 1964 raised enough money for two kindergarten play centres. With a self-imposed tax on cigarettes, the Canadians contributed six thousand dollars for a maternity hospital and baby clinic for the Jabaliya Refugee Camp, as well as to a new Canadian medical centre for refugees operated by the United Nations Relief Works Agency at Khan Yunis.[38] A memorial fund for Palestinian refugee children was created in the name of Trooper R.H. Allan, who was shot by Egyptian troops while he was on patrol. The admission charged to watch inter-unit baseball games went to a children's ward at the hospital at Rafah.

But thoughts of home were always in the minds of the

peacekeepers. A poem written in 1957 by a member of UNEF, Private Robert Buckberry, Royal Canadian Ordnance Corps, sums up the common feeling of those on peacekeeping assignments:

THE MAGIC WORD

The word was out and all about
Our hearts were beating fast
It could not be . . . we could not see
How it had come at last!

The word was plain, was told again
On lake, canal and sea
No gift so fine, nor faith divine
was ever brought to me.

The word was true, and stories grew
Amid the heat and sand.
Not stories told of wine and gold
Or of the promised land.

But tales of wives and happy lives
Of cars, and TV screens;
On every face there was a trace
Of some nostalgic dreams.

This magic word
Is often heard
Wherever soldiers roam.
Within each heart
there is a part
That ever dreams of — HOME.[39]

Among the reasons why individuals could be returned to Canada before completing their tour were physical and mental illness, including alcoholism, compassionate grounds, a criminal offence or just general unsuitability. Any man discovered to be homosexual would be sent home. Anyone considered to be a coward would be ostracized by his peers and had to be removed. There is the story of one inebriated private, who was repatriated when his commanding officer spotted him attempting to copulate with a donkey. Overall, morale was satisfactory.

A WINDING DOWN OF UNEF I

In 1958, after UNEF's advance into the Sinai and its deployment along the International Frontier and Armistice Demarcation Line, the contingents of Colombia, Finland and Indonesia were withdrawn. To offset this decrease in strength, the contingents from Denmark/Norway, India and Sweden were reinforced. There was increasing pressure to replace military personnel with less costly local employees; consequently, by May 1967 the total number of military personnel was only 3,378.

Canada's external affairs minister, Lester Pearson, was awarded the 1957 Nobel Prize for peace for the creation of the first United Nations Emergency Force in 1956. Although 'Mike' Pearson deserved the award, the concept of such a force did not suddenly arise out of a vacuum; it evolved. A UN peacekeeping force in various forms had been proposed since the end of the Second World War. As the reader will see, Canada had participated previously in observer forces in Kashmir and Indochina. This award to Pearson, the first and only Canadian to receive it, also marked a form of recognition to Canada and the efforts of its representatives in helping to try to maintain peace.

For nearly ten years UNEF carried out observation and

patrol duties. Along the border between Syria and Israel raids and terrorism began to escalate. In November 1966 Egypt signed a mutual defence pact with Syria. The storm clouds of war were appearing once again in the Middle East.

3

THE WITHDRAWAL OF CANADA AND UNEF I FROM EGYPT

AS IN 1956, ARAB-ISRAELI tension had reached a critical level in 1967. The Palestine Liberation Organization (PLO) emerged in 1964 as a coordinating group for the Palestinians forced out of Israel and wanting their own Arab state. A terrorist campaign was initiated. The main guerrilla force of the PLO, al-Fatah, used Israel's Arab neighbours as bases for its attacks. This brought Israeli reprisals.

In the Arab world, President Gamal Abdel Nasser saw Syria growing in prestige as it pursued a policy of leading the fight against Israel. As well as training and arming Palestinians, the Syrians shelled Israeli farming communities on the plains below the Golan Heights. Syria appeared to be in the forefront of the struggle for the Palestinians in the Arab world.

Al-Fatah's acts of terrorism and sabotage, from its Syrian bases in 1966, inflamed Israeli opinion. An Israeli military raid against Jordan using tanks in November 1966 brought Arab League proposals for the withdrawal of UNEF. There were border clashes between Israel and Syria including an air battle on 7 April 1967. Further clashes were likely. The failure to see a new Middle East war brewing was not due to any lack of danger signals, but rather to a failure to read those many signals.[1] The Canadians were quite unaware what was about to happen although the withdrawal of their reconnaissance squadron in 1966, as a cost-saving measure, presaged the departure of the rest of the force.

President Nasser entered into a military alliance with Syria. When Soviet intelligence and Syrian President Hafiz al-Assad informed him that Israel was intending to attack Syria, Nasser moved his forces into the Sinai to Gaza. Jordan's King Hussein met with the Egyptian president in Cairo on 30 May 1967 and belatedly signed a mutual-defence pact with Egypt. Jordanian troops were placed under Egyptian command.

At ten o'clock on the evening of 16 May a military courier handed the UNEF commander, Major-General I.J. Rikhye, a career officer from India, a message from General Mahmoud Fawzi, chief of staff of the UAR[2] armed forces, demanding the withdrawal of UNEF forces from Egypt's border with Israel. General Rikhye was also informed that Egypt would take control of Sharm el Sheikh, thus gaining mastery of the Strait of Tiran and the Gulf of Aqaba as well as El Sabha, a strategic hill mass straddling the central approaches to the Negev. Rikhye refused to comply immediately but informed U Thant, the secretary-general, of the situation. U Thant ordered that the UNEF positions still be maintained. At noon (New York time) on May 18, the secretary-general received a request from the Egyptian government for the complete withdrawal of UNEF. Seven hours later, instructions were sent to the commander of UNEF to withdraw the force.

On 17 May Yugoslav camps located at El Quseima and El

Sabha found themselves behind UAR army positions. On 18 May at El Sabha, Yugoslav sentries — those not at a CBC "concert-party" — lost their observation post occupied by Egyptian soldiers the previous day without offering any resistance. President Nasser placed his forces on the international frontier. Next morning UNEF contingent commanders were informed that a withdrawal was to be carried out, and policing operations ceased.

At first it was thought RCAF aircraft of Air Transport Command would be allocated for the withdrawal but Canada was informed that Egypt would not permit military aircraft to land. Preparation then began for evacuation of the Canadian force by the Royal Canadian Navy[3] or possibly even by commercially chartered ships and aircraft.[4]

This was serious news. In case of hostilities there would be little possibility of commercial aircraft or ships entering a war zone. The Canadians could be stranded defenceless in the midst of the probable fighting. Casualties were a distinct possibility. On the positive side, the entertainment group with the CBC concert-party had been able to leave and a convoy managed to evacuate the Canadians from Sharm el Sheikh.[5]

On Thursday, 18 May, a Canadian Caribou aircraft on service with the UN was harassed by two Israeli fighters as it was travelling from El Arish to Gaza, and tried to force it to land in Israeli territory. On board was an Egyptian army captain and General Rikhye, who refused to allow the diversion. It was only with difficulty that Flying Officer R.J.V. Simpson of the RCAF was able to reach the landing field at Gaza.[6] Simpson later received a Queen's Commendation for bravery and his co-pilot was awarded one for service in the air.[7]

On Friday morning, 19 May, General Rikhye received U

Thant's instruction to withdraw in a dignified and orderly manner.[8] In order for the evacuation to be carried out, all contingents had to be concentrated. Three days later, prior to a visit by U Thant, Egypt took control of Sharm el Sheikh and announced a blockade of the Strait of Tiran.

Wing Commander J.W. Fitzsimmons, commander of 115 Air Transport Unit, flew General Rikhye to Cairo for a meeting with U Thant and President Nasser on 23 and 24 May. He was present for the discussions and kept the Canadian ambassador and military attaché informed. During the discussions Nasser told U Thant that Canada had undermined its own position in the Middle East. In particular, reference was made to Prime Minister Pearson's warm welcome of the then Israeli President Zalmar Shazar to Canada on 21 May. A visit to Canada by President Lyndon B. Johnson on 25 May further persuaded President Nasser that Canada was on the side of the United States and Israel.[9]

Three Canadian warships were proceeding towards the Mediterranean to retrieve the Canadians and their equipment when, on 27 May, President Nasser demanded of the secretary-general a "complete withdrawal and departure of Canadian forces immediately and not later than forty-eight hours from the time my cable reaches you."[10] The Egyptian note of 27 May indicated that Canada's attitude and the dispatch of destroyers had inflamed Egyptian public opinion. Faced with this demand, U Thant agreed to the request. In reality, only a few Egyptians knew about the Canadian warships[11] as no such information had appeared in the Egyptian media. The Canadian government's bias in favour of Israel was the excuse given by the Egyptian press to demand Canada's withdrawal. The lack of contingency planning by the UN had forced Canada to move its ships towards the Mediterranean and near the Azores in case no other means of evacuation was possible. Fortunately, as events were later to show, Nasser luckily gave Canada — and Canada alone — the opportunity for a timely withdrawal.

CANADIAN PLANS BECOME REALITY

The new Egyptian demand for Canada's immediate withdrawal was made known to the Canadian government at 1:00 p.m. (Ottawa time) on 27 May.[12] As a result firm arrangements were begun. Air Transport Command would supply C-130 Hercules and Yukon aircraft. The aircraft would land at Pisa, a stopover point already frequently used for NATO and UN operations. The place of departure for the Canadians was to be El Arish, Egypt having given its approval. The withdrawal was to commence on the morning of Monday, 29 May. At 11:00 p.m. (Ottawa time) that Monday the sea evacuation plan was cancelled.[13]

Late on Saturday night, 27 May, General Rikhye informed Colonel D.H. Power, commander of the Canadian Base Units, of the new Egyptian evacuation demand. The Canadian Base Units of UNEF had some ten years accumulation of regimental and unit equipment. Although much of the heavy items such as vehicles were left behind, important communications equipment was saved. In approximately twenty-five working hours from 29 to 31 May, eighteen flights of Hercules[14] aircraft withdrew about seven hundred men and 232,110 pounds of equipment. (The Canadians were able to obtain an extra working day to evacuate passengers and freight.)

The commander of the Canadian contingent, Colonel Power, followed a course of action that best ensured the safety of

69

his men. He was faced with a variety of instructions and he discerned the most suitable alternative. The transfer of his men and equipment from Rafah Camp to the El Arish Airport with much of their equipment in a short space of time was no small feat. The speed of Air Transport Command in reacting to this crisis was outstanding.

THE EVACUATION FROM EL ARISH

As usual, a beautiful sunrise welcomed the Canadians that Monday, 29 May 1967. Also greeting the Canadians very early that morning was the noise of a C-130 from Trenton, Ontario, as it flew over the Canadian quarters to El Arish Airport. That day, Flight Lieutenant Michael Belcher, among the last Canadians left behind, witnessed their residence known as "the Marina" transformed into bedlam. As the Canadians hastily departed, Egyptian workers and house boys went on a looting rampage. Everything that was moveable, even Christmas decorations, disappeared. Nearby, Mike Belcher observed the road outside the camp gate clogged with T-34 and T-54 Russian tanks on their way toward Gaza with Egyptian troops enthusiastically chanting, "Tel Aviv in three days" as they passed.

Late that afternoon the commanding officer finally retrieved Belcher who had managed to destroy ciphers, codes and classified documents. Together, in a UN staff car, they headed for the El Arish Airport ignoring Egyptian roadblocks and obstacles. At the airport they scampered aboard the last Caribou with the last evacuees and, as they took off, bade adieu to Egypt. As they flew off, the CO called Belcher forward and said with a smile, "I just looked down at our headquarters building and YOU forgot to lower the flag."[15]

THE SIX DAY WAR

With Arab armies on her borders, the Gulf of Aqaba closed to her ships and the Arab media calling for the destruction of the Jewish state, the Israelis struck first. On 5 June, the Israeli air force launched a preemptive strike against Arab airfields, first in Egypt, then Jordan, Syria and Iraq. With air superiority from the outset, Israeli forces were able in six days to capture the Sinai Peninsula from Egypt, the West Bank of the Jordan River including East Jerusalem from Jordan and the Golan Heights from Syria. A cease-fire eventually was established and UNTSO was called upon to supervise the new cease-fire lines.

UNEF AMIDST HOSTILITIES

No sooner had the Canadian unit left Rafah Camp than looting by civilian inhabitants of the region also began. It took Brazilian troops about two days to restore order. The other national contingents of UNEF began to make arrangements to leave. Only an advance withdrawal party of the Swedish battalion and about half of the Yugoslav contingent had been evacuated when the war started. The casualties of the Indian and Brazilian contingents during hostilities provide an indication as to what might have happened to the Canadians had they remained. During the fighting, Indian casualties totalled fourteen killed and twenty wounded. The Brazilian

71

battalion, which had taken over from the Canadians at Rafah Camp, had one soldier killed by machine-gun fire. The casualties were accidental and the consequence of UN forces being in a battle zone next to Arab forces. The UN force was finally evacuated through the Israeli port of Ashdod, not off the beaches near Gaza as planned by General Rikhye. Although Rikhye had been unable to complete a phased withdrawal by train from Gaza to Port Said, he succeeded in concentrating the bulk of his force on the Gaza beaches where most of the UNEF troops were safe from the fighting.[16]

CONCLUSIONS

Although Canadian troops with UNEF were placed under the control of the UN, the responsibility for their withdrawal and safety became that of their own country. Fortunately, the armed forces at the time had the aircraft to effect a speedy and safe evacuation. One thing that this episode did point out was the need for direct global communication especially between Air Transport Command at Trenton, Ontario, and 115 Air Transport Unit, and between National Defence in Ottawa and Canadian forces in Egypt. The status of forces agreement had deprived the Canadian contingent of a direct radio communication link with Canada—apart from a "ham" set which could only be used for personal messages. Official messages had to be relayed through the Egyptian system of radio, telegraph or telephone. The separation of authority between 115 Air Transport Unit under headquarters Air Transport Command and the 700-man Canadian contingent located a short distance away under Colonel Power, created a communication problem when the time came for the Canadians to withdraw.[17] Fortunately, this was overcome. Recent liaison visits from staff officers at headquarters in Ottawa had helped make the final evacuation easier as a result of knowledge of the area and personal contact established by officers at both ends of the chain of command.[18]

Some three years prior to the Canadian forces ignominious exit from Egypt, the Canadian government sponsored an international conference on peacekeeping. In response a good number of speeches were given on the subject, highlighting past problems and suggesting likely solutions. Among the many problems that Canadian military personnel pointed out were the necessity of dealing with a mixture of equipment that created logistical difficulties and the variety of languages among force members. A more important requirement was an adequate intelligence unit. These recommendations were ignored for the operation of UNEF I; however, intelligence for the Canadians was improved for UNEF II.

The United Nations Emergency Force cost Canada some five million dollars annually or approximately fifty-five million dollars during its existence. Thirty-two Canadian servicemen lost their lives in the Middle East, seven of whom were killed while on duty.

The multilingual, multinational nature of the force from so many different parts of the world created problems. But these were overcome. It was the way the force was organized that caused the most aggravation. The structure of UNEF was scattered, with its headquarters based at Gaza and a large unwieldy command structure. In spite of weaknesses, the force did function, and served a useful if temporary purpose.

After ten and a half years of successful service, the Canadians had to abruptly pull out. They left behind a record so creditable that they were asked to contribute again in 1973.

Today, a UNEF medal remains the only concrete reminder for many of the year of their lives devoted to preserving peace in that troubled area of the world.

The expulsion of the Canadians from Egypt and the abrupt termination of UNEF I came as a shock to many people in Canada. It led to a disillusionment with the concept of peacekeeping and with the United Nations. The negative results of that experience have persisted.

4

UNITED NATIONS YEMEN
OBSERVATION MISSION

WHILE CANADIANS KNEW ABOUT UNEF, there was, during its existence, another peacekeeping sideshow about which most were unaware. This may have been because Canadian attention was also diverted by another large-scale peacekeeping operation in the Congo. Trouble arose in Yemen and Canada again contributed peacekeepers, but on a smaller scale.

INTRODUCTION

The Yemen Arab Republic is situated in the southwestern part of the Arabian Peninsula. It consists of a narrow coastal plain along the Red Sea next to a rugged interior comprised of mountains rising as high as 12,000 feet. Its eastern region is largely desert. The hot climate and barren, rugged terrain do not make life the most pleasant for its inhabitants. The

Canadians of 134 Air Transport Unit, supporting the peace-keeping operations in Yemen, found it a tough assignment and would agree that the area merits its title as "the country God forgot."

BACKGROUND

In 1962 the two major Arab states contending for power and influence in Yemen were Egypt, or the United Arab Republic under President Nasser, and Saudi Arabia under a monarchy, the House of Sa'ud. In September the monarchy in Yemen was overthrown by a pro-Egyptian army leader, Colonel Abdullah al-Salal, who later became the president. President Nasser promptly recognized the newly proclaimed Yemen Arab Republic. The United Nations and the United States both recognized the new republic in December.

While the new revolutionary government controlled the cities and towns in the centre, the south, and on the western sea coast of Yemen, the intensely royalist tribesmen resisted the new regime. They controlled the northwest and southeast mountains and the deserts of the east. To contain and possibly overthrow the new government in Yemen, Saudi Arabia assisted the Yemeni tribesmen with arms and other military supplies. In turn, Nasser's United Arab Republic sent arms, military personnel and supplies to help consolidate the new regime.

Early in 1963, the UN secretary-general, U Thant, became alarmed at the intensification of fighting in Yemen. After negotiations with Saudi Arabia, the UAR and Yemen, the secretary-general reported on 29 April that each of the three governments party to the dispute confirmed their acceptance of identical terms of disengagement in Yemen. While Saudi Arabia agreed to end all support and aid to the royalist forces and deny its territory to them, the UAR undertook to begin a phased withdrawal of its troops from Yemen and cease further military activities. In addition, it was agreed that a demilitarized zone would be established twenty kilometres or just over twelve miles on each side of the Yemeni-Saudi Arabian border, and UN observers would be stationed to check on compliance of the terms of disengagement. The observers would also be able to travel freely to certify that the UAR and Saudi Arabia were conforming to the terms of the disengagement.[1]

At the end of April, Major-General Carl von Horn of Sweden, chief of UNTSO in Jerusalem and formerly with the UN force in the Congo, along with Major E.R. Sharpe, a Canadian, proceeded to assess the situation and the requirements. On 3 May 1963 Air Chief Marshal F.R. Miller, chairman of the chiefs of staff, was advised that Canada would be asked to assist in air operations in Yemen. Members of the Canadian forces working with UNEF and UNTSO helped establish the operation and organize UNYOM headquarters.[2]

On 10 June, U Thant announced to the UN Security Council that there would be no cost to the UN for the mission in Yemen as the UAR and Saudi Arabia had agreed to split the costs.[3] While this sounded optimistic, in reality neither party was adhering to disengagement terms. It was hoped, nevertheless, that once the observer team was there, it would constitute a face-saving device for the Saudis and Egyptians. The UN force for the Yemen, composed of troops withdrawn from UN operations in the Congo and the Middle East, numbered about two hundred. It began to arrive on 13 June 1963. General von Horn was named head of the mission. He established his headquarters at Sana in the former monarch's palace and named Colonel Branko Pavlovic, a Yugoslav, his second-in-command.

The headquarters for the United Nations Yemen Observation Mission was established at Sana, Yemen. A 100 to 125-man Yugoslavian reconnaissance unit from UNEF originally had one troop based at Najran (Nijran), one at Quizan (Jizan), both in Saudi Arabia, and one at Sada, Yemen. Three observers were stationed at Sana and three at Al Hudaydah (Hodeida) in Yemen. A headquarters for the RCAF air unit was set up at Sana (134 Air Transport Unit), with detachments at Najran and Quizan. A logistics base for the operation was located at Gaza.

A Caribou and an Otter aircraft assigned to an advance party from 115 Air Transport Unit, based at El Arish, departed on 11 and 12 June respectively. Their safety became precarious with the bombing of airstrips at Quizan and Najran on 15 June. On 16 June, the Caribou suffered light damage from ground fire.[4] RCAF personnel were advised to carry side arms.

Squadron Leader A. I. Umbach of Ottawa, commander of 134 Air Transport Unit, and four others departed from Trenton, Ontario, on 18 June 1963 and arrived at Aden, South Yemen, two days later. The main body left on 22 June. A Yukon transported the RCAF personnel to Pisa and a C-130 to Aden.

Four Otters were based in Saudi Arabia, two at Quizan and two at Najran and they were used to carry out air patrols to observe ground activity, such as the flow of arms. Two Caribous were based in Sana where they were primarily employed in logistic support to the mission outposts within Yemen as well as transport and liaison to neighbouring countries. In spite of the aircraft, the size of the UN force was inadequate for the job.

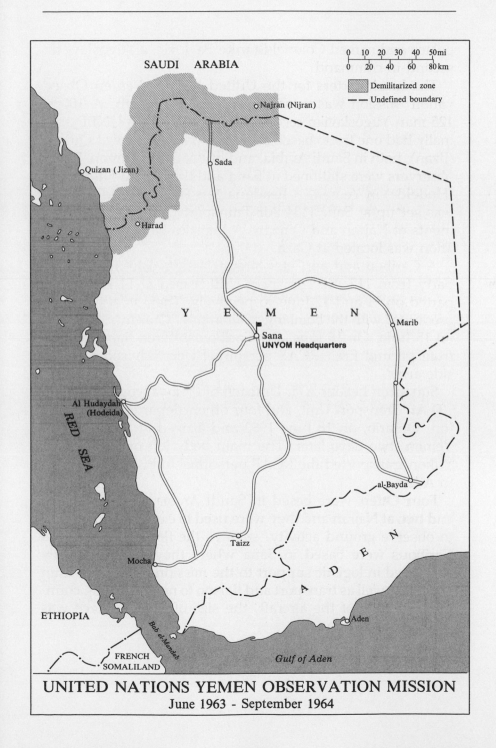

UNITED NATIONS YEMEN OBSERVATION MISSION
June 1963 - September 1964

THE FIRST MANDATE

The UN civilian staff at Sana was approximately fifty and in the whole area it was ninety-six. Accommodation was acquired at Sana in the oddly-shaped, crowded rooms of a hotel converted from a battle-scarred, mud-brick building that had formerly housed the monarch's concubines. An attraction for a while was the main gate of Sana adorned with heads of unfortunate politicians and criminals.

The official date of the implementation of UNYOM was 4 July 1963. That was the arrival date of most of the 114 Yugoslav reconnaissance troops equipped with jeeps and light trucks from UNEF. The Canadian air contingent of fifty officers and men was in place by 20 July.

Patrols were begun to familiarize the pilots with the area, but it was soon found necessary to fly the Otters in pairs because of poor air-to-ground communication and for mutual assistance in case of trouble. The featureless terrain and low visibility also made navigation difficult. There were also problems in communications with Egyptian control-tower operators who spoke very little English. In addition, if UAR aircraft were departing from or arriving at an airfield, UN aircraft were not permitted to fly to or from it at the same time. At Quizan the men were quartered in a former meteorological office and subjected to intense heat. At Najran only tents were used as shelter and the men suffered from constantly blowing sand and dust. Air patrols from Sana began early in the day because it was essential to get back before three o'clock when storm clouds would close the airfield and it would invariably rain for a brief period.

The RCAF ground crew operated under extreme conditions of heat and sandstorms and all repairs were carried out in the open. Dust and sand penetrated clothing and all parts of the aircraft making their maintenance very difficult. Living conditions and frustration at the UN's inability to curb the fighting caused the morale of the Canadians to decline. The initial diet of packed rations did not help. None of the local meat and vegetables were medically acceptable. This problem was solved by the importation of fresh rations via a weekly North Star flight from El Arish and supplemented by fresh vegetables and some fruit imported from Ethiopia. The rocky terrain hampered outdoor sports so card games were played inside to pass the time.[5] The men were crammed together, three, four and more to a room, and could not leave their quarters from sunset to dawn because their safety could not be assured.

Incidents involving aircraft bear testimony that hostilities had not ceased. The Otters based at Najran were fired upon on 16 and 17 August, one of the Otters having its starboard wing creased by a rifle bullet. Between 23 and 26 August both Otters based at Najran and one of the Caribous were hit by ground fire. As a result of poor UN organization, there were shortages of gasoline, spare parts, and even food.

At the end of the month General von Horn resigned as commander. Among his reasons were insufficient air and logistical assistance from UNEF I in Egypt, poor administrative support from UN headquarters, inadequate leave for UNYOM personnel and a shortage of medical facilities. Von Horn also felt hampered from being allowed to make official contact with the Yemeni royalists.[6]

The Second Mandate

UNYOM continued to operate through September and October 1963 in its second mandate. Due to Saudi Arabia's lack of firm commitment to continue financial support, there was some uncertainty as to whether the operation would continue. The UAR and Saudi Arabia finally agreed to finance the operation for another two months. The new commander of UNYOM was Major-General P.S. Gyani of India.

While the Canadian Caribou aircraft were used principally on logistic, liaison flights and reconnaissance, the Otters were used on daily patrols in the Quizan and Najran areas. However, there was growing doubt about the value of Otter aircraft that did not have oxygen equipment for flying at high altitudes.

Canada was requested to continue its air unit and three staff officers for two additional months beyond 4 November — the anticipated termination date of UNYOM — and Ottawa agreed. The necessity of providing additional Caribous to replace the Otters in Yemen was also apparent. The Otters were becoming a burden due to their continuing and extensive maintenance requirements and were found to be unsuitable for the assignment in Yemen. Air patrols were ineffective because they could only observe traffic by day. For climatic reasons, overland travel was customary during the hours of darkness when it was cooler.

The Third Mandate — Reorganization

Upon another extension of UNYOM in early November 1963, the secretary-general named Pier P. Spinelli, the director of the European office of the UN, as special representative of the secretary-general in Yemen and as head of UNYOM to succeed General Gyani. Spinelli's appointment signalled a change in the complexion of UNYOM from an observer to a more political role. A political solution, not observing or reporting, was required.

The Yugoslav contingent was withdrawn, the final group leaving on 25 November, but the number of military observers was increased to almost twenty-five. Canada's air contribution was also changed. Personnel were reduced and Otter aircraft were replaced by Caribous. The nature of their assignment also shifted from air patrolling to logistic support. 134 Air Transport Unit became a detachment of 115 Air Transport Unit at El Arish, Egypt.[7]

A December visit by Flight Lieutenant Peter Kelly, a medical officer from Air Transport Command, Trenton, to investigate the living conditions and health of the Canadian contingent, helped open the eyes of higher authorities. Complaints were substantiated that security of aircraft and personnel accommodation was totally inadequate in Yemen.

A report to RCAF headquarters from Air Transport Command, Trenton, Ontario, on 20 December summed up the frustration:

There is a feeling in UN circles that Canadians are an easy touch and more malleable than other nationalities . . . . We seem to them to be capable of existing on promises . . . . We begin operations with less than adequate United Nations provided facilities and equipment. The worst example of this is Yemen where living conditions of RCAF personnel are simply described as atrocious. The degradation of Canadian standards of hygiene, health, sleeping and eating is too much to expect of Canadian servicemen in peacetime operations . . . . We in the RCAF have reached the peak of our endurance in the filthy living environment of Yemen . . . .

The third extension of the UN mandate in Yemen resulted in continued Canadian participation in UNYOM until early September 1964.[8] The air staff officer of UNYOM initially resisted the removal of any RCAF aircraft and personnel from Yemen, but later agreed as the conflict resulted in an increasing threat to the lives of the men. On 15 September the last RCAF aircraft left Yemen and returned to Trenton, Ontario. Thus ended Canada's active participation in this peacekeeping operation totalling one year and three months.

UNYOM was finally terminated as a result of Saudi Arabia's decision not to continue funding or to abide by the mission's terms. The UAR had no objections to the ending of UNYOM as it was unwilling to stop its intervention.

CONCLUSION

Following the UN withdrawal on 4 September 1964, the dispute continued. After the defeat of the UAR in the Israeli-Arab War of 1967, UAR troops were withdrawn from Yemen. Saudi Arabia also reduced her support for the royalists. By 1970 the civil war had come to an end and the Yemen Arab Republic took control of its own destiny.

5

UNITED NATIONS PEACEKEEPING FORCE

IN CYPRUS

BACKGROUND

IN GREEK MYTHOLOGY, CYPRUS is known as the island of love. Historically, however, the island has been a battlefield for thousands of years. Greek culture and language were first introduced about the fifteenth century BC. Cyprus was subsequently ruled, conquered and colonized by a wide variety of powers such as Assyria, Egypt, Persia, Greece, Rome, the Arabs, the Crusaders and the city states of Genoa and Venice. The Ottoman Turks began to settle on the island in 1571. Great Britain annexed Cyprus on the outbreak of the First World War and made it a Crown colony in 1925. The movement for union with Greece increased after the end of the Second World War. A terrorist campaign against British rule eventually led to an agreement signed in London on 19 February 1959. It provided for the setting up of an independent Cypriot republic within a year. Britain was to retain sovereignty over military bases at Dhekelia and Akrotiri.

At the time of its independence from Britain in 1960, Cyprus had a population of about 650,000. Of these 78 percent were Greek-Cypriots, 18 percent Turkish-Cypriots, and 4 percent minorities divided into small communities. Tension had been growing between the Greek and Turkish communities following independence but mutual hatred was centuries deep.

A PEACEKEEPING FORCE

On 30 November 1963, the president of the republic, Archbishop Makarios, attempted to amend previously agreed constitutional arrangements. He argued that the existing constitution was causing the two communities to draw further apart rather than closer together. Makarios' proposals included: the abolition of the veto power of the president (Greek) and vice-president (Turk); the abolition of separate majorities required from either community in their House of Representatives in order to enact certain laws; the establishment of unified municipalities; the unification of the administration of justice; and the reduction of the agreed proportion of Turkish-Cypriots in the public service and military forces.

Trouble soon erupted. There was vicious communal violence in December of that year and again in early 1964. British troops based in the south of the island were interposed as a stopgap solution. The imminent threat of invasion by Turkish armed forces and the likelihood of war between Greece and Turkey were countered by UN mediation. As an interim measure, on 4 March 1964, the Security Council gave approval to a resolution establishing a temporary peacekeeping force. The Soviet Union had objected to interference by NATO.

On 11 March, Turkey announced that it was intervening unless the UN force was on the island within a few days. Paul Martin, Canada's secretary of state for external affairs, flew down to New York on 12 March to meet U Thant. On Friday the 13th, Martin made a series of telephone calls to various capitals, and by 6:00 p.m. U Thant was announcing that a UN force would be constituted. The same evening, in emergency session, Parliament authorized the dispatch of a Canadian contingent. Some of the troops, however, were en route even before Parliament gave its approval.[1] An order in council subsequently authorized a contingent not exceeding twelve hundred at any one time.[2] Originally, it was believed the Canadians would only be required on Cyprus for three months.

The advance party with the Canadian contingent commander Colonel E.A.C. Amy, flew to Nicosia arriving on 15 March 1964. They were followed the next day by RCAF Air Transport Command's first flight with part of an 1,100-man contingent composed of the 1st Battalion, Royal 22e Régiment, and the reconnaissance squadron of the Royal Canadian Dragoons. Heavy vehicles and materiel along with ninety-five personnel arrived two weeks later aboard Canada's only aircraft carrier, HMCS *Bonaventure*. Three weeks after the Security Council's original resolution of 4 March, the Canadian contingent became the first to be operational. The suddenness of the Canadian move helped convince Turkey to call off an invasion or possible air and naval attacks.[3] It was not until the end of June that the entire UNFICYP force was assembled.

HMCS *BONAVENTURE*

The *Bonaventure, Magnificent*'s successor, departed Halifax on 18 March in a heavy snowstorm with men of the "Van Doos" (Royal 22e Régiment), the Royal Canadian Dragoons and the Royal Canadian Army Service Corps, along with sixteen Ferret scout cars, thirty-six trucks and trailers, two jeeps and 160 tons of army stores as well as aviation fuel. The soldiers wore running shoes instead of boots with steel cleats or hobnails for fear a spark might ignite fumes from the aviation fuel. Apart from two civilian stowaways found smoking in the back of a truck, the journey through heavy seas was uneventful. One of the stowaways was a baker running away from his wife and five children. The stopover at Gibraltar on 25 March lasted only five hours. The aircraft carrier then speeded on its way arriving at the port of Famagusta, Cyprus at the end of March. Under a balmy Mediterranean sun, men and vehicles were put ashore.[4] The Canadian contribution included force headquarters troops as well as an infantry battalion and a reconnaissance squadron. The force's first assignment was to patrol Nicosia and a hundred-square mile area in the north central part of the island.

STATUS OF THE FORCE

Every peacekeeping operation had its particular difficulties. The Congo peacekeeping mission was the most complex in terms of role and operations. The force in the Sinai was better organized than the one in the Congo but the UN effort in Cyprus was probably the most ordered of all. UNFICYP took the longest space of time to become operational. It also had the help of the British forces there for headquarters' staff assistance, organization and logistical backing. In contrast, UNEF I and II as well as the Congo force were much more hurriedly organized and dispatched.

The status of forces agreement for UNEF I formed the basis for a similar agreement on Cyprus. Terms included the right to use force in self-defence as well as exclusive criminal and disciplinary jurisdiction over its members by the soldiers' parent state.

Under the terms setting up the peacekeeping force in Cyprus, its commander was to report directly to the secretary-general, who, in turn, was to report to the UN Security Council. A mediator was also to be appointed to seek a permanent solution to the situation. UN forces were organized to replace British troops stationed at two British sovereign bases as well as others flown from Great Britain. Some of the British troops remained as part of the UN force. The arrival of troops from Canada and later, Denmark, Finland, Ireland and Sweden did not stop all the violence.

1964-1974

The UN forces were powerless to disarm the combatants. Their presence, however, prevented major operations by both sides. Consequently many lives were saved. In spite of sporadic fighting and killings, an uneasy truce came to prevail between Greeks and Turks on the island and, as a result of the stalemate, UNFICYP's mandate was repeatedly extended.

The Canadians were the first troops to arrive from abroad and begin work as peacekeepers in April 1964. In the initial deployment of troops in Cyprus, the Canadian contingent

(Cancon) was deployed along a "Green Line,"[5] a buffer zone set up by British troops to separate Greek- and Turkish-Cypriots in Nicosia. Portions of the line were later manned by Danish and Finnish troops. Two companies of the Van Doos moved into deserted homes, stores, factories and apartment buildings between the combatants. This Canadian occupation confirmed the Green Line which came to be respected by both factions, even though each tried to encroach on the other's territory.

The main centre of tension, the Nicosia Zone, came under a Canadian commander, Brigadier A.J. Tedlie of UNFICYP. He reported to General P.S. Gyani. Goodwill on all sides enabled a rather hodgepodge UNFICYP organization to function smoothly.

Every soldier who has served on peacekeeping duty can remember the particular circumstances at the time of being called out. Lieutenant Jacques Grenier of the Van Doos recalled that he was about to be married, and as a result of a sudden recall, his wedding and a large reception had to be cancelled on short notice. Brigadier Tedlie wrote how he learned of his appointment:

One day in early April 1964 while commanding 2nd Infantry Brigade Group I was watching infantry-tank cooperation training in the area of Gust Point at Camp Petawawa, Ontario. My radio operator, Corporal Evans, was chatting away on the wireless set when I heard him say 'I'll fetch Sunray' (or the commander). It made me shudder as it usually was a prelude to news of an accident at the worst and a disagreement between participants in the exercise at best. Evans told me that the vice-chief of the general staff wanted me to phone him. Within the half hour I was on the phone with Major-General Paul Bernatchez. His message was short and to the point. Headquarters of the United Nations in New York had requested that Canada supply a reinforced brigade headquarters to replace the British 16th Parachute

Brigade headquarters who were now exercising control of United Nations forces operating in the vicinity of Nicosia.

As is true with all military operations our preliminary information was scarce and sometimes contradictory . . . . We were advised that the planes flying us to Nicosia should be combat loaded and ready for immediate action on landing. This caused quite a laugh on more than one account. First, was the impossibility of loading a Yukon aircraft to allow immediate combat readiness on touch-down. The second, was preparing a plan of how we would leave the aircraft. I had a personal problem in that I had to ask Gordie Wetherup, a valuable addition to the Brigade Staff to load my pistol for I had forgotten that fine art in my desk-bound years . . . . After make-shift attempts to look warlike, we were formally met upon landing by a welcoming party consisting of Arthur Andrew, the Canadian high commissioner, along with other UN and Canadian dignitaries . . . . It was not at all what we expected.[6]

Living conditions for the Canadians were difficult at first. When the Van Doos and the Royal Canadian Dragoons arrived they slept under the stars and later in abandoned buildings but mostly in tents. They ate British rations and organized their own recreation. The Canadian support echelon, located in a tented camp to the north of Nicosia Airport, was called Troodos Road Camp. The British troops supplied reconnaissance personnel who guided the Canadians as they dashed about the island in those early days in British-marked vehicles to demonstrate the UN presence and show the UN flag.

Most of the Canadian heavy equipment was transported by the *Bonaventure*. Some lighter vehicles, such as jeeps, were flown to the island aboard Yukon aircraft. Both the Royal Canadian Air Force and the Royal Canadian Navy gave outstanding support.

Both Greek- and Turkish-Cypriots initially greeted the Canadians with cheering and flowers.[7] Warrant Officer 2 E.P Carey of the Royal Canadian Dragoons claims he received a rosebush in the face. When the Van Doos tried to dismantle a Turkish roadblock, Turkish women threw sticks, stones and mud. A settlement was eventually negotiated.[8]

Perhaps the most exciting time for the Canadians from 1964 to 1974 was when they first arrived on the island. The Canadians' blend of diplomacy and toughness helped solve many a troublesome situation. In mid-April 1964, Major Patrick Tremblay, of Quebec City, commanding C Company of the Van Doos, found himself between a cross-fire of Greeks and Turks in the mountains dominating the road to the Greek-Cypriot port of Kyrenia. When the Turks refused to stop, he ordered sixty rounds of .30-calibre fire in their general direction. After that, they were more cooperative.[9]

The 1st Battalion of the Royal 22e Régiment under Lieutenant-Colonel J.A. Woodcock took over responsibilities in Nicosia as well as the Kyrenia area near the end of April. The Van Doos were kept very busy trying to separate battling Greeks and Turks. At times the Canadians faced bullets, threats and insults from both parties.

There were many instances of individual heroism. One example was a reconnaissance patrol led by Company Sergeant-Major Georges Ouellet of Levis, Quebec. He received the British Empire Medal for rescuing twelve Greek-Cypriot farmers from Turkish gunfire and successfully negotiating a cease-fire on 10 April.

Trying to keep the status quo or stop fighting was not easy. One of the most frustrating tasks was to prevent both sides from building new fortifications and improving their positions. "Delta Force," a mobile multinational reserve group, was created to meet and deal with incidents and tensions as they developed. Surprise and speed were used to dismantle new positions.

To help offset the buildup of heavy arms and equipment

by either Greek- or Turkish-Cypriot forces, Canada provided an anti-tank platoon equipped with jeep-mounted, 106-millimeter recoilless rifles. The unit of about twenty-five men arrived on 15 August and, along with a troop of Ferret scout cars, was held in reserve by Nicosia Zone headquarters.

On 21 September 1964, the Turks blocked the strategic Kyrenia road which linked Nicosia to the port city of Kyrenia and included the Kyrenia Pass. After much negotiation, agreement was reached on 23 October to reopen the road to Greek-Cypriot traffic. The Canadians were among the UN troops who then provided escorts from Nicosia to Kyrenia and back.

In December 1964 Finnish troops relieved the Canadians in Nicosia who had been assigned this key Nicosia-Kyrenia road. One Canadian company was sent to Oneisha Farm, one to Kyrenia and the other remained between Greek and Turkish forces. By September 1965, the situation in and around Nicosia had stabilized and the Nicosia Zone headquarters was disbanded to allow the more efficient use of available manpower.

The Canadians' main problem area was the Green Line. The Canadians were in shooting and even shouting distance of both opposing forces and this required more interpersonal skills of negotiation and communication than, for example, with UNEF I where the antagonists were much further apart.

From the battalion headquarters of the Royal 22e Régiment, an abandoned apartment building in downtown Nicosia, there was not much of interest to see. Homes and shops on either side of the Green Line had been abandoned by their owners and taken over by Greek and Turkish soldiers. The real power on the island lay not so much with the politicians but with those who controlled the military forces. As

Brigadier Tedlie wrote to his wife on 1 October 1964 near the end of his stint:

What a panic, most, if not all, caused by the gross stupidity of those in power in New York . . . . Day after day, night after night, I prepare new plans knowing that none of them could possibly be implemented as the [UN] political leaders are not dealing with the people who hold the power but with those who are nominally in charge . . . . The whole thing is getting me down to the point that I can't wait to see the last of it.

After more than two years of living in abandoned buildings or tents, the Canadians were able to obtain the use of buildings formerly housing the RAF next to the Nicosia Airport west of the city. This was a substantial improvement as they received solid sandstone huts, proper messes, a medical examination room and sufficient warehousing as well as operations rooms. This became Camp Maple Leaf, the home away from home for Canadian units. The site of the camp was subsequently moved and moved again. Recreational facilities were limited but leisure time could be spent by counting airplanes, bird watching and bar hopping.

Recreational facilities were gradually improved for both leave periods and non-working hours. A swimming pool was built and tennis courts were repaired. Leave centres were set up off the island as well as in its northern and eastern sections. A library, movies, swimming, scuba diving and boating became available. Bus trips were offered to various tourist sites on Cyprus. The Canadians established themselves as congenial hosts. Cocktail parties, dinings-in and mess dinners helped create a harmonious atmosphere with the other contingents.

Although there was a high degree of cooperation among the different national contingents, not all problems could be resolved. At one point the high rate of venereal disease was discussed. Wayne Sparks from Debec, New Brunswick, who served with the UN Military Police in 1965-66 recalls:

The Finns, Danes and Austrians were all for inspection of certain 'houses' by detecting and treating those affected. The British and Canadian representatives nixed the idea because of political implications. The Irish resisted on religious grounds.[10]

As a result, there was no resolution of the problem.

For most of those who served six months with UNFICYP the tour was uneventful. A typical excerpt is taken for 27 February 1965 from the war diary of the Reconnaissance Squadron of Lord Strathcona's Horse:

0800 The squadron completed its battle efficiency test except for a small group who still have to attempt the 2 mile run . . . .

0830 The weekly rotation of troops took place.

1200 The weekly maintenance flight arrived from Canada bringing parcels and papers for the squadron.

1215 The morning convoy totals were:
1. One car, 1 truck and 1 MC [motorcycle] escorted to Kyrenia.
2. Five cars, 2 vans, 4 trucks and 2 MC escorted to Nicosia.

1500 Four personnel from the squadron departed on seven days leave to Beirut.

1630 The squadron softball team was defeated 8-5 by a team from HQ Nicosia Zone.

1730 The afternoon convoy totals were:
1. Forty-one cars, 1 bus, 1 van and 3 trucks escorted to Kyrenia.
2. Three cars, 1 bus and 1 van escorted to Nicosia.

1830 The squadron movie was *Carry on Admiral*.

The strength of the Canadian contingent reached a high

of over 1,100 in 1964-1965 of a total force of 6,500. As tension had subsided by 1969, UNFICYP was reduced by about half and reorganized. The Canadians were relieved of their northern patrol task and returned to their earlier assignment of manning the Green Line in Nicosia. Two infantry companies and the reconnaissance squadron were withdrawn. Vehicles, such as the Ferret scout cars, were no longer required and were reassigned to duties elsewhere. When hostilities broke out anew in July 1974, the Canadian contingent's operational strength numbered approximately 480. At the request of UN headquarters, Canada increased its contribution to some 950. This contribution was reduced to 790 in late December 1974 and the Canadians became responsible for Nicosia East and the airfield. By 1978 the Canadian contingent was further reduced to some five hundred as it was before the 1974 crisis, and the Canadians were given responsibility for one of the five sectors along the cease-fire line including Nicosia.

UNFICYP has varied in strength from its beginning on 27 March 1964. At its peak in that year it consisted of 6,500 soldiers. From 1965 to 1968, troop numbers averaged around 4,500; from 1969 to 1974 they were about 3,500. In addition, a UN civilian staff served as political and legal advisers, administrators, secretaries, procurement and public-relations officers.

During the years 1964 to 1974, UNFICYP's main concern was to prevent a recurrence of serious fighting. There were, however, numerous small battles between both communities. The most serious occurred in November 1967 near Kophinou. The Greeks were led by General Georgios Grivas, the military mastermind of the guerrilla campaign of 1955-1959 to oust the British, gain independence for Cyprus and eventually union with Greece. Negotiations brought about a Greek withdrawal and averted a threatened invasion by Turkey.

The Greek-Cypriots constantly strove to impose their view of a unitary state and majority rule and eliminate the separatist features in their previously agreed constitution with the Turkish-Cypriot community. The Turkish community preferred independence with their own separate territory. While talks and incidents continued and little progress toward a solution was made, what developed was a form of partition of the island. The Turks controlled a number of enclaves, the most important being located on the east coast at Famagusta in the port area, and in the region between Nicosia and Kyrenia.

INVASION

On 20 July 1974 this stalemate was broken. Turkey invaded Cyprus. The invasion was in response to an attempt by the military regime in Greece to bring about *enosis* (the union of Cyprus with Greece) by means of a military coup on 15 July that temporarily toppled Archbishop Makarios's government. On 20 July, a Turkish force of some six thousand troops and forty tanks was ferried to Cyprus by the Turkish navy, disembarked in the Kyrenia area and moved south to Nicosia. By the time a final cease-fire went into effect on 18 August, Turkey had some 40,000 troops with about four hundred tanks in Cyprus and controlled the northern 40 percent of the island. This relatively easy conquest was made possible by Turkey's military superiority and its proximity to Cyprus as compared with Greece. The Greek junta of political generals failed to respond adequately to the chain of events that they had provoked in Cyprus. This, coupled with the Turkish victory, brought about the downfall of the junta and the restoration of democracy in Greece. Turkey's use of military force to achieve its end in spite of the presence of UNFICYP demonstrated to the countries in the area the ineffectiveness of the UN forces in preventing war.

For the Canadian Airborne Regiment which began its tour of duty in April, everything was quiet until the coup of 15 July followed by the Turkish invasion at 4:55 a.m. on 20 July. Apart from some soldiers in the Kyrenia leave area, most of the Canadian troops were in the Nicosia area, those on duty manning the Green Line. That day, the Canadian paratroopers in observation posts were caught in the cross-fire and in the interests of safety evacuated most of their posts.

Major Clayton Samis, who was on Cyprus from April to December 1974, relates his recollection of the invasion:

On Saturday morning, July 20th, I received a call at 0430 hrs. advising me that we were placed on "Red Alert" and that I was to report to the joint operations centre immediately for orders. I hurried over and learned that a Turkish invasion was in progress along the north coast in the Kyrenia area.

At 0700 a dramatic illustration of the invasion occurred as I watched the Turkish airborne operation from the upper floor of the Ledra Palace Hotel. Turkish aircraft were dropping parachutists north of Nicosia. It was a beautiful, still cloudless morning and watching the sky fill with parachutes was an awesome sight, especially to our Canadian Airborne Regiment members.

Throughout the morning sporadic firing continued increasing in intensity, and punctuated by key machine-gun fire and heavier explosions. At about 1230 hrs. we received three mortar rounds in Wolseley barracks, and our first injuries . . . . I told everyone to start digging. One thing I did discover was that when there is danger, it is no problem to get troops digging. Getting them to stop digging however is another story. A little later in the afternoon, I had to order

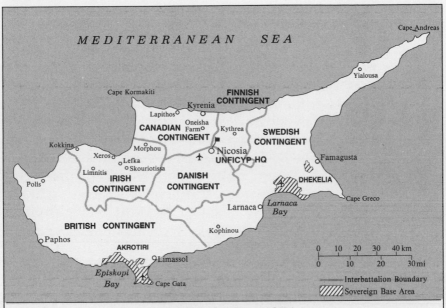

CYPRUS - Pre 1974
Deployment as of 1965

CYPRUS - Post 1974
Deployment as of 1987

some dirt put back in two trenches. The occupants had dug down so far that they couldn't see out.[11]

One of the key installations at Cyprus was the international airport, located just west of downtown Nicosia. Camp UNFICYP was not far from its terminal building. The UN had tried unsuccessfully to have the airport declared neutral. When it was discovered that the Turks were massing in nearby woods, Colonel C.E. Beattie, deputy chief of staff of the UN forces Cyprus and commander of the Canadian contingent, set out early on the morning of 23 July with a driver and a British soldier to try to head off the attack on the airport buildings held by the Greek-Cypriots. Beattie made his way to an amusement park in the area where Turkish troops were holding prisoner over thirty men, women and children. The Turks agreed to release the women and children. The attack went in anyway but Beattie managed to arrange a cease-fire. After much negotiation, the UN was given possession of the airport. The Commanding Officer of 1 Commando Group, Canadian Airborne Regiment, and of the Nicosia district, Lieutenant-Colonel D.S. Manuel, had also played a major role in helping place the Ledra Palace Hotel, in downtown Nicosia just inside the Greek side of the Green Line, under UN control. These negotiations as well were carried out in the midst of the fighting. During the invasion there were other examples of acts of courage and coolness under fire on the part of Canada's peacekeepers.

While most of the airborne unit was located in downtown Nicosia at Camp Maple Leaf, members of the logistics company and others under Major David Harries, based at UNFICYP headquarters at Blue Beret Camp (nicknamed Blueberry Camp), took up defensive positions at Nicosia International Airport and were responsible for helping secure the airport for UNFICYP. The British sovereign bases on the southern part of the island remained secure and a possible exit in case the situation really deteriorated. The airport at the British base of Akrotiri remained open to UNFICYP flights during the conflict.

Colonel Beattie and his staff did an excellent job of transforming peacekeepers back into soldiers, for the blue flag of the UN no longer had the same restraining effect. Armoured personnel carriers were needed to move troops about and weapons required to prevent intimidation by the heavily armed Turkish forces. Moving a sandbag or placing a magazine on a weapon was previously considered a provocative act. Men of the Airborne Regiment proved very adaptable to the new situation. The logistics company at Blue Beret Camp also faced a massive job of feeding hundreds of Greek refugees who took safety there from Turkish troops.

For several days UNFICYP troops at considerable risk to themselves and in spite of casualties were able to help in escorting some of the civilians to safety during the fighting. These included Greeks, Turks, diplomats and tourists. Both sides, however, came to realize stranded civilians could be exploited and thus held on to them as hostages.

In Nicosia the UN resorted to gunfire to rescue two wounded Canadian soldiers from the no-man's land of the Pedhieos River.[12] Captain Normand Blaquière and Sergeant Joseph Plouffe with a white flag and bullhorn had tried to escort some stranded Turkish-Cypriot soldiers back to their lines, but Blaquière was hit in the legs and Plouffe in the face. Greek-Cypriot machine gunners prevented the Canadians from rescuing them. The Canadians and a British armoured scout car from one of their sovereign bases — the Canadians did not then have a reconnaissance unit or armoured vehicles — then knocked out the machine-gun post and rescued the pair. This was one of the few instances in which live fire was returned by peacekeeping forces on Cyprus.

Both Blaquière and Plouffe were decorated. Blaquière received the Medal of Bravery and Plouffe the Star of Courage. Captain Alain Forand, who led the rescue party, also received the Star of Courage and Corporal J.R.M. Whelan, Private J.M. Belley and Private J.G. Pelletier the Medal of Bravery. Their citations are given in Appendix C.

As a result of the fighting the Canadian government agreed to double the size of its contingent. Some four hundred more troops of the Canadian Airborne Regiment and a reconnaissance troop from the Lord Strathcona's Horse, with their armoured personnel carriers and reconnaissance vehicles, arrived during the first week of August and had to be accommodated.

Captain W.F. Gee of the airborne artillery gives his recollections:

We of the first main reinforcement flight arrived at RAF Station Akrotiri on a dead black night where our maroon berets were taken away and small arms ammunition issued . . . . The closest most of us got to direct small arms fire was during the first week of August while we were on standby with our mortars in the downtown area. Indelible memories will always remain with me of walking as fast as decency permitted down an ill-lit street to take over the midnight duty officer shift. Even in daylight the walk was made in the fervent hope that the Greek-Cypriot .30-calibre would not take that particular time to be insolent to the Turkish .50-calibre.[13]

The Turkish invasion of the island resulted in the flight of about 200,000 Greek-Cypriots from the northern part of the island southward across a buffer zone of 135 miles separating the Turkish and Greek-Cypriot forces. In turn, an estimated

37,000 Turkish-Cypriots moved north to the area held by Turkish troops.

North of the Green Line, the Turkish-Cypriots live in the 37 percent of the island that only they and Turkey recognize as the Turkish Republic of Northern Cyprus. South of the line is the internationally recognized Republic of Cyprus populated by Greek-Cypriots.

As a result of the Turkish invasion the total UNFICYP force was increased to 5,000 men in August, then decreased to 4,300 men by the end of 1974. While previously the mandate was to separate Greek- and Turkish-Cypriots, the new task was to man a buffer zone running through the island separating the Greek-Cypriots from the Turkish regulars.

Unfortunately, there were two Canadian fatalities. In the evening of 6 August, an investigating officer, signaller and driver went to check a report that Turks, not far from the Ledra Palace Hotel, were laying wire in contravention of the cease-fire agreement. At the scene a shot was fired in the dark hitting the signaller, Private Gilbert Perron. Perron died shortly after. On 19 September, Claude Berger, a paratrooper, was also killed by a sniper while on a humanitarian mission to feed livestock abandoned by refugees. These two deaths cast a somber shadow over the contingent. As well as the two killed, seventeen Canadians were wounded during the fighting.

A small Canadian medical facility on the island has been named in honour of Gilbert Perron and Claude Berger. There is also a cenotaph at Sector IV's headquarters with a tall wooden cross listing the names of some twenty Canadians "who gave their lives in the service of peace with the UN in Cyprus."[14]

The breakdown of peace talks in Geneva in mid-August 1974 led to a further round of fighting for several more days with the initiative being taken by the Turkish forces on the island. Again, a major concern of UN troops was to avoid getting hit in the crossfire. The Turks wanted UN troops out of the areas of Cyprus they had captured and this request was obeyed. Of particular help during the second stage of the fighting was the availability of Canadian armoured personnel carriers and Lynx vehicles. Their presence permitted the evacuation of UN personnel from areas under heavy fire. With the end of the fighting, the UN reinstituted armed patrols and peace once again returned to the island with Greek-Cypriots now in the south and Turkish-Cypriots in the north.[15] UN positions in the northern part of the island bypassed by Turkish forces were later permanently abandoned.

The Canadian peacekeepers had reacted as best they could to a rapidly changing situation. Perhaps their most important role was carrying out humanitarian tasks such as helping civilians stranded in isolated pockets. While the events of 1974 demonstrated that in a crisis UNFICYP could not keep the peace, its presence did help to bring the situation more quickly under control and perhaps was a deterrent to an enlargement of the fighting. UNFICYP had been so cut back to save costs that when an invasion came it could certainly not frighten an attacker.

From 1964 to 1974 the situation in Cyprus had been relatively stable. Many local disputes had been resolved and procedures developed for dealing with incidents. Like Nasser's previous pullout order to UNEF I, the military coup and subsequent Turkish invasion caught the peacekeepers unprepared.[16]

Leslie Gelb, a *New York Times* reporter, and others claimed that the United States government and the Central Intelligence Agency had foreknowledge of the coup that overthrew

Archbishop Makarios. The British knew. This information may or may not have been known to some Canadians on Cyprus.[17] There have been rumours that Colonel Beattie was told about a Turkish invasion well in advance. This is untrue. The airborne unit just happened to be on Cyprus when the Turks invaded.

Although there was some apprehension in intelligence circles that Archbishop Makarios might be overthrown in Cyprus, there was much conflicting information. The installation of Nikos Sampson as the next president of Cyprus, a former terrorist who favoured union with Greece, unleashed an unexpected chain of events. In the past Turkey had threatened and had even intervened in a limited way but had never actually invaded the island on a large scale. For example, in the summer of 1964 Turkish-Cypriots had established a bridgehead in the Kokkina area in the northeast part of the island where arms and men were brought ashore. The Greek-Cypriots attacked it in strength in early August that year. Outnumbered and out-gunned, the Turks on Cyprus faced a major defeat. In response, Turkey sent F-100 aircraft several times to bomb and strafe the Greek positions. The UN Security Council managed to obtain a cease-fire and prevented an invasion.[18]

1974

After the Turkish invasion in 1974, the Canadians were again given responsibility for the Green Line (now fixed and impermeable) running through Nicosia. Patrol duty alternates with standing guard. Guard stations have become a favourite meeting place for Cypriot children who can be both a source of amusement and a nuisance. Canadian ingenuity has also prevented many small incidents from escalating. For example, a Canadian observation post that was abandoned in an area that had become quiet was reoccupied by Greek-Cypriot militia. Efforts at persuading them through discussion to vacate the post were in vain. They quickly left, however, when the Cancon commander had a cesspool truck empty its contents in the trench around the observation post. The trench was later recovered with earth and the post reoccupied by the Canadians.[19]

Warrant Officer George W. Norman of the 1st Battalion of The Royal Canadian Regiment served in Cyprus from October 1966 to April 1967 and on a second tour from December 1974 to May 1975. During the latter he kept notes and a few highlights are included to offer the reader some insight as to the life of an average soldier there:

17 November 1974

My second tour of Cyprus is approaching . . . . It will be a tour of tension. The Turkish army has invaded Cyprus . . . . As a Canadian professional soldier, I look forward with pride and honour to serving . . . .

30 November

. . . . Airborne Regiment had a farewell party.

17 December

Corporal Watkins, Corporal Ritchie and Roman Catholic padre got shot at. Watkins had three shooting incidents on this tour. Each time he would return to the barracks a nervous wreck. I gave him some rum and he always went out in good humour next day.

21 December

Regimental birthday . . . . Greek stripper hired. She didn't strip but Brigadier-General . . . , Brigadier-General . . . , Lieutenant-Colonel . . . and Chief Warrant Officer . . . did to undershorts. Stripper looked at her watch. Said she was paid only for two hours and she left . . . . Master Corporal Findlay and three from the Regiment returned from refugee relief.

05 January 1975

Sergeant Doug Hilchey took me to our former location in the Kyrenia Pass area. What a change from 1966-67! Buildings were burnt out, etc . . . .

20 January 1975

Greek show in mess in evening. Man, could those two skinny Greek girls eat. They ate plate after plate after plate . . . . they sang horribly.

02 April 1975 (Lahr)

Heard Captain Ian Patten was killed in Cyprus yesterday.

23 April 1975

19 men on order over drugs. Caught by undercover Mountie posing as cook. Worst cook we ever had.

16 May 1975

Royal 22e Régiment in control.

Within the buffer zone, UNFICYP has exclusive control of all military, economic and other activities. The composition of UNFICYP in 1987 is 2,388 soldiers as well as volunteer civilian police officers (none from Canada). The civilian police, originally 175 now thirty-six, as well as the military forces are backed by thirty-five UN civilian staff and 472 Cypriots. There are five sectors assigned to the forces of the different participating countries. Britain, with the largest military contribution (760 soldiers), mans an eighteen-mile stretch of the buffer zone in Sector Two; Canada, with 515 soldiers, is responsible for Sector Four, mainly in Nicosia. The working language among contingents is English.

Although there is a Canadian officers' mess, the UNFICYP Officers Club where officers from all contingents can mix, is the more popular. For other ranks the sergeants' mess or the bright lights of Nicosia offer a break from their regular duties on the island. Generally, relations between UNFICYP and the Cypriots are good, particularly because the money spent by UN peacekeeping troops helps sustain the local economy.

A generally sunny climate and excellent beaches offer the tourist a welcome holiday in Cyprus. Apart from a few brief periods of hostilities, Canadian forces who have served there can attest to the island as an almost ideal tourist spot.

Should the Canadians who had served on Cyprus some ten or even twenty years ago return to the island, they would notice more commercial development especially on the southern part of the island. Cyprus has become a popular vacation spot for Scandinavians and other Europeans seeking warmth and sunshine during their colder months. Canadian servicemen have found young women vacationers there to be quite friendly and appreciative of their efforts to preserve peace in the world.

For most Canadian peacekeepers with UNFICYP whose average age is twenty, a peacekeeping assignment in Cyprus is their first mission outside Canada. To prevent homesickness, Canadian beer and cigarettes are imported and a military video-camera crew record and send greetings from wives and girlfriends. An escape from the cold Canadian climate to "Nipple Beach," a topless beach near Limassol, is a temptation that many young Canadian soldiers cannot turn down.[20] For most of their twenty-year stay on Cyprus, the Canadians have been in the Nicosia area. As a result leave areas for their use have been set aside along the coast.

A serious problem which Canadian peacekeepers have faced and overcome on the island is that of traffic accidents. Narrow winding roads, the driving habits of the Cypriots, the sun, slippery roads after a heavy rainstorm or even from grape juice during the harvest, caused serious accidents. Speeding and drinking exacerbated fatalities. A good number of minor accidents were not reported. In late 1974, while transporting the unembalmed corpse of a Greek woman in an open box from a hospital in Nicosia back to her village a Canadian truck driver nicked the side of a building. As it was New Year's Eve and the corpse was about four days old, the driver was in no mood to stop except for required road blocks. UN decals were put on the truck to hide the damage. With better-trained soldiers currently in the forces, and improved roads such as a four-lane highway to Limassol, traffic accidents have shown a marked decrease.

The Canadians have taken an active interest in charitable ventures on the island. Over the years Canadian peacekeepers have contributed substantially to the Kyrenia Red Cross Hospital as well as to crippled children and most recently to the mentally retarded.

Relations between the Canadian soldiers and the Greek and Turkish population on Cyprus are generally good. The majority of contacts at the official level are also cordial. There was one minor incident in 1966-1967 that temporarily damaged relations between some Canadians and several members of the Greek National Guard. A Canadian soldier dumped a large shipment of rancid canned sardines over a cliff with the word "poison" printed in red all over the boxes. The Greek National Guard came across the sardines and thinking this meant "fish" in French ate the sardines. Fortunately there were no deaths, but a number of Greek-Cypriots believed that the Canadians had tried to poison them.

CONCLUSION

The Canadian peacekeepers have been on Cyprus for over twenty years. While their presence has helped strengthen the island's economy, Cyprus has given the Canadians who have served there a renewed appreciation of their Canadian identity and of their own country. As Lieutenant-Colonel Robert Mitchell who commanded the 2nd Regiment, Royal Canadian Horse Artillery in Cyprus from October 1985 to March 1986 remarked: "Seeing what the Greek- and Turkish-Cypriots did to their beautiful island in the Mediterranean makes one all the more aware and grateful for the peace and stability we enjoy in Canada."

Lieutenant-Colonel H.W. Mulherin, who commanded the 1st Battalion of the Canadian Guards on Cyprus from October 1964 to April 1965, believed that, "Cyprus has been valuable training . . . even though the job goes against the grain of army training. The soldier has learned to be diplomatic; instead of fighting he must use patience and persuasion."[21] The tour offers experience and more independence for young officers and other ranks. By contributing to the peacekeeping force on Cyprus, Canada helps to prevent war between two fellow NATO members, Greece and Turkey.

The Canadians are currently responsible for keeping the peace between the Greek- and Turkish-Cypriots in the old city of Nicosia. The Canadians' main task in Nicosia is to watch the Green Line which has, since 1974, become a permanent fixture separating Greeks and Turks. Prior to the Turkish invasion there was a greater flow of people and goods through the line. As of 1987, there is only one gate through the Green Line in Nicosia that permits entrance to or exit from the Greek and Turkish sectors of the island.

Boundaries and positions have become so fixed that it has become impossible to change anything. A sandbag added or removed can lead to protracted negotiations until the status quo is restored. Trees cut in the summer of 1985 were wired back in place soon after.

The movement of an observation post even a few feet necessitates endless negotiations and reams of paperwork. Some claim that Cyprus has become another *raison d'être* for the UN, which has made the forces there into one of its bureaucratic creatures. Some of the Scandinavian troops, in fact, have become professional peacekeepers and a tour on Cyprus is part of their way of life.

What exists in fact and what is stated officially by the UN about Cyprus are different. According to the official version, UNFICYP is there as a temporary measure until Greeks and Turks can resolve their differences. In fact, the island is partitioned almost like East and West Germany. The chances that the island can become one country again are remote. All parties concerned, including the UN, seem to have a vested interest in maintaining the status quo.

There are those who generally disparage peacekeeping and its effectiveness. As for Cyprus, I believe the UN presence there is worthwhile. If one takes the time to read the unit war diaries and talk to veterans it becomes apparent that their presence is vital. There were numerous incidents between Greeks and Turks that could have easily triggered a serious resumption of fighting. By their presence UNFICYP has saved lives by preventing serious incidents from escalating.

While participation in peacekeeping operations has given Canada a high international profile it has required the financial support of its taxpayers. The normal operating expenses of the Canadian Forces have been absorbed by National Defence. With UNFICYP, where contributions to its upkeep are voluntary, Canada has often paid many additional expenses. In considering costs, however, any estimates of costs of peacekeeping wane in comparison to the likely costs of any war.

*N Secretary-General Dag Hammarskjöld (left) and Major-General E.L.M. Burns,
mmander of UNEF (centre), confer with Canadian troops.*

Dominion Day celebrations, UNEF, 5 July 1960. The camel race at Rafah Beach.

Canadian personnel burn confidential files at Rafah Camp prior to their departure, M
1967.

embers of the advance party at Troodos Road Camp, Cyprus, 20 March 1964.

lonel Clayton Beattie visits an
servation Post on Cyprus, summer
74.

A member of The Royal Canadian
Dragoons leads a traffic convoy between
Nicosia and Kyrenia, April 1965.

Camp Shams, 16 December 1973.

Garbage collection at Camp Shams, Egypt, December 1973. It was eventually discovered that stolen valuables were being hidden in a compartment in this cart and smuggled out of the camp.

ving quarters, 'Camp Roofless,' Golan Heights, June 1974.

ivate J.W.S. Simard, a vehicle mechanic with the Canadian logistics company, eives some personal attention from entertainer, Lillian Stillwell, with the Rothman's ow, Golan Heights, 12 January 1976.

Departure for the Congo.

A typical scene in the Congo. Canadians attempting to create something out of chaos. Here signallers install a telephone system at UN headquarters, Leopoldville.

Three signallers at work on the motor of a truck converted into a mobile radio station, Luluabourg, September 1960.

...utenant-Colonel H.H. Angle in Kashmir on the Pakistani side of the cease-fire line, ...49.

...e delivery of a jeep to UN observers at Kargil, India.

*Lieutenant-Colonel Frank Campbell (foreground) and Captain Robert Shepherd prepa
for Vietnam by trying on their summer shorts, 25 January 1973.*

*Captains I.E. Patten and F.M. Thomson investigate an incident not far from Xuan L
South Vietnam, March-April, 1973.*

6

UNITED NATIONS EMERGENCY FORCE II

INTRODUCTION

ON 17 JULY 1967, AS A cease-fire came into effect, UNTSO personnel were assigned observer posts on the Golan Heights and along the Suez Canal to supervise new cease-fire lines. The United Nations Security Council passed Resolution 242 which called for Israel to withdraw from territories of recent conflict but also seemed to confirm Israel's right to exist within secure and recognized boundaries. However, an enduring peace remained as remote as before.

The Israeli occupation of territories with large Arab populations only exacerbated Arab hostility. The violence continued. The Palestinian Liberation Organization increased the scale of its attacks resulting in quick retaliation by Israel. Egypt embarked on a war of attrition. There were commando raids and sporadic firing across the Suez Canal. In response, the Israelis constructed defensive positions, the so-called Bar-Lev Line, along the east side of the canal. This phase ended with a cease-fire in 1970.

Meanwhile, power was changing hands in the area. In

Israel, Golda Meir took over as prime minister in 1969. Muammar al-Qaddafi came to power in Libya that same year. President Nasser died on 28 September 1970 and was succeeded by Anwar Sadat. The Organization of Petroleum Exporting Countries (OPEC), dominated by the Middle East producers, increased the price of oil and began using oil to help them achieve political aims.

The situation of "no war, no peace" could not last. Throughout 1973 tension between Israel and her Arab neighbours had been growing. There were aerial clashes between Israel and Syria. The Egyptians increased their military strength on their side of the Suez Canal.

President Sadat was anxious to regain the Sinai and avenge his country's humiliating defeat in 1967. He met with neighbouring Arab states to coordinate military plans. Over-confident Israeli leaders dismissed Arab troop movements as annual military manoeuvres. When war broke out again on 6 October 1973 (the Yom Kippur War), the Israeli forces were caught off guard.Surprise attacks on Israel by Egypt and Syria were initially successful, but eventually the Israelis gained mastery of the situation. There was the threat of direct intervention by the Soviet Union as well as by the United States.

Effectively employing modern Soviet equipment, the Egyptians crossed the canal and sliced through the Bar-Lev Line. The Israelis retreated, regrouped, then counter-attacked along the southern part of the canal. They established a bridgehead on the west bank.

UNEF II

Fighting between Israel and Egypt ceased with a week remaining in October and a truce was established under the auspices of the United Nations. A disengagement agreement was worked out and a new United Nations Emergency Force, UNEF II, was created on 25 October 1973 to ensure that its terms were followed. Canada's role was to help meet the service requirements of the new peacekeeping force. Contingents from Austria, Finland and Sweden, serving with a peacekeeping force on Cyprus, were the first to be transferred to the cease-fire lines.

An eleven-man evaluation team, headed by Canadian Brigadier-General Douglas Nicholson, helped assess the logistic requirements for the entire UNEF II force. Nicholson, formerly of the Royal Canadian Army Service Corps, continued as commander of the Canadian contingent until 21 January 1974. Negotiations on what Canada would provide proved ongoing and continued even after the departure of the first group at the end of its six-month tour. From nothing, the Canadians quickly created a logistical support system. At first its headquarters was at the racetrack at Heliopolis, a suburb of Cairo, named Camp Shams. Canada and Poland were to divide logistical responsibilities. A Polish logistic contingent was to be responsible for medical support, engineering, repair of Eastern bloc equipment and transport functions. However, because the Israelis refused to allow the Poles into areas held by them, the Canadians were forced to assume additional transport duties. The Canadians became operational much sooner and did the work of the Poles for a number of months.

In early November, Canada agreed to provide a signals unit and the air movement of the Canadian soldiers began on the tenth of that month. Some twenty flights airlifted 481 troops, forty-three vehicles and 115 tons of equipment in three days — one of the largest peacekeeping airlifts in such a short time. The entire operation was a great accomplishment by Air Transport Command. Later in November, Canada agreed to provide a supply company, a maintenance company, a postal detachment, a military police detachment, a movement control unit and an air transport unit. 116 Air Transport Unit was comprised of two Buffalo aircraft and some fifty technicians to help provide logistical support for the entire force (later to average about four thousand) drawn from twelve other UN members. By early January the force included Canada (1,012), Poland (803), Sweden (626), Finland (615), Austria (600), Indonesia (550), Peru (497), Panama (409) and Ireland (290). Senegal (fifty) and Ghana (four) had advance parties in Cairo. The Irish contingent was withdrawn in May 1974 to help at home.

The Early Period

The first Canadians to arrive at Camp Shams initially slept in front of the betting windows under the grandstand. Next tents were erected on the grassy racetrack strip between the tote boards and the track. License plates had to be switched among vehicles as the Egyptians had only approved certain plate numbers to bring in supplies from the airport to the camp. An excellent field kitchen was organized first using field rations then later locally purchased foodstuffs.

The signallers had a major task of trying to establish good internal communications within the camp. They also installed a link to Canada. The service unit successfully or-

116

ganized maintenance, supply and other service functions, and acquired a warehouse at Alexandria for storage of rations. The initial stages of getting organized proved the most trying of this undertaking. Although having supplies in greater abundance, these Canadians were not as organized as their predecessors with UNEF I.

The two major Canadian units were 73 Service Battalion and 73 Signal Squadron. (The number "seventy-three" indicated the year of their formation.) There were also some forty Canadians who joined the UN headquarters staff to oversee communications and logistics. One of the early tasks of the Canadians in mid-November was to deliver food and water under UN auspices to the encircled Egyptian Third Army in Suez city.

Between 26 November and 6 December, a second group of Canadian Forces personnel was airlifted to Egypt, and 1,100 all ranks were in place by February 1974. During July and August the headquarters of both UNEF II and the Canadian contingent in the Middle East were moved from Cairo to Ismailia. Most Canadians were located at El Gala Camp (an airfield) on the outskirts of Ismailia, some at Cairo, some at Port Said, and some in the Sinai Desert buffer zone. The average size of the Canadian contingent at El Gala Camp was approximately eight hundred. Originally, it also supported the UN Disengagement Observer Force along the Israeli-Syrian border.

National Defence had been preparing various options as to what it might be called upon to provide. Perhaps the troops would be reinforced on Cyprus or elements of the standby Canadian Airborne Regiment could be sent to Egypt. Once again, however, Canada's role in UNEF II would be to provide service support and a new unit had to be created.

Captain Anthony McCormack, a logistics officer at National Defence Headquarters then on a French language training course, found himself given two days notice to report to Canadian Forces Base Kingston. Specialists in various fields were hastily assembled. The only previously formed unit was the 1st Canadian Signal Regiment, which made up an important element of the Canadian contribution to UNEF II. In Egypt, McCormack found himself initially kept busy trying to sort out rations, ensuring for example that Moslem troops were not given pork rations.

The code name for the Canadian contribution to UNEF II, Operation Danaca ("Canada" jumbled), accurately reflected the state of Canada's peacekeeping effort, at least in its early stages. One of the first actions taken by the Canadians was to establish security around the perimeter of their camp. Armed pickets of the Princess Patricia's Canadian Light Infantry made regular foot patrols through the night. It was discovered, however, that intruders would slip through the barbed wire and later return after the guard had passed. That problem persisted until the arrival of Nepalese troops in February 1974. After these Gurkha troops were assigned the responsibility for security, intrusions ceased. Their method of night patrol was to have a guard armed with a rifle pass but to have another Gurkha armed only with a *kukri* (knife) stealthily following about a hundred yards behind. The Canadians with UNEF I had experienced that same security problem.

This peacekeeping force should not be considered a carbon copy of UNEF I. While UNEF I had been established by the General Assembly, UNEF II was created by the Security Council with the approval of both the United States and the Soviet Union. This time the Security Council ensured that it would be consulted and would decide the question of termination. There was no desire for a repetition of UNEF I's withdrawal at the unilateral request of Egypt. The Soviet Union, which considered Canada a close ally of the United States, had insisted that its own ally, Poland, share logistical duties with Canada.

GETTING ESTABLISHED

Major Donald Banks served with communications at UNEF II headquarters from November 1973 to about mid-March 1974. Excerpts from the log he wrote are evidence of a general feeling of frustration:

13 Nov 1973 — Very difficult to convince staff to make a decision . . . .

17 Nov 1973 — Telex still not in; trouble with contractors — no lines available within city. (What a bloody way to work!)

19 Nov 1973 — Line crew of the city system arrived today on a bicycle (real big time). Still no Telex . . . . Still no furniture . . . .

20 Nov 1973 — The bloody switchboard has problems again . . . . There's all kinds of [UN] officers but no one to do the work. I'd sell my soul for a few clerks right now.

29 Nov 1973 — Received message . . . concerning Telex circuit to Canada. Bell Canada requires information on exact termination of equipment this end before operating. (Seems peculiar since circuit has been in operation for approximately four days already.)

11 Dec 1973 — Today is our anniversary — we've been here one month. The time isn't passing as quickly as we had hoped. Everyone misses their families and this often results in short tempers . . . .

119

Frustrated in his efforts until mid-December to receive approval for using certain radio frequencies from Egyptian authorities, Banks finally offered the Egyptian general responsible a bottle of Scotch and two cartons of American cigarettes. In no time he had received approval. The Canadians learned that a gratuity was usually necessary in order to get prompt action.

The first several weeks were not the easiest. Soon it was Christmas, which proved a hectic time for all chaplains and cooks. A Christmas dinner of turkey and all the trimmings was served by the officers and senior warrant officers according to general military tradition. Trees that had been shipped in from Germany were trimmed with decorations made from pull-tabs from beer cans and a few locally purchased ornaments. For many who were there it remains a most memorable Christmas.

Excerpts from the minutes of a meeting of senior Canadian officials there give some indication of the problems at Camp Shams:

7. . . . . Pits used for liquid garbage or water . . . must be pumped out and the contents disposed of under local contract. Draining from the pits into the soil is slow and gradually ceases after a few hours use.
8. Although there are some 25 toilets in the racetrack buildings serious problems were encountered because the plumbing was not designed to take toilet paper . . . .
10. Temperature drops rapidly after sunset making the heating of tents and messes necessary. Additional heaters are required.
11. Hygiene is a matter of concern and involves inadequate ablution, latrine and messing facilities. The large number of flies serve as carriers of disease . . . .[1]

Gastroenteritis was not uncommon. Sports activities were

curtailed as shower facilities were almost nonexistent. In spite of innumerable difficulties and obstacles, the Canadian troops coped.

No matter how bad things were or became Canadian servicemen usually did not complain officially to the press. The controversy over unification was an exception. Media interest in peacekeeping was aroused by one incident involving UNEF II.

The senior medical officer had made arrangements to have two major civilian hospitals cater to Canadian needs until the arrival of a small twenty-bed Canadian hospital with a surgical room and facilities as well as attendant surgeons and anesthetists. Two Canadian soldiers were badly injured in a traffic accident and had to wait six hours for treatment. One subsequently died. After returning from the autopsy, the junior medical officer there, Major J.P. Vezina, informally criticized his superiors to a member of the press at Camp Shams for not sending a Canadian medical unit earlier to Egypt. He also complained about the standard of the standby Egyptian medical facilities and the living conditions of the Canadian troops. As a result, he was sent home by the commander of UNEF II and returned to his former duties at CFB Valcartier Hospital. During the ensuing fuss raised by the media, the chief of the defence staff, General Jacques Dextraze, gave a press conference and read a prepared statement, part of which follows: "I shall not tolerate, by members of the Armed Forces, any public criticism of the government, the United Nations, or any other national contingent participating in any United Nations Emergency Force."[2] That continued to be National Defence policy.

Master Warrant Officer D.R. Mathews, formerly with UNEF I, who served with vehicle maintenance from 1 December

1973 to 10 May 1974, kept a detailed diary and some of his observations are presented:

29 December

As a senior NCO in charge of thirty men, I have spent the last month clucking over them like an old mother hen and encouraging them to improve and do anything (within reason) to make things easier and more comfortable for themselves in their living quarters. They were just nicely developing into homogeneous entities when the whole house of cards came tumbling down.

The Brigadier got on the rampage and wanted everything in every tent to be nice and uniform. Naturally, a Brigadier's whim or suggestion gets magnified as it passes each link in the chain of command. By the time it gets down to the men, the original idea has been blown all out of proportion.

Needless to say, my people were highly agitated at all the orders, directions and changes they had to make over a two-day period. Morale took a decided nose-dive to the point where one small spark would have triggered off a donnybrook. All tents are definitely crowded so one can imagine how easily feelings could be upset.

If our senior officers had recognized the conditions, tried to relieve the congestion by putting up more tents and thinning the occupants out, the personnel concerned would have recognized the effort as improvements and would have accepted directions for uniformity.

8 January

The equipment and logistics situation continues to be a point of concern and embarrassment to this contingent . . . . The Canadian contingent here has all the expertise in the world but the oldest and worst equipment to work with. The other contingents nearly all have newer and better equipment than we have but in some cases haven't the foggiest idea how to operate or look after it properly.

We don't have to prove our abilities as peacekeeping — that's well established, but we don't have to look like country cousins while doing it. National prestige has its place and it is going to cost money.

This author for one is very disillusioned to see the depths to which the Canadian Forces have sunk. We are poorly equipped, poorly clothed, poorly housed and above all poorly disciplined. The only saving grace is that through all our muddling inefficiency, we still get the job done.

24 February

To some of the younger members of my crew, service in the UNEF has proven to be a traumatic experience. The state of limbo between war and peace in a foreign land has shattered a lot of pre-conceived ideas that many of them had. The transition from a modern, clean, up-to-date society to one of nearly total filth and abject poverty has had its effects. The first couple of months were hard on everyone's nerves. Waiting for equipment to arrive, adapting to a new climate and a strange society are all trying experiences.

30 March

The Canadian contingent is now doing the very best it can and with what resources are at hand. Material, parts and supplies are slowly building up to where we can better fulfill our original roles in our various fields — i.e. communications, supply and maintenance. Unfortunately, recent events have brought to light a number of severe accusations against the Canadians from other contingents. We've been accused of not being able to do the job we were sent here to do and that we should do as we did in Vietnam — pull out and go home.

The Canadians volunteered to to a job. None of us proclaimed to be experts at everything we are asked to do and yet others still complain. I for one would be quite content to turn my job over to a member of any other contingent and go home and I'm sure every Canadian soldier here feels the same way. But we are here and we will do our best.

The Finns could do our role but won't. The Swedes don't want to be here at all. The Poles are here for political reasons only. The Austrians could do our role but their general attitude turns people off. The Irish criticize anything and everything but having some knowledge of their maintenance procedures — well I doubt if they would be successful. It is also quite obvious the Indonesians, Ghanaians, Senegalese or Panamanians couldn't do our role either as they just aren't trained or equipped to the calibre required.

18 April

There are still many problems to solve, many of which could have been solved long ago if it were not for the bureaucratic UN staff over here. Our logistics people could have had the force far better organized and operational on a far more efficient scale if they could have been able to implement their policies and directives without hindrance at every detail. New York UN headquarters is not much help either as they are completely divorced from the scene of action and just can't possibly envisage our problems. To this date not one high ranking official has visited this camp site to see just how the force is making out. We have been thrown into the field and left to sort out this mess for ourselves.

The United Nations needs a standing armed force, highly trained and highly equipped for instant deployment to any part of the world for peacekeeping duties. But that is a pipe dream at best . . . . So we stumble along, doing the best we can, trying to accomplish the role we were sent to do. The next time a peacekeeping force is required they should send over the UN delegates first and the troops later. A lot of problems would be solved long before the soldiers got there.

27 April

The pending move to Ismailia has always been foremost in our minds as its part of the long range planning for the UN force. In the past week we have been told to "be prepared" for a move by 15 May. How can you "be prepared" to move when no detail of how a move is to be done has been issued. You just don't go and pick up a camp this size and move it 130 kilometres in one day. It will take several weeks to move this camp properly and several months to get settled in again in Ismailia. [He was right.]

The airforce unit of 116 ATU is a typical product of the air element in a land force environment. They arrived with all their own tentage, set up in their own area, all ranks together. We are supposed to be

124

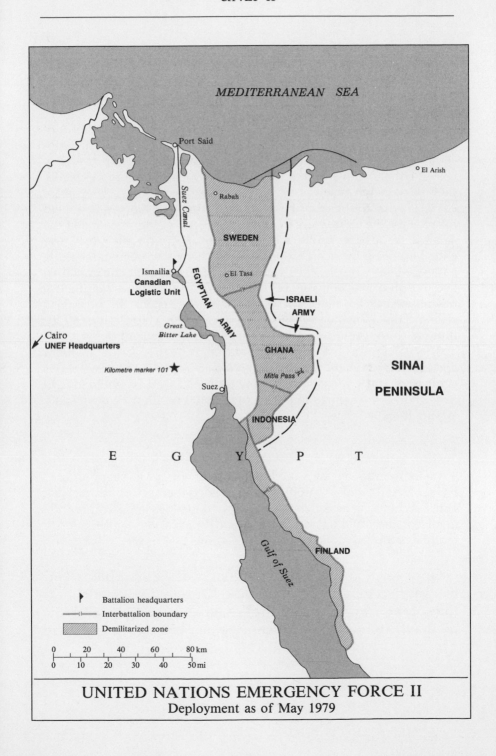

MEDITERRANEAN SEA

Port Said

El Arish

Rabah

SWEDEN

Suez Canal

Ismailia
**Canadian
Logistic Unit**

EGYPTIAN ARMY

El Tasa

**ISRAELI
ARMY**

Cairo
UNEF Headquarters

Great
Bitter Lake

Kilometre marker 101 ★

GHANA

Mitla Pass

**SINAI

PENINSULA**

Suez

INDONESIA

E   G   Y   P   T

Gulf of Suez

FINLAND

▶   Battalion headquarters
⊢—⊣—   Interbattalion boundary
▨   Demilitarized zone

0   20   40   60   80 km
0   10   20   30   40   50 mi

UNITED NATIONS EMERGENCY FORCE II
Deployment as of May 1979

integrated in the Canadian Forces but the only thing really integrated is the uniform.

2 May

There are stories going around that the Poles want to pull out of their Middle East role. As far as the UN officials over here are concerned the Poles are tolerated but that is about all. In some ways they brought this on themselves. They were two months on site before they declared themselves ready to perform any work. They were charged with the responsibility of supplying and operating a field hospital for the entire force but never did get it going. As a result the small field hospital brought over by Canadians for their own use ended up being the main hospital for the entire force. The same thing happened with the Canadian dental unit. Consequently the Canadian field hospital is running out of certain drugs and supplies but the UN has refused to buy the material necessary to restock the pharmacy claiming that some of the drugs asked for are not necessary. A nice thing to think about when you're sick in a strange land.

The Poles put on a highly organized production of deployment and settling in when they arrived in Camp Shams. Their camp and equipment was a model of what any unit in any army would love to have. When it was time to put on the show though they were sadly lacking in experience.

15 May

In six months all the varied elements of this peacekeeping force have solved their major problems and melded themselves into a viable entity. When one considers the varied nationalities and backgrounds involved, the building of a multi-national peacekeeping force in six months is indeed an accomplishment of the first order.

Once the Canadians had settled in at Camp Shams and life was becoming routine, Brigadier-General Donald Holmes, the second commander of the Canadian contingent and formerly of The Royal Canadian Regiment, ordered everyone under him to learn, on a certain day, a second skill not related to his job. As a result, telephone communication quickly broke down as many decided to become switchboard operators. Holmes chose to learn to drive a road grader and succeeded in building a road to nowhere, or in coming close to levelling Camp Shams as some tell it.

There is the true story of a high-ranking Egyptian military delegation who appeared one day at Holmes' office with a sheath of air photos demanding to know why all the Canadian mortars were aimed towards their military academy. Holmes studied the photos, restrained his laughter, and then escorted the delegation around the camp showing them our "P-tubes" (urinals improvised from shell casings or map tubes). The only reason they were pointing toward the academy and the overlooking apartments was Canadian modesty.

Ismailia

General Holmes proved to be a wise choice to command the Canadians. His previous experience as a military attaché in Poland and his knowledge of Polish proved invaluable. For example, in negotiating with the Poles the best location for their contingents at El Gala Camp, Ismailia, about eighty-five miles east of Cairo, Holmes first selected the worst section of the camp. The Polish commander had a secret discussion among his staff and then insisted on having that site. The Canadians obliged and received their actual preference.

A great deal of renovation was required at the former British base at Ismailia. The Canadians restored the water supply and a considerable number of residential and operational buildings. The airfield was improved and C-130 Hercules flights came in weekly from Lahr, Germany.

Canada's signallers were a key element in the entire operation providing radio communication among UN units as well as at the Ismailia airfield. A communications centre there monitored all UN flights in the Middle East and supplied a link with Canada.

Canadian signallers were first deployed in mid-November 1973, when a team was assigned to Suez city. They encountered shells of burnt-out vehicles along the highway as they entered the town, half of which was reduced to rubble and without electricity and water. On the Egyptian side of the Suez Canal the Canadians were assigned a villa. On the Israeli-occupied side of the canal they lived in tents. By mid-December over seventy Canadians had been deployed to front-line positions on either side of the canal including Rabah and Ismailia.

Peace Efforts and the Canadians

First had come a cease-fire then, as a result of an agreement in January 1974 at Kilometre 101 (so-called because it was at the 101st kilometre on the road from Cairo to Suez), a disengagement zone just east of the canal was created between Egyptian and Israeli forces. It thus became possible for UNEF II to man and control a firm disengagement zone. There was also to be a restricted zone on either side of the buffer zone with UN military observers detached from the UN Truce Supervision Organization to check fixed levels of troops and weapons. UNEF II was deployed across the Sinai in a narrow strip from the Mediterranean to the Red Sea with eventually four infantry battalions from Sweden, Indonesia, Finland and Ghana. The January agreement proved to be a step to a more permanent peace. The deployment took until early March with some Canadian officers involved in telecommunications, liaison, map reading and the location of positions.

Excerpts from the personal diary of Captain L.M. Juteau, a Canadian signal officer, UNEF II Forward Headquarters, offer a better idea of what it was like to be there:

27 January (Sunday) 1974

Five Canadians left Cairo (Camp Shams) at 1030 hours for Kilometre 101 where disengagement negotiations between the Egyptians and Israelis were taking place. The five Canadians, all members of 73 Canadian Signal Unit were:

a. Captain L.M. Juteau
b. Master Corporal R.W. Jennex
c. Corporal J.E. Campbell
d. Corporal J.L.R. Jean
e. Private C.D. Waddell

The trip to Kilometre 101 had been difficult. Many vehicles carried soldiers who were shouting and waving and giving "peace signs." It was obvious that they felt immense relief and elation on the eve of the beginning of the Israeli withdrawal back across the Suez Canal. The start of the withdrawal would finally free the Egyptian Third Army which had been trapped around Suez by the Israeli force that had crossed the Suez Canal. From Kilometre 101 explosions could be heard and pillars of smoke seen off in the distance towards Suez as the Israelis destroyed equipment and ammunition.

28 January (Monday)

At 0900 the Israelis took down their flag for the last time. The day was generally without incident. Then at 1800 hours the Egyptians started firing in celebration. When we reached the outskirts of Suez, the firing was bad enough to force us to turn back. The Finns reported several hits on their OPs [observation posts] and one wounded soldier hit in the knee by a rifle bullet.

29 January (Tuesday)

I later travelled into Suez city where I saw hundreds of Egyptian soldiers wandering aimlessly about. I saw a whole column of Israeli armour that had been destroyed while entering the city. I then went to the waterfront area where the Egyptians have set up a display of captured Israeli equipment. As we were about to leave, we noticed a sudden commotion. It was the arrival of the Egyptian war minister and the governor of Suez. They went into an auditorium. The UN photographer and I boldly made our way in. We sat in the front row and watched as frenzied Egyptian soldiers cheered and raved at the dignitaries.

18 February (Monday)

At 0915 this morning I drove to the Swedish lines on the other side of the Israeli positions. This was the first time that I had driven through the Israeli lines on this side of the canal. I was amazed to see females near the front. There were quite a few mingling with male soldiers . . . . Most wanted their pictures taken with us.

21 February (Thursday)

Another interesting and historic day. We drove to the Israeli canal crossing. They were moving back hundreds of vehicles across the canal. All the vehicles carried pennants, flags, balloons or something to show how the men felt.

24 February (Sunday)

What a night. The wind picked up and blew the hell out of our tents. They blew down in the night and we finished the night in vehicles. First thing in the morning we found a good building, cleaned it out and moved in.

27 February (Wednesday)

The biggest problem of the day was the Indian battalion's ration situation. They are sloppy (by our standards) and unsanitary. I took the 7 Canadians in this location off their food for fear of illness.

1 March (Friday) 1974

I saw plenty of Israeli equipment and deployments. The Israelis have a number of novel ideas. One is not digging in too deeply. Armour, artillery and infantry in depth are left in the open but camouflaged. This enables them to move quickly. Water and gas trucks contain tanks that are independent, light and removable. If hit and the vehicle is disabled, the tanks can be moved to another vehicle.

I saw one position where the Israelis had counter-attacked the Egyptians. Nine Egyptian tanks were knocked out, all facing away from the Israeli direction of advance. They were running away. I later saw a shot-down Egyptian fighter. It looks as though it was shot down by cannon fire. That is apparently another Israeli tactic. All Phantoms have cannon mounted in them for the day of the dog fight is not over in the Middle East. Too many planes in too small an area means close contact against which missiles (air-to-air) are awkward.

Col. Gat, the Israeli liaison officer, also explained how the crossing of the canal was done. The Israelis had to break through the Egyptian forces in the east bank first. One force pushed the Second Army northwards and one pushed the Third Army southwards to create a gap which they sliced through. A company of paratroops in rubber boats crossed and established a small bridgehead. 14 tanks crossed on rafts to assist. Several convoys brought barges down and some were hit by Egyptian artillery fire. The operation was touch and go for several hours.

4 March (Monday) 1974

Tomorrow at 1200 the operation ends. I will go to Ismailia with the radio crew. The others go to Cairo. It's a shame to finish for the operation was beginning to grow on me.[3]

The mediation efforts of Henry Kissinger, the US secretary of state, brought about a further agreement between Egypt and Israel in September 1974 that was completed in February 1976. An enlarged buffer zone further to the east was created. The United States provided personnel and electronic surveillance equipment on ground just west of the Mitla Pass.[4]

IMPROVEMENTS TO UNEF II

After eight years of idleness as a result of the Six Day War, the Suez Canal was reopened in 1975. Waiting time to cross the canal then ranged from minutes to hours. The most frustrating travel for the Canadians often proved to be between El Gala Camp at Ismailia on the west side of the Suez Canal and El Tasa, the forward logistics camp set up in September 1976 in the demilitarized zone to the east.

The main Canadian UNEF II camp at El Gala eventually received recreational facilities. As in UNEF I, an AM radio station was set up as well as a ham-radio station. There was also a small cable-TV network broadcasting some five hours of taped television programs from Canada. The messes, however, were the main social centres of the camp.

The border with Israel was open which permitted the Canadian soldiers to visit Israel readily. This relative ease of travel to Israel had been unavailable to UNEF I. There were also more air-conditioners in use as compared to UNEF I. About a third of the Canadians with UNEF II had air-conditioned quarters. An air-conditioned bus was also purchased in West Germany with private funds to take the Canadians on excursions. A tour of duty was normally for six months rather than a year as in UNEF I.

132

For the first time female members of the Canadian Forces formed part of the UN contribution. Their number grew to some fifty at El Gala Camp. There were also some women on duty at Lod Airport, Tel Aviv, a control point in cargo movement. Major-General J.P.R. LaRose, who commanded the Canadian Contingent United Nations Emergency Force Middle East (CCUNEFME) in 1975-1976 found that, "their presence did not reduce our effectiveness and did indeed add a significant human touch."[5]

TRAGEDY

In June 1974 the United Nations Disengagement Observer Force was established between Israel and Syria. The Austrian and Peruvian battalions were taken from UNEF II along with a Canadian logistics company and a Polish transport platoon. On 4 June of that year a third Buffalo aircraft was requested for service in the Middle East with 116 Air Transport Unit at Ismailia. On 9 August, while on a routine flight from Ismailia via Beirut to Damascus, a Buffalo of this unit was shot down by missiles over Syria near the Syrian-Lebanese border with the loss of all nine Canadians aboard. The Syrians claimed it had been mistaken for an Israeli aircraft. A subsequent investigation revealed the Syrians to be trigger-happy and the Buffalo aircraft to be flying ahead of schedule. To mistake a slow-moving UN transport aircraft for an Israeli jet fighter, however, was a serious error. It was rumoured that the Syrian battery commander paid for this mistake with his life. The Canadian government claimed and received financial restitution from the UN.

Termination of UNEF II

The signing of the Middle East Peace Treaty between Egypt and Israel, on 26 March 1979 in Washington, signalled the end of UNEF II. As the Soviet Union would have vetoed a renewal, the Security Council allowed UNEF's mandate to expire on 24 July 1979. The Canadian contingent's peak strength was then about 850 of a UN force that numbered some 4,200 on average.

No. 73 Service Battalion of 425 personnel was tasked with carrying out the closure of all the outpost sites in the buffer zone, including an advanced logistic detachment of the unit at El Tasa on the east side of the Suez Canal. Initial planning began in July. The job of closing four major battalion sites and their satellite outposts in the Sinai took some three weeks. It required long hours on the part of the Canadian team to appraise UN items on site and subsequently to return to warehouse any material worth salvaging. Operations in Ismailia were completed gradually so as to permit the Canadians to leave Egypt no later than 1 November 1979. By that time the battalion's strength had been reduced to just enough to fill one Boeing 707 aircraft. Eight servicemen remained behind to assist with the close-out of the force. They left on 21 December 1979.

Lessons

UNEF II provided a good training lesson for planners at National Defence. One lesson learned as a result of UNEF II was not to send so many individuals without their units. They were creating a team from people who had never functioned together previously. Some of those sent were desk-bound bureaucrats totally lacking in field-craft experience or skills. Some careers suffered as a result of a shaky performance. As those responsible for service to the entire UNEF II force, the Canadians should have been more willing to share initially scarce items, such as wood, with the rest of the force. The arrival of Hercules aircraft with supplies exclusively for the Canadians and not for other contingents created resentment. As with UNEF I, some Canadian senior officers proved unwilling to share items in short supply with junior ranks. While with UNEF I a coveted early appliance had been an air-conditioner, with UNEF II it was a kerosene heater. Chemical toilets and mosquito netting also were in short supply. The excellent cooperation of Air Transport Command and of Canadian Forces Europe at Lahr helped to quickly overcome deficiencies.

Canadian military personnel reestablished their reputation as the best scroungers. They were the first to lay their hands on UNEF supplies and also attempted to waylay some items destined for other contingents. Major L.W. MacKenzie of the Princess Patricia's Canadian Light Infantry recalls how he and two others tried to intercept the Polish contingent's supply of high-quality vodka. Unfortunately, the Polish captain they courted at Alexandria harbour for one day was delivering military supplies to the Egyptians and could not help. The correct ship with the vodka was berthed alongside. The Canadians never did manage to intercept that vodka.

Although the initial mounting of a peacekeeping operation proved stressful, it was not the same type of pressure as in wartime. For the senior officers such as Colonel G.D. Simpson, deputy commander of the Canadian contingent for the first seven months, the experience was a challenge. Meeting and overcoming the problems that developed at the outset of the operation "kept the adrenalin pumping" in spite of long hours. To be working at something worthwhile and historically significant provided strong motivation in contrast to routine duties and military exercises.

Each peacekeeping operation not only proved a good training school; it was also a sociological laboratory where Canadian troops had to function within their own contingent as well as work along with those from other countries. Canadian troops had a tendency to complain. That is not to say that their complaints were not justified. Although morale is difficult to judge, I would deem the overall morale of the Canadians with UNEF II to be on a par with that of UNEF I.

CONCLUSION

UNEF II bears the unique distinction of being the only peacekeeping force in the region that was terminated with a peace treaty. It can be argued that UNEF II would not have been politically successful without the experience of UNEF I. In contrast to UNEF I, UNEF II ended with the prospect for peace being relatively good. In that direction Egypt and Israel had made substantial progress.

7

UNITED NATIONS DISENGAGEMENT
OBSERVER FORCE

IT WAS NOT UNTIL THE END OF May 1974 that Henry Kissinger was able to obtain a disengagement agreement between Israel and Syria on the Golan Heights and to separate both sides. The Security Council then authorized a United Nations Disengagement Observer Force (UNDOF) to supervise the cease-fire. Both the United States and the Soviet Union sponsored its creation. A 1,250-man force was created from contingents already with UNEF II. By June 1974 UNDOF was operational and continues today. Military units from Austria, Canada, Peru and Poland occupied an area of separation. The Canadian contingent was comprised of a logistics company, a signal troop and some staff officers employed at UNDOF headquarters in Damascus. As in UNEF II, Canada and Poland shared the support role. The logistic contingents did not carry any weapons.

A year after UNDOF's creation, the Peruvians were withdrawn and replaced by additional Austrians, themselves replaced in September 1975 by Iranians. In March of 1979, the

Iranians withdrew and the Finns took their place. An armed battalion of Austrians and one of Finnish soldiers then manned and patrolled the area of separation. The Austrians, with their headquarters on the Syrian side, assumed responsibility for the northern section and the Finns, with their headquarters located on the Israeli side, took over the southern section.

In contrast to the chaos surrounding the setting up of Camp Shams, the establishment of Camp Ziouani on the Golan Heights, near Qneitra, was well organized. Excerpts follow from the log of Major D.G. Porter, the commanding officer of the Canadian logistics company there from June to November 1974, who was responsible for establishing the Canadian camp:

4 June

Convoy proceeded in dark at 2:00 a.m. Route: Cairo, Ismailia, Rabah, Gaza, Tel Aviv, Tiberias, Qneitra.

25 June

The first civilian Druze employees have started working in the kitchen. A few Druze inhabitants have red or blond hair and blue eyes. Legend has it that the Crusaders were responsible for the blond hair and blue eyes.

26 June

With the Israeli withdrawal and the return of many former Syrian inhabitants to Qneitra, the population suddenly grew to some 20,000. Streets were impassable. I dispatched a couple of armoured personnel carriers for use by the military police as they saw fit but primarily as transportation if the crowds (which also contributed a fair number of al-Fatah guerrillas) forced them to withdraw to the safety of my camp. Fortunately, the Syrian anger (on account of the devastation of the town) was mostly directed at the Israelis. All the MPs and myself got as we moved around were a few rock-throwing incidents. After the initial week of occupation by the Syrians was over, the tempo died down and the population reduced to about 300-500 . . . . This was suspected to be the base from which al-Fatah launched their future excursions in this area against the Israelis.

29 June

Water truck and wrecker involved with a terrorist on Mount Hermon. He wanted a ride into Israel with my vehicles. Austrians turned him over to Syrian "civilian police."

4 July

Israelis and Syrians are still blowing up mines. So far four Austrians and twenty Syrian civilians have been killed by mines.

11 July

Two Russian military advisers and one Syrian lieutenant-colonel killed by mines yesterday.

21 July

Communications link with Cyprus still being maintained in spite of heavy firing there.

24 July

Israeli forces' main worry was the slow occupation by the UN of Israeli positions vacated on Mt. Hermon . . . . This is strong al-Fatah area and the Israelis do not want them to move into those positions.

11 August

Stopped by six al-Fatah soldiers near the border. One shoved a Kalashnikov machine-gun in my gut. Not supposed to be any armed troops except UN and police in buffer zone.

139

12 August

At Damascus, the Syrians to show their own regrets (at the shooting down of the Buffalo and the killing of all nine Canadians aboard) post an honour guard. I shall never forget the sight as the bodies are loaded. The armed Canadian guard faces the Syrian guard. If the order had been given, our guard would have charged with bayonets fixed!

23 August

Captain Rick Prest stopped by a gun in the gut. Second time UN stopped that way in Qneitra — mine was first.

26 August

Lt. Willy Smith has temporarily become an officer in the Canadian Forces but is normally an officer of the Austrian army. His real name is Wilfried Koller. It appears that he and his platoon turned back an entire convoy of Syrian government cars. A convoy containing the Syrian defence minister, his chief of staff and senior military officers were out for a sight-seeing tour of the territory just handed back by Israel. Under the UN agreement, no traffic of any sort was allowed on this particular road in the buffer zone. Although the convoy turned around under the pressure of Willy's pointed pistol and the levelled rifles of Willy's platoon, they weren't too happy about the incident. On their return to Damascus they issued instructions for Willy to leave Syria. Willy was moved across the border into Israel to finish his tour with the Canadian logistics company. The Syrians had previously been told by UN officials that he would cross into Lebanon. The Syrians waited for him there in vain . . . .

CANADIAN INVOLVEMENT

Headquarters for UNDOF is at Damascus. Most of the Canadians, whose strength has varied from initially 120 to 230,

140

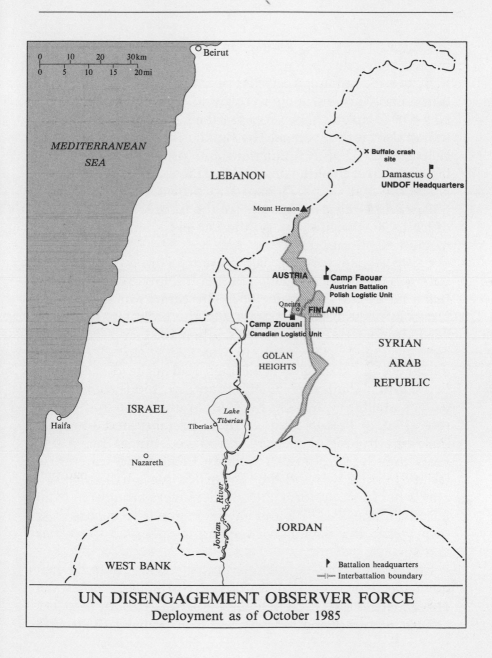

UN DISENGAGEMENT OBSERVER FORCE
Deployment as of October 1985

are situated in Camp Ziouani in Israeli-occupied territory, immediately adjacent to the area of separation. As of 1987, there are 190 Canadian logistics personnel at Camp Ziouani, thirty signallers and some ten other Canadians out of a total UNDOF complement of 1,335. For the Canadians a six-month tour of duty is the average. The signal unit mans the message centre at UNDOF headquarters and provides a signal detachment to each of the operations centres. The logistics unit is stationed at Camp Ziouani and provides supply, maintenance and transport services for the force. Since the arrival of UNDOF, the situation on the Israeli-Syrian front has remained stable and quiet.

Camp Ziouani was originally a French Foreign Legion post dating from the 1930s, then a Syrian military camp that was flattened by the Israelis in 1967. The camp was nicknamed Camp Roofless because so many of the buildings had been shelled and were without a roof when the camp was originally occupied. The UN camp was first a tent city. Badly damaged and crumbling buildings had to be demolished. Former inhabitants such as snakes and scorpions were forced to seek shelter elsewhere. Leftover ammunition and explosives had to be removed. In 1975 prefabricated plywood buildings from Turkey were introduced but within a few years they were rotting. A wooden theatre and warehouse facility burnt down and the roof of the mess hall collapsed after a heavy snowstorm. Atco trailers were brought in from Ismailia in the late 1970s and have remained. To ensure their own well-being Canadian engineers overhauled the water and sewage systems.

Hard work by the Canadians eventually made Camp Ziouani quite liveable. Minefield warnings, restrictions across the area of separation, the visibility of armed troops and the carcasses of burnt-out military vehicles along the highways are constant reminders that the area is a likely location for any renewed conflict.

One of those who helped organize UNDOF in its early years was Lieutenant-Colonel Georges Boulanger, the chief logistics officer from November 1975 to May 1976. When he took over the Iranians had replaced the Peruvian contingent. The location of the headquarters in Damascus in relation to the location of the contingents — two in Israel (Canadian, Iranian), two in Syria (Austrian, Polish) — rendered movement very difficult at times. On some occasions while visiting the units located in Israel, Boulanger or his men were not able to come back until the next day. Accordingly he warned, "Always carry a toothbrush!"[1]

Boulanger contributed towards improving organization. Originally, the chain of command was not too clear. The Canadians on the Golan Heights were detached from their battalion in Ismailia with UNEF II but did not belong to UNDOF. Numerous meetings were set up and finally the Canadians were placed under the UNDOF commander, much to the latter's delight. With the expiration of UNEF II's mandate, this arrangement became official.

Originally, all supplies came from Egypt. As the Polish transport company was not permitted to travel in Israel, the Canadians were given this task. Colonel W.J. Yost of Wyoming, Ontario, helped arrange to have all supplies arrive at Syrian ports, freeing the Canadians from major transportation duties. The Poles then assumed the responsibility for moving supplies through Syria.

Canadian Private Robert Howie reported in the summer of 1978:

Our detachment of 4 personnel is situated in the once thriving city of 37,000 called Qneitra. Only a few buildings remain standing. A grim reminder of the '73 Israeli-Syrian War. All around lies rubble and evidence of the carnage and waste that war brings. We operate vehicle control from Damascus to Tiberias. One must always know who is where and going where. Three radios, 24 hours a day, 7 days a week, who says it's easy? Not us! Sun, wind and heat; we have it all. But our sanity remains. UNDOF Sigs lives![2]

Like their predecessors with UNEF I and II, the Canadians on the Golan Heights have contributed time and money to charitable projects in the region,[3] including the House of Peace Orphanage on Jerusalem's Mount of Olives built and operated by Polish sisters. There are other examples such as the delivery of vital supplies from Damascus to Beirut by several truck convoys on behalf of UNICEF in the summer of 1982. These were the first relief shipments to reach Beirut since it was attacked by Israeli forces. Major Wayne De Wolfe led the first convoy, and Captain Charles Gilbert the second, through a diversity of fighting forces.[4] The latter was caught in an artillery duel between Israeli and Syrian forces in the eastern outskirts of Beirut. Fortunately, no one in the convoy was hurt.

Social activities begun with UNEF I have continued. Canada Day and Christmas remain important social occasions. During the latter holiday, there are visits by entertainers from Canada. Skits are also performed by members of the force.

Life on the Golan for a Canadian soldier becomes rather routine. Canada Day activities, medal parades (receipt of UN medals), entertainers from Canada, visits by Canadian and other dignitaries, and trips to nearby cities and countries provide diversions. More enduring are the friendships made. Weather also offers variety. While members of UNEF II faced the heat of the Sinai desert, those with UNDOF are located on gently rolling hills with an almost steady wind in the summer. In the winter there is rain, snow and constantly gusting winds. The dominating geographical feature there is Mount Hermon with its snow-covered peak.[5]

For those going to the Golan Heights, the trip is a tiring one. There is the flight from Canada to Lahr, West Germany, then on to Larnaca, Cyprus, and finally to Damascus. The final phase of the journey is a bus ride to Camp Ziouani.

An old joke played on many new arrivals from Canada, nicknamed "pinkies," has been to bring the new replacements to an old dilapidated building and inform them that this will be their home for the next six months. Still in a partial state of shock, they are taken to the mess for introductions and correctly informed as to their accommodation. By the time a Canadian on a typical six-month tour has mastered his job and begins to feel familiar with everything, it is time to move on and make way for his replacement. Although the Canadians comprise only about one-sixth of the 1,250 to 1,300-member force, thousands have served with UNDOF since its inception.

8

LEBANON

LEBANON HAS DOMINATED THE NEWS in recent years. In the course of the last three decades that country has been transformed into an epicentre of violence. This change did not come about suddenly but as a result of failure to resolve long-standing problems that were festering below a superficially peaceful surface.

During the Second World War, Lebanon obtained its independence from France. The country was considered a land populated by merchants, not fighters. Its capital, Beirut, was an oasis in the Middle East, a city noted for its nightclubs, lavish hotels and sandy beaches with bikini-clad women amidst a Moslem sea of religious fervour. Canadian servicemen from UNEF (and for a while from Cyprus) could spend very enjoyable leaves there. Business flourished. The Lebanese authorities even made an effort to see to it that Canadian servicemen were not fleeced in bars or by currency traders. Lebanese civilian police would investigate and remedy complaints.

What transformed a cosmopolitan city like Beirut into a chaotic battleground and devastated country was caused by external events, internal politics and foreign powers. The original division of power between Lebanese Christian and Moslem inhabitants was a census which gave the Christians a 6 percent overall majority. However, the emigration of Christian Lebanese, a higher Moslem birthrate and the arrival of Palestinian refugees since 1948 reduced the Christians to a minority.

Several successive events combined to end the tranquility that prevailed in what was once described as "the Switzerland of the Middle East." As a result of the Suez Crisis in 1956 and the ensuing Egyptian-Israeli war, the Sunni Moslems in Lebanon became upset by the failure of their pro-western government to sever diplomatic relations with Britain and France. The anticipated reelection for an unconstitutional second term of the pro-Western president, Camille Chamoun, a Maronite Catholic, and charges of a rigged parliamentary election exacerbated the discord. The formation of the United Arab Republic, consisting of Syria and Egypt, at the beginning of February 1958 and of the Arab union of Jordan and Iraq two weeks later marked the onset of internal strife in Lebanon. Virulent propaganda from Cairo radio, coupled with fear, suspicion and the infiltration of some saboteurs from Syria, helped to inflame the Moslem population.

UNITED NATIONS OBSERVATION GROUP IN LEBANON

In response to an appeal to the UN from the Lebanese president to halt intervention by the United Arab Republic, a resolution was approved by the Security Council (with the exception of the Soviet Union, which abstained) to send an observer group known as the United Nations Observation Group in Lebanon (UNOGIL). Its headquarters was in Beirut. The observer group's initial members were an Ecuadorian civilian, an Indian civilian and a Norwegian air force officer, Major-General Odd Bull. UNTSO provided the early observers and a Canadian army major, Major G.D. Mitchell, was one of those seconded from UNTSO for duty in Lebanon. On 21 June 1958, five majors and five captains arrived from Canada as the number of observers was increased to over a hundred to be deployed throughout the country. Patrols by jeeps and aircraft looked for evidence of foreign intervention. An initial report by the force on 1 July noted that there was no foundation to claims of any massive infiltration.

On 14 July the Lebanese situation was further complicated by a coup that overthrew the pro-Western monarchy in Iraq. Both Jordan and Lebanon asked the West for protection. The next day US marines landed on the beaches of Beirut and two days later British troops were flown into Jordan at the request of King Hussein. There was considerable apprehension on the part of the USA and Britain as to the stability of certain governments of the region, particularly of the oil-producing states and sheikdoms bordering the Persian Gulf.

The turning point in the Lebanese situation came with the election by the Lebanese parliament of General Fouad Chehab as the new president on 31 July. As he was the most universally acceptable of all the possible candidates, fears and tensions diminished. Like the army he headed, Chehab was neutral and disliked violence and fighting.

The UN force in Lebanon reached a strength of 591, of whom seventy-seven officers and men were Canadian. Forty-nine posts were manned by UN personnel, all unarmed. The presence of American forces (5,790 marines and 8,508 soldiers) in the Beirut area did not make things easier for the

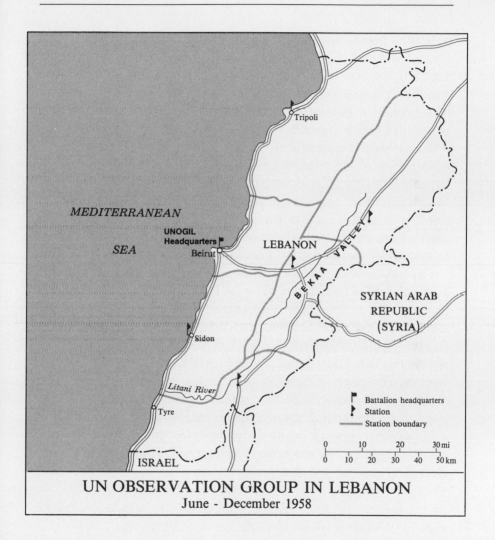

UN OBSERVATION GROUP IN LEBANON
June - December 1958

UN observers although it likely shocked the Lebanese political leaders into seeking a solution to their political confrontation. For the UN observers, conditions at each post varied. In remote areas such as the Bekaa Valley, observers were occasionally fired on, frequently stopped by armed men and sometimes robbed.[1]

In August the situation began to wind down. That month a battalion of US marines was withdrawn. At the end of the month, 120 Syrian commandos left the Moslem sector of Beirut and returned to Syrian territory. On 15 September a second American battalion left. UNOGIL was increased as the Americans departed. The last American troops embarked in late October. General Chehab had taken office as president on 23 September and in mid-October Prime Minister Rashid Karami created a cabinet of two Christians and two Moslems that proved satisfactory. Although there was still some violence and discord, the crisis had passed. This was confirmed at the end of November by UNOGIL's report that its assignment was completed. By 10 December 1958 the force had been withdrawn.[2]

The 1958 crisis in Lebanon was largely forgotten. However, internal strife again erupted in Lebanon in April 1975 and became more prolonged and bloodier than anyone would have imagined. At the time of writing this account the prospect of peace seems remote.

UNITED NATIONS INTERIM FORCE IN LEBANON

The creation of peacekeeping forces on the Egyptian and Syrian frontiers with Israel did not prevent the escalation of violence along the Israeli-Lebanese frontier. Using Lebanon as a base, the Palestine Liberation Organization waged a campaign of terror into Israel bringing increased levels of reprisals. This culminated in an Israeli invasion on 14 March 1978 when its forces attacked Lebanon and occupied a four to six-mile security belt on the Lebanese side of the border. That frontier area was eventually turned over by the Israelis to a Christian militia force when the Israelis left Lebanese territory on 13 June that year.

The Israeli penetration of Lebanon as far as the Litani River brought about the establishment by the Security Council of a four-thousand man peacekeeping force, the United Nations Interim Force in Lebanon (UNIFIL), on 19 March 1978. Among its objectives were the withdrawal of Israeli forces, the restoration of peace and security and the return of the area to the control of the Lebanese government.[3] Canada responded modestly yet positively to the UN request for assistance by agreeing to provide signallers for six months only. Canada's supply of communications personnel was being strained as UNEF II was also in operation.

A Canadian signal troop was at first seconded from the United Nations Emergency Force II based at Ismailia. This group was relieved during the last week of April by men mainly from the 1st Canadian Signal Regiment at Kingston, Ontario. Administrative and logistical preparations by the UN proved to be inadequate. Some of the national contingents arrived without internal-communications equipment. To fill the gap, the Canadians purchased urgently required equipment from an Israeli firm.

Captain Blaine Williams, an air force communications officer, arrived about 23 March in southern Lebanon with 73 Canadian Signal Troop, a detachment from 73 Signal Squadron of UNEF II. Williams witnessed the early organization and growth of UNIFIL for a month prior to the arrival of the signallers from Canada. He recalls various incidents:

We were to be self-sufficient with the exception that each nation which hosted one of our detachments was responsible for the feeding and physical protection of that detachment. Because we had to supply our own detachments with fuel for generators, in some cases water, mail, spare parts, etc., we had a supply vehicle. In this way we could supplement the meagre rations that some detachments received. Originally, the detachment of 3 young Canadian city boys that first provided communications for the Nepalese battalion was presented with 3 freshly killed chickens each day — not cleaned. Meanwhile the detachment providing communications for the French battalion was faced with daily decisions regarding which wines to use with their sumptuous meals . . . .

A favourite game played by the Palestine Liberation Organization (PLO) which used to annoy us to no end was to follow us on our supply run for miles. The favourite patrol vehicles for many of the smaller PLO factions were pickup trucks and repainted, obviously stolen, UN vehicles. Most of these vehicles were refurbished with machine guns or recoilless rifles mounted in the back. The situation was aggravated by the extreme youth of many of these PLO participants. Well-armed youths of not more than 10 or 12 years of age seemed to favour these annoying follow-the-leader games . . . .

Like most Canadian military personnel in similar circumstances, I wore the Canadian flag with more than just pride. It also offered considerable comfort as you realized its worth as a passport and peacemaker. Although our vehicles were UN blue and white and we had UN insignia and flags on our uniforms and vehicles, the largest flag we carried was on a pole attached to our vehicles; and it was always a Canadian flag.[4]

Lieutenant B.W. Drummond of Kamloops, British Columbia, who was among the early signallers in Lebanon from UNEF II, adds a recollection:

The UNTSO officers were happy to have Canadian troops in the area as we were armed while they were not. Warrant Officer "Turk" Deschamps and I would make tours of the UNIFIL area of operation visiting our radio detachments at the various contingents. We became quite familiar with passing through check-points. Generally, the first thing a militiaman or PLO type would do at a check-point was open the jeep door and push a rifle in at us. This procedure was, of course, intended to be intimidating. We counteracted by having my submachine gun, loaded and cocked, cradled casually in my lap pointing directly at the soldier's crotch . . . .[5]

Camp Pearson at Naqoura, Lebanon, named after the late Nobel Prize winner, provided tents for those working at UNIFIL headquarters. The camp was set on bulldozed flatlands that extended to the shore of the Mediterranean. The camp's purpose was to support the signal detachments scattered among the various national contingents. Living conditions away from headquarters were usually more spartan. The only incident involving Canadians and any factions in Lebanon occurred on 12 July, when three Canadians of a mobile repair team were captured by the Palestinian Liberation Organization along with forty-nine other UN troops. After being held for three hours, they were released unharmed.

Among the Canadians with UNIFIL some 30 percent had served previous tours with the United Nations elsewhere. For most, however, this was their first exposure to land mines, small-arms fire and, especially, marauding forces. Members of this and other recent peacekeeping forces came mainly from a younger generation of service personnel who had not seen action in the Second World War or Korea. Exposure to the conditions in Lebanon, as well as living with other national contingents under difficult conditions, gave the Canadians invaluable experience.

Beginning in April 1978, ninety Canadian signallers assisted UNIFIL. To help cope with the violence involving Lebanese Christians and Moslems, Israelis and Palestinians, UNIFIL's strength was increased in May from four to six thousand. The number of Canadians rose to a maximum of 120 in June and that level was maintained. With a communications system established and in light of the recurring serious cycles of violence, the Canadian government decided to withdraw its signallers in October as scheduled.[6]

The following excerpts from the diary of one Canadian signal detachment attached to the Nepalese battalion (Nepbatt) give additional insight of what it was like to serve in Lebanon:

28 Apr 78

This is the first entry. Members of the detachment are: Master Corporal M.B. Forbes, Private K.S. Kendricks, Private E.P. Grehan, Private T.W. McIntyre.

3 May

Everything is quiet here. There is shooting all around us but none in our area. There were 4 people killed in the fight last night.

16 May

We got a new UN Military Observer today, a Canadian captain. It seems he has bad luck wherever he goes. Six cars were blown up outside his apartment so he was moved to some outpost. The first night he was mortared so they sent him to Tyre. You guessed it, they were attacked last night by the PLO. Now he is here for a rest . . . . Ha, ha. It seems that if anything is going to happen, it should, by rights, happen with him here.

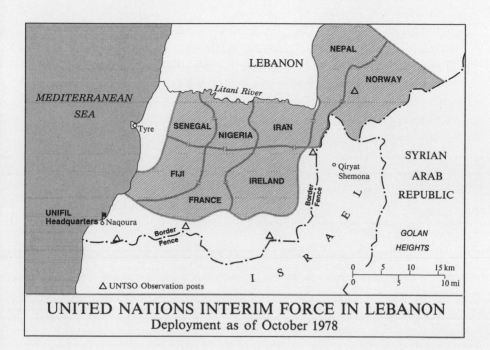

UNITED NATIONS INTERIM FORCE IN LEBANON
Deployment as of October 1978

19 May

Last night the PLO and Christians shot the shit out of each other. It was the heaviest fire fight to date.

9 June

Gary might not wake up tomorrow as he mistook two Gurkha sergeants for me and Mike and threw a cup of water on them from the balcony. They seemed to take it in good humour . . . but?

12 June

Right now we don't know where we're moving to. Back to Canada would be a good idea. My feelings are quite simple, they should corner off this part of the world and just blow it sky high and start over again. The longer you're here, you can see how childish the situations are.

155

21 June

We had another movie, *Saturday Night Fever*. Another great success. If this keeps up I should be able to go into the Nepalese army as a colonel . . . . Lots of fun was had by all.

07 Sept

A lot of shelling today and there are no lights on tonight.

08 Sept

. . . . We drank Scotch all night, listening to traditional Nepalese army songs . . . . Everyone sang . . . . All in all it was a once in a lifetime evening.

15 Sept

Today we were quite nervous; for today we were presented with our medals. Our parade square was a total success. The general congratulated us for a very fine parade.

27 Sept

We were invited to the Commanding Officer's (CO) bungalow for a farewell party. As I write this on the morning of the 28 Sep my head is still pounding. We were presented by the CO with a jeweled and velvet knife along with insignia of Nepal. We presented the CO Nepbatt with a plaque from the 1st Canadian Signal Regiment. All in all a very successful evening.

30 Sept

Today we pack up and get ready to go. We will leave at 0800 tomorrow.

31 May 1979

We all got home in good shape. The move turned out good and everyone has some good and bad memories of Lebanon.[7]

With the departure of the Canadian signal unit, UNIFIL became the only peacekeeping force in recent UN history without Canadian participation. The subsequent heavy death toll as a result of ambushes or clashes with military forces operating in the area and the lack of progress in bringing peace has proved the wisdom of that withdrawal.

A second more serious invasion into Lebanon was launched by Israel in June 1982, this time as far as Beirut. UNIFIL was forced to watch or move aside as the Israelis advanced. The troubled situation in southern Lebanon calls for an impartial presence but whether UNIFIL can ever fulfill this role effectively remains to be seen; indeed, an impartial presence throughout all of Lebanon would be useful.

9

MULTINATIONAL FORCE AND OBSERVERS

IN VIEW OF THE CERTAINTY OF A veto by the Soviet Union in the Security Council, UNEF II's mandate was allowed to lapse in July 1979. The United States had encouraged Egypt and Israel to make peace that year at Camp David and a peacekeeping force was felt to be necessary along the Israeli-Egyptian frontier. Consequently, an independent peace-keeping force was established outside the United Nations that remains in operation today.

The peace treaty between Israel and Egypt had foreseen a role for United Nations forces in the process of a gradual withdrawal of Israel from the Sinai. With the expiration of UNEF II's mandate, all that remained was the US Sinai Field Mission which, together with UNEF II, had been monitoring the September 1975 Egypt-Israel disengagement agreement. To replace UNEF II and effectively monitor the disengagement zones, the Multinational Force and Observers (MFO) was created on 3 August 1981 and began its duties in April 1982.[1] It was to act as an observer not a buffer force. As well, a naval component to patrol the international waterway in the Gulf of Aqaba was formed as part of this force. The Sinai

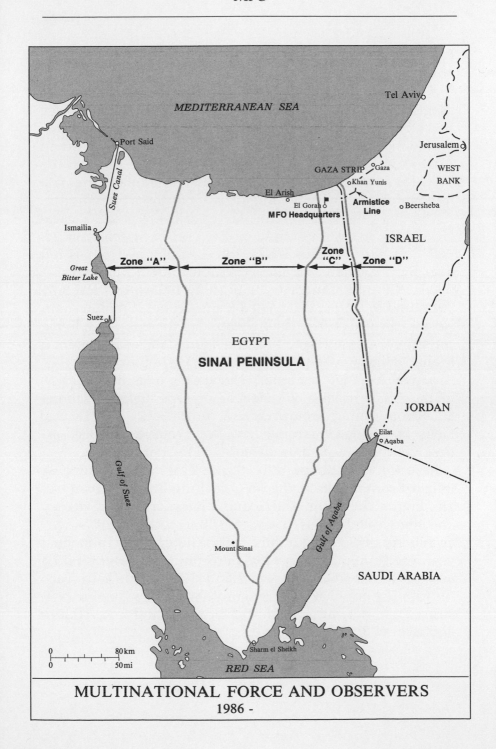

MULTINATIONAL FORCE AND OBSERVERS
1986 -

Field Mission was disbanded to then become the civilian observer component of the MFO.

A 140-man Canadian helicopter contingent participates in a logistics and reconnaissance role for the Multinational Force and Observers. It provides both communications and transportation of men and supplies. The Canadians replaced an Australian unit in 1986. Canada has agreed to serve in the MFO for a period of two years and thereafter may terminate its commitment by providing twelve months written notice.

The first Canadian unit to take up duties was 408 Tactical Helicopter Squadron from Edmonton on 31 March 1986. As with the two previous UNEF forces, unlocated mines left over from previous fighting continue to be a hazard. As a result, the nine Canadian Twin Huey helicopters are only permitted to land in designated "safe" zones. Sudden sandstorms can also cause a crash. In spite of the problems, living conditions are quite good for the Canadians at El Gorah, a former military base just south of the Gaza Strip.[2]

As well as 408, other units participating on a rotating basis in the MFO include 403 Helicopter Operational Training Squadron from Gagetown, New Brunswick, 427 Tactical Helicopter Squadron from Petawawa, Ontario, and 430 Tactical Helicopter Squadron based at Valcartier, Quebec.

In addition to Canada, other countries which are providing military contingents to the MFO include Britain, Colombia, Fiji, France, Italy, the Netherlands, New Zealand, Uruguay and the United States. They contribute equipment as well as military personnel for the 2,600-member force. In the first year, the United States paid 60 percent of the direct funding and subsequently Egypt, Israel and the United States each contributed one-third. Considerable work was done to construct buildings, observation posts, roads and a naval dock at Sharm el Sheikh for the MFO.

160

The Multinational Force and Observers are stationed in Zone C (see map) and man a line of observation posts and checkpoints along the international boundary. Their task is to ensure that both parties adhere to specific limitations and levels of forces in the various zones provided for in the 1979 peace treaty. Criminal and civil jurisdiction over members are vested with their respective national states.[3] The fate of this force will, like their predecessors, depend on what transpires in the Middle East in the future.

PART
II

SOUTH ASIA

10

INDIA AND PAKISTAN

ASIA, THE LARGEST CONTINENT IN BOTH size and population, covers one-third of the world's land surface and has about three-fifths of its people. It includes part of the Middle East. This birthplace of great civilizations contains nations with people who differ greatly in ancestry, religious beliefs and ways of life.

The twentieth century has seen the end of colonial rule there by European powers. Quarrels, some of them long standing, brought strife to the continent. To help contain these Asian conflicts, Canadian military personnel became peacekeepers and observers. It was as a result of a dispute between India and Pakistan that Canadian military personnel first became involved in trying to keep the peace.

UNITED NATIONS MILITARY OBSERVER GROUP IN INDIA
AND PAKISTAN

In August 1947, India and Pakistan became independent
dominions. The State of Jammu and Kashmir (referred to
here as Kashmir) was free to accede to India or Pakistan. The
accession became a matter of dispute between the two countries and fighting broke out. The dispute was referred to the
United Nations. In early 1948 the Kashmir problem was de-
bated in the Security Council, whose president was General
A.G.L. McNaughton of Canada. As a result, a UN commission for India and Pakistan (UNCIP) was formed to investigate and, if possible, mediate the conflict. UNCIP sent a
military mission to the area. The commission submitted a
proposal for a cease-fire and truce, known as the Karachi
Agreement of 1949, which was accepted by both sides. Under
this arrangement a new United Nations Military Observer
Group in India and Pakistan (UNMOGIP) of some thirty-
five observers was created to observe the cease-fire line and
determine whether there was any violation by either side.
Initially, Canada sent four officers as observers in February
1949 to Kashmir. They were for a time replaced regularly by
others. The total number of UN observers fluctuated to as
many as a hundred.

The first chief military observer was Canadian, a reserve
officer, Brigadier Henry H. Angle[1] who was appointed 10
January 1950. (He had previously served on the United Nations Commission for India and Pakistan from February to
October 1949.) Brigadier Angle helped establish a UN control
headquarters located in Srinagar, on the Indian side of the
cease-fire line, from May to November and in Rawalpindi,
Pakistan, for the rest of the year. Some UN military observers
were attached to the military headquarters of both India and

166

Pakistan as well as to local outposts occupying strategic points in Kashmir. Unfortunately, Brigadier Angle's effective contribution was ended when he was killed in a plane crash on 17 July 1950. Other Canadians who served as chief military observer were: Colonel J.H.J. Gauthier, 4 January to July 1966; Lieutenant-Colonel P.A. Bergevin, 19 June 1977 to 8 April 1978; and Lieutenant-Colonel P.P. Pospisil, 9 April 1978 to 3 June 1978. At that time Canada's contribution had been reduced to one observer.

RCAF Participation with UNMOGIP

At the outset UNMOGIP had one C-47 Dakota aircraft. Then 102 Kashmir Unit was formed in 1964 to provide a Canadian air element. The first Canadian aircraft sent to the area was on 15 June 1964, when a Caribou along with three RCAF officers and five technicians took over.

As a result of greater tension in 1963, the number of UN observers had increased to forty and Canada's contribution rose to nine officers. From 15 June 1964, the addition of 102 Kashmir Unit, with three RCAF pilots and five Canadian technicians, made the Canadians the largest national group in UNMOGIP. Australia, New Zealand, Denmark, Norway, Sweden, Finland, Belgium, Italy, Chile and Uruguay also contributed between one and five military observers each.

UNMOGIP's Activities

One of the first tasks of the military observer group had been to mark a clear cease-fire line along Kashmir's southern, western and northern borders. The observers then took up strategic positions in fixed posts on both sides of the line. As the cease-fire line ran through arable land in the valleys, incidents often originated with farmers. Until 1965 the group reported troop movements and helped resolve minor disputes along with Indian and Pakistani officers. The force could only report cease-fire violations; it had no power to enforce a cease-fire. Thus, like its counterparts in the Middle East, the group would be powerless if large-scale fighting broke out.

On average during this tour some eight, ten or twelve observer stations — half on each side of the border — were manned throughout the year. In addition, some northern stations were open only in the summer after the snow had left. Each station had military observers from different countries. The numbers at each would be less during the summer months in order to man the northerly posts. During a twelve-month tour an observer would normally find himself at a new station every three months. There were also about eight observers usually employed at headquarters and on liaison duties in New Delhi.

Investigation of a complaint could be difficult, particulary if the incident occurred in an isolated area at an altitude of thousands of feet above areas reachable by jeep. For those very few who enjoyed arduous hiking, such an assignment was ideal. Often a week passed by the time an observer could reach the point of complaint.

Living conditions at Srinagar or Rawalpindi were quite good. Life on a cool houseboat on a Srinagar lake during the summer was pleasant, especially with the availability of a batman for menial chores. Accommodations at field stations ranged from a cement-block building to a former Rajah's palace.[2] However, living conditions were generally quite primitive in the outposts.

An observer was granted compensatory time off during his tenure. Visits to New Delhi and the Taj Mahal outside Agra proved popular. Some visited Calcutta out of curiosity. For at least one Canadian, Major Malcolm Hyslop, the poverty there was worse than expected. The sight and smells of people living on the street, even being left to die, was shocking.

UNITED NATIONS INDIA-PAKISTAN OBSERVATION MISSION

Minor clashes along the the India-Pakistan frontier led to renewed hostilities. In the desolate Rann of Kutch, on Pakistan's southern border with India, Indian and Pakistani regular troops clashed in April 1965. By August the fighting had also spread to Kashmir along the line patrolled by UNMO-GIP. Early in September the Security Council called for a cease-fire which both nations accepted on 20 September. The cease-fire came into effect eight days later and the deployment of observers followed. Under the terms of the Security Council's resolution, a United Nations India-Pakistan Observation Mission (UNIPOM) was established, "to ensure supervision of the cease-fire and the withdrawal of all armed personnel." Since UNMOGIP's authority was limited to Kashmir, UNIPOM was given operational authority from the Rann of Kutch to Kashmir along a thousand-mile segment of the India-Pakistan western frontier, where the new hostilities were taking place.

A Canadian, Brigadier-General Bruce F. Macdonald, formerly commanding the United Nations Nicosia Zone in Cyprus, was appointed commander of UNIPOM with the rank of major-general at the end of September 1965. The Canadian government also provided an RCAF Air Transport Unit (117) to support UNIPOM to be based at Lahore, Pakistan, with three Caribou and three Otter aircraft, as well as some ten additional officer observers from all three services. UNIPOM's headquarters were set up at the stadium and in the administrative buildings of the National Horse and Cattle Show in Lahore, Pakistan, and at Amritsar, India. Almost a hundred military observers, some of whom were on loan from UNTSO and UNMOGIP, served under General Macdonald. Military observers manned stations on each side of the cease-fire line. Initially only two radio sets were available and local telephones had to be used for communication, sometimes with up to a twenty-four hour delay for connections. Gradually vehicles, communications and all other equipment were obtained from various parts of the world. In February 1966, following a peace conference at Tashkent, the two opposing armies withdrew to their own sides of the international border and on 22 March UNIPOM was disbanded. Only UNMOGIP was left to monitor the cease-fire in Kashmir. UNIPOM's mission was a success and helped to restore peace to the region.

Originally Canada sent reserve and then later regular army officers on peacekeeping duty to India-Pakistan. As integration neared, National Defence changed this role from a predominantly army to an air force support role for the observer group. Eventually, that role was reduced to one aircraft to support UNMOGIP.

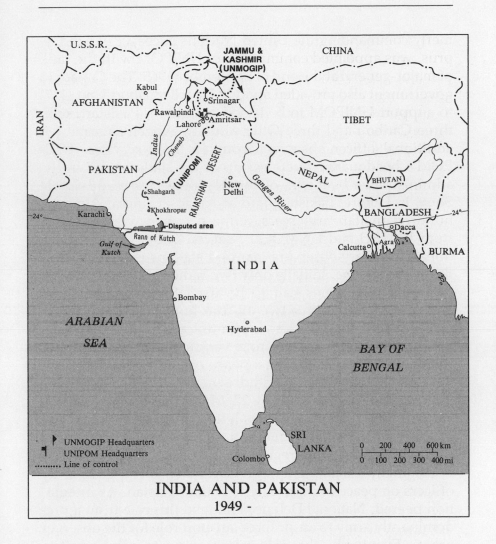

INDIA AND PAKISTAN
1949 -

RCAF Participation with UNIPOM

In September 1965, 117 Air Transport Unit was formed to assist UNIPOM. Two Caribous, from Trenton, Ontario, reached Lahore, Pakistan, on 3 October. They joined a Caribou and Otter aircraft formerly with UNMOGIP. Two other Otters arrived in early October, making a total of three Caribous and three Otters manned by twelve pilots. One Caribou was damaged on landing at Khokhropar, Pakistan, and although it was repaired with parts from an UNMOGIP Caribou bombed at Srinagar by the Pakistan air force on 8 September 1965, it could no longer be used for operations.[3]

While the Canadians had previous experience in the mountainous northern Kashmir area with UNMOGIP, all had to familiarize themselves with the barren Rajasthan Desert in the central southern portion of the international border. By October 1965, No. 117 Air Transport Unit, now composed of about a hundred officers and men, became responsible for flying and servicing the aircraft for both missions. In addition, Canada supplied the senior air adviser for UNIPOM from November 1965 to March 1966. Hercules C-130 flights from Marville, France, carrying freight and personnel for UNEF were extended on a fortnightly basis to go on with supplies to Lahore.

For many of the men of 117 Air Transport Unit, their assignment with UNIPOM was not a hardship.[4] They were proud to be wearing the blue beret of the UN and considered what they were doing to be a challenge. Temperatures, such as 95 degrees Fahrenheit in Pakistan, were offset by good accommodation at the Hotel International in Lahore, complete with central air-conditioning, a swimming pool and meals for seven dollars a day.

While it is not possible to present a detailed account of life

172

on every peacekeeping assignment, the following excerpts from 117 Air Transport Unit's diary give an indication of some of its experiences:

Friday 24 Sept 65

Shocking bloody news — off to Kashmir on Monday. Confusion everywhere — medicals to get, dental check, inventories to clean up, clearance to sign, pay to arrange, and in only three days . . . .

Monday 27 Sept 65

Arrived at Trenton 5 PM . . . issued first part of kit — blue beret . . . . Almost feel like 007 Agent on another mission.

Tuesday 28 Sept 65

Received rest of our tropical kit — wow short pants and all!

Sunday 3 Oct 65

Touch down in Bahrain approximately 0100 hr in unbearable heat and the stink is terrible.
So this is Pakistan — sure is a strange looking country.

Monday 4 Oct 65

Rented buses, if that's what you call them, providing transport to and from the site at airport. They drive like maniacs around here, on the left side too.

Wednesday 27 Oct 65

Bad accident with Caribou 5320 on landing at Chor. Nose wheel collapsed and she ran off runway. No real estimate of damage . . . .
Quite a few of the troops sick today with upset stomachs.

Saturday 30 Oct 65

Boys have to do inspection on Caribou outside — no hangar space available. Otter had to go out to rescue, Caribou 5325 down with an oil leak.

Another pay day — so lots of boys are out shopping, sure can buy lovely souvenirs around here.

Ball game was cancelled in afternoon — too many of our guys working.

Wednesday 3 November

Reports of an Otter being forced down in desert with oil leak. I guess they are having problems with the Otters using too much oil on their trips.

Saturday 6 November

We had another social night in the lounge tonight with a good size crowd, only one problem — our bloody bar ran dry at about 2300 hrs. What now?

Thursday 11 November

Remembrance Day in Pakistan. It has been a while since our guys spent the day the way they have. All our planes are out except the Caribou on inspection.

Monday 15 November

Third Caribou (5325) shook up today, hit a bird on landing, pilot said was as big as a Harvard? Apparently it made quite a mess . . . .

Friday 19 November

Lots of the boys out golfing today. It is a shame we are not back home with all the snow?

174

Wednesday 24 November

Apparently there is scads of mail and parcels aboard the Herc on Sat, for the troops. We're also to receive the Grey Cup film, should be good.

Saturday 27 November

Here comes Santa Claus — Oh brother! Who's going to sort all the presents that arrived on the Herc today.
Received our football games, both East and West finals.

Saturday 25 Dec.

Man we had a wonderful dinner today. Just like home. Turkey with all the trimmings.
Everyone sang carols after dinner, plus the officers put on a skit which was A-1. Leading Aircraftman Pouliot was the new Commanding Officer for the day and did very well.

27 — 29 Dec

Normal unit operations. With the stress on rest in off duty hours.

31 Dec 1965 — End of Year

Had a real bang-up New Year's Eve. The hotel sponsored the dance; good crowd, excellent time.

March 1966

March was the month that . . . saw the end of 117 Air Transport Unit Lahore. During the first 10 days the Otters and Caribous continued operations. Despite this, a good start was made in packing materials for shipment back to Canada. The battle of forces of total sea-lift vs total airlift ended in a compromise. One Yukon flight was authorized to part Lahore 18 March with the main party of 50 personnel plus baggage and some aircraft spares. Three C-130E flights were authorized for the first week of April to airlift the three Otters back to Canada. A rear party of 12 men with Flight Lieutenant M.S.

Tasker as Officer Commanding will remain at Lahore until arrangements to sea-lift the equipment is completed and to carry out the administrative, supply, and accounting details entailed in closing a unit. They expect to complete their task by the end of March . . . .

Temperatures during the month rose to 100 degrees F. in the sun so all personnel will leave with healthy tans.

UNMOGIP CONTINUES

After the withdrawal of 117 Air Transport Unit, a Caribou continued observation and supply flights in Kashmir where flying was a challenge. Whether facing flocks of vultures, navigating treacherous valleys and mountains, attempting to land on makeshift airfields, a pilot had to be constantly alert. He had to act as navigator, meteorologist and air-traffic controller. Fortunately, the Caribou proved an ideal aircraft for the Himalayas.[5]

A tour of duty for a Canadian ground observer usually was of one year's duration for the officers posted to UNMOGIP. Essential requirements for an observer were an even disposition, patience and the ability to get along with officers of other nationalities. A tour for a ground observer was spent at a variety of field stations along the cease-fire line between India and Pakistan. At one end of the armistice line were the Himalayas with peaks in the 18,000-foot range, while at the other extreme was the desert with temperatures of 120 degrees Fahrenheit. What remained with an individual after the tour were memories such as crossing gorges on narrow rope bridges, Himalayan peaks, new friends or enemies and stories of contacts with the people and military personnel of the area.[6]

On return from one year's duty with UNMOGIP in July

176

1970, Lieutenant-Colonel G.F.B. Ritchie gave some insight into what it was like for the fifty or so UN observers of whom nine were Canadian and the eight Canadian airmen.[7] Ritchie made clear that the term "observer" was a misnomer as the UN posts were not precisely forward with the opposing front-line units but back at formation headquarters. The role of the observer then became one of "investigator" when he was called upon to look into and report upon a complaint.

THE EMERGENCE OF BANGLADESH

In 1971, civil war erupted in East Pakistan (Bangladesh) and there was renewed fighting between India and Pakistan in November and December. One of the casualties was a Canadian twin-engine Otter on duty with UNMOGIP, destroyed on the runway at Rawalpindi on 5 December by a Hawker Hunter aircraft of the Indian air force. Fortunately nobody was hurt. With total air superiority and popular support, India quickly defeated Pakistani forces while fighting a holding action in the west. Following the war Bangladesh obtained its independence and a weaker Pakistan emerged.

A new truce line was established in Kashmir between India and Pakistan. Thereafter Canadian participation in UNMOGIP was gradually reduced. From 1972 to 1978 the Indians became less cooperative, for to them the war had ended the boundary problem to their satisfaction. Thus, a token number of observers remained on the Indian side, the majority being kept busy on the Pakistani side of the border with Kashmir. Treatment and hospitality for these unarmed UN observers, however, was as best as the Indian or Pakistani armies could manage within reason. Since 1979, Canada's contribution to UNMOGIP has been limited to a Hercules aircraft to assist in the movement of the peackeeping headquarters twice a year between Srinagar, India and Rawalpindi, Pakistan.

11

INDOCHINA

INTERNATIONAL COMMISSIONS FOR SUPERVISION AND CONTROL

FOLLOWING THE SURRENDER OF JAPAN in 1945, France attempted to regain control of its colonial empire in Southeast Asia. Its efforts were resisted chiefly by the forces of Ho Chi Minh's Viet Minh, whose most notable victory was at Dien Bien Phu. In 1954 the Geneva Accords ended the fighting and brought about the division of Vietnam, approximately on the 17th parallel (along the Ben Hai River), with the Communists in the north and a weak non-Communist government in the south. To supervise and report violations of the cease-fire agreements signed on 20-21 July 1954, three International Commissions for Supervision and Control were created — one for Cambodia, one for Laos and one for Vietnam — also referred to as the International Control Commission (ICC) or International Commission. Canada, India (chairman) and Poland were the countries which agreed to provide the commissions, which reported to Britain and the Soviet Union, the co-chairman of the Geneva Conference.

The three countries supplied delegations, each headed by civilian commissioners, assisted by military and political advisers. In early August, at a conference in New Delhi, Canada, India and Poland agreed on the organization and expenses. Fixed and mobile unarmed teams composed of an equal number of officers from each delegation were assigned to various strategic locations. The commissions for Cambodia, Laos and Vietnam had their headquarters in each capital.[1] While the latter was the largest and most significant of the three, it was not responsible for nor did it direct activities in either Cambodia or Laos. It was hoped that the Vietnam commission might supervise free elections in 1956, leading to the eventual reunification of North and South Vietnam.[2]

Separate cease-fire agreements empowered each commission to establish fixed and mobile teams comprised of an equal number of officers from each country. Fixed teams were to be located at points of entry for military supplies (five in Cambodia, seven in Laos, and fourteen in Vietnam), and included mobile elements. Teams were to control the entry of weapons of war into the three territories (four after the division of Vietnam) and keep arms at status quo levels as of 1954. The total number of observers and staff rose to 960 in its first year of existence.

The three international commissions were in Indochina by 11 August 1954, the date on which the cease-fire was to become complete. The first Canadian military personnel had arrived from South Korea in early August and approximately 150 Canadian service personnel and members of the Department of External Affairs from Canada landed in Indochina three weeks later. Most of these were stationed in Vietnam. Three-quarters of the Canadian personnel on the three commissions came from the Department of National

Defence. The Canadian Army provided most of the service personnel. The RCN and RCAF each supplied three officer observers.

By the end of 1954 there were some two hundred Canadians on the commissions. About 150 military personnel carried the main burden of work required to supervise the cease-fire agreements and the exchange of prisoners of war and refugees. While there was initial success in supervising the movement of military forces to their respective areas, there would be less progress in stemming the flow of war materiel.

What the ICSC observer in Southeast Asia quickly became aware of was the low sanitation standards. Immunization and antibiotics could generally control diseases such as malaria but many observers with the ICSC contacted some form of dysentery. Water could be purified by means of a foot-operated filter pump, a Lyster bag to store the water, and tablets added to kill any remaining bacteria. Fresh meat was available.[3] As a result of sanitation discipline, the overall health of most of the Canadians was good. Life for those based in Hanoi and the other capital cities, however, was much better than at the team sites.

With the withdrawal of the French forces from their Indochinese colonies and the return of the Viet Minh forces to North Vietnam, the situation became tranquil. After its first three hundred days or so the mobile teams were disbanded. The fixed teams, numbering two representatives from each country, were generally reduced to one or disbanded in some places. This episode was essentially a minor one in the overall story of Canada's military history but for most who served there it was a memorable experience.

Once France withdrew from its Indochinese possessions, the United States gradually intervened more and more to prevent Communist elements from taking control of the region. Doubts as to the value of the commissions in Cambodia, Laos and Vietnam grew. While each ICSC would issue reports or complain about the lack of cooperation from the governments of these countries, it had no means to change the situation.

CANADIAN LEADERSHIP

Heading the Canadian delegation as commissioner for Vietnam was Sherwood Lett, a distinguished veteran of both world wars. During the first year, Major-General W.J. Megill, the senior military adviser to the Canadian delegation in Vietnam, was based with his staff in Hanoi. The late Major-General R.E.A. Morton served mainly as the senior military adviser in Laos. In Cambodia, Major-General T.E. D'O. Snow, the senior military adviser there, also served as commissioner from June 1955. It is worthwhile noting that Canadian military personnel combined the qualities of diplomats as well as soldiers and acquitted themselves well in this role.

ICSC CAMBODIA

The commission for Cambodia began operating in August 1954. The twenty Canadians, mostly military, on the commission in Cambodia were outnumbered by the Polish complement of forty and the Indian group of 120, which were augmented by extra employees. Major A.L. Maclean, who was based in Kampot from September 1954 until August 1955, observed that life on an inspection team was similar

182

to being stranded on a desert island with a few colleagues. "Isolation, loneliness, clashing personalities, and eventually boredom, were the main enemies to combat."[4]

What remains vivid for most who served in Indochina are the good times. The following poem about life in Cambodia with the commission will give some insight to the novice and bring back many memories to those who served there:

WHICH OF THESE WILL WE THEN REMEMBER?

When we've been home for quite a spell
And shot our line, and shot it well;
When thoughts flash back on memory's train,
Because of a word, or a pouring rain
To Cambodia and our position
On the International Commission;
And to our thoughts we fully surrender,
Which of these will we then remember?

. . . the uniforms from the *Fantasie*,
Or a 'tasty' leg of *poulet roti*,
Or a trip by train to Battambang,
Or a ride in a jeep to Kompong Chhnang,
Or the morning after with *bière trente-trois*,
Or the night before with *soupe chinoise*,
Or a week-end at Chhup, at the rubber plantation,
Or Norodom Sihanouk's abdication?

Or a stay at Kep with a swim in the sea,
Or a visit to a *Bonzerie*,
Or the first full view of Angkor Wat,
Or the monotony of being caught
In the whirl of cocktail parties, all
Held on the terrace of Hotel Royal,
Or the Joint Commission at Svay Rien,
Or a Chinese meal at the Quoc Minh?

Or breakfast aboard SS *Sunon*

Berthed at the dock on the muddy Mekong,
Or a cyclo ride around Phnom Penh
With the cyclist shouting *"femme, femme,"*
Or writing an essay, or discussing reports,
Or the Cambodian Army's very short shorts,
Or the funny sensation on first eating crickets,
Or hopefully buying lottery tickets?

Or paddy fields, or coconut palms,
Or Calcutta beggars asking alms,
Or riding an elephant or a mule,
Or discussing the merits of a team at Snoul,
Or learning how to wear a sarong,
Or a Canadian conference sing-song,
Or our Hanoi arrival last September,
Which of these will we then remember?[5]

The teams were initially kept busy trying to ensure that the Geneva Accords were followed. The Viet Minh were persuaded to leave the country. Khmer Resistance Forces and local opposition elements were disbanded and permitted to return to their homes without retribution. By March 1955 monotony had set in on the commission as most of the work had been completed.

In March 1955, Prince Norodom Sihanouk abdicated the throne in favour of his father. This permitted the prince to organize his own political party and to hold a free election — one of Cambodia's obligations arising from the Geneva Conference. The election of September 1955 gave Sihanouk and his party the majority of the votes.

The ICSC remained in Cambodia at the insistence of that country's government. The Canadian delegation was represented there only in token form from 1958. The Cambodian commission finally withdrew on 31 December 1969 at Prince Sihanouk's request.[6]

ICSC Laos

The 1954 agreement for Laos envisaged a political settlement between the Royal Laotian government and the Communist-supported Pathet Lao dissidents, by which the latter would be reintegrated into the national community. Pending such a settlement the Pathet Lao forces were to be concentrated in the two northern provinces of Sam Neua and Phong Saly. The international commission's principal tasks were to control the withdrawal of foreign forces, the release of prisoners of war and civilian internees, and to supervise the points of entry for military personnel and war materiel.

The commission was initially kept busy supervising the exchange of prisoners of war and the release of civilian internees. It also investigated minor military clashes that took place during the regroupment process. With the cease-fire established, the commission became involved in promoting negotiations between the Royal Laotian government and the Pathet Lao. Finally, the two sides reached an agreement.

Brigadier Frederick Clifford replaced Major-General Morton as the senior Canadian military adviser in Vientiane and served there from September 1955 to September 1956.[7] Under him there were some twenty-five service personnel. Further Canadian service on the ICSC for Laos was discontinued from 1958 to 1961 when the commission there was adjourned[8] as a result of a temporary lull in the conflict.

Excerpts from the war diary of the military component of the Laotian section may offer some insight into what life was like for a Canadian military observer in that part of the world:

Vientiane — 7 September 1954

Major E.B. McCorkell evacuated to French military hospital, Saigon, owing to an ear infection. Everyone is sorry to see him go, but envious of his opportunity to leave this evil-smelling town for the relative luxury of Saigon.

Sam Neua (Xan Neu) — 2 December

The team . . . received a delegation of villagers who had come to submit a complaint. It appears one woman nursed her baby throughout the conference even while registering her complaint. She received the closest attention!

Phong Saly — 19 March 1955

A very strong meeting was held today with the Administrative Committee. Requirements put in as early as February had not even been remembered let alone met . . . . The boys [Laotian help] are dirty, indolent and inefficient. The "head boy" is as useless as the proverbial appendages to the bull's stomach . . . .

Captain P.R.W. Petrick, of the Signal Corps from Kingston, served as a teamsite member with the ICSC from September 1956 to September 1957. He offers some of his recollections:

My first teamsite was at Dong Hoi, North Vietnam, not far from the 17th parallel dividing North and South. It lasted three months. Travelling was often quite onerous — 200 miles over some of their roads in a beat-up jeep was no picnic. I spent the next three months from December to February in Tan Chau, South Vietnam. It is located on the Mekong River just south of the border with Cambodia. On the last day before leaving I managed to convince the Vietnamese liaison officer that he should invite me to dine with him for a real Vietnamese meal. It was wonderful. I gobbled up everything . . . . By about 7.a.m. I had been to the john about fifteen times. Then it [dysentery] got bad. I just stayed on and didn't move — not even when the administrative officer's girl friend, who had stayed overnight, had to have a widdle. Fortunately . . . the doctor was able to get cracking im-

186

mediately. Talk about a sore blow hole! Quite an experience . . . then it was on to various sites in Laos from March to September.

My next teamsite was at Muong Peun, a village in northern Laos just to the south of the area controlled by Pathet Lao but still in Royal Laotian territory. This place was lousy with fleas (no pun intended) and we were almost raw half-way to our knees. Everything came by air because Muong Peun was in the hills with nary a road in sight for at least 20-30 miles. The tents where we lived were hell when it rained.

In April, after my stay in Muong Peun, I went to Vientiane. I lived in the "Bungalow," a two-storey place, built more or less like a hotel. My room had a bit of a shower facility but since no water ever got up into the reservoir on top of the building, there was no such thing as running water. So you see, toilets (the few that were there) didn't get flushed all that often. To add insult to injury, it was at this time when I got prickly heat as the temperature every day for 3 weeks stood at 115 degrees to 120 degrees Fahrenheit and it used to cool down to 90 degrees at night.

In about 1954 or even earlier a company of the paratroopers of the Royal Laotian Army were dropped to dominate the airfield near Sam Neua (Xan Neu). They missed by several miles and landed on another mountain where they were immediately contained by the Pathet Lao. This was the Houei Thao or Houay Tou teamsite. By the time I was sent there in June 1957, there wasn't a tree left and hardly even any grass on the mountain top. Women and children had moved up to be with their men. All food and other supplies were air dropped by a regular plane about once a week. Sometimes we walked in and out, other times we made the change by helicopter, when it was in working order. All four of us (Indel, Candel, Poldel and interpreter) lived in a hole in the ground about four feet deep, covered by a tent. This was not a good posting. One of our officers almost went off his rocker and had to be evacuated.

In Vietnam most of the flying travel between Saigon and the teamsites was done by a DC-3. In Laos, most of it was done by Beavers and Otters. There also seemed to be three de Havilland Dragons. They were built in the early '30s and should have been retired long since. It was a real challenge to work up enough guts to climb into one as you quickly noticed the oil leaks and repaired fabric on the wings. One did, in fact, crash at Sam Neua, killing the pilot and at least two Indian passengers aboard.

After spending June and July there it was finally on to Luang Prabang, the royal capital. At this final phase of my tour, there was good accommodation, good food and something to do . . . . [9]

In Laos, supplementary elections and the formation of a coalition government in late 1957 brought a temporary peace. On 19 July 1958, the ICSC for Laos adjourned itself and withdrew. The collapse of the coalition government led to political realignment and the reconvening in 1961-1962 of the Geneva Conference on Laos. The ICSC for Laos was formally reestablished 23 July 1962 with broader powers but without means of enforcement. The ICSC for Laos was given its own independent means of transportation; however, no fixed teamsites were assigned. It proved less effective than the 1954 ICSC. In May 1966 the Canadian delegation consisted of nine civilians and nineteen military personnel. At the end of December 1969 Canada withdrew its ICSC delegation from Vientiane; thereafter a member of the Canadian delegation in Saigon, usually the commissioner or the next in command, represented Canada at ICSC meetings in Laos.

With the Paris peace accords for Vietnam, there was hope that a peace settlement would also take place in Laos. In July 1973, the international commission for Laos was again revived. Canadian representation on this revived commission consisted of one officer of the Canadian Forces and one from External Affairs, the commissioner. However, it became clear by January 1974 that the commission was going nowhere. The Canadian mission was withdrawn 15 June 1974, twenty years after the original Geneva Conference, and the ICSC for Laos ceased to function.

ICSC Vietnam

When the International Control Commissions first began, they functioned quite well. They helped save face on both sides. They were to supervise the cease-fires, the withdrawal of French troops at the very outset as well as the movement of refugees. In Vietnam, Communist sympathizers went north and many Catholics moved to the south to avoid living under communism. It quickly became clear that the international commissions lacked power to enforce any of their decisions. They could only report to the co-chairman of the Geneva Conference, Great Britain and the USSR.

As instructed, the Canadian military observers embarked upon this operation determined to be impartial and objective. On the other hand, the Poles were often one-sided. The Indian chairman grew increasingly frustrated at the futility of trying to reach any consensus.

For Canadian military personnel who served with the ICSC in North Vietnam in 1954-1955, there was much to observe. There was the flight of French colonials and troops leaving with whatever they could take with them. This hasty departure caused some temporary chaos due to the absence of trained local Vietnamese. French sympathizers or those who opposed the new regime in the North were often liquidated or "re-educated."

Ho Chi Minh impressed Canadians, such as Major Charles G. Provan of Kingston, as a brilliant yet ruthless individual with a theatrical flair. For example, during a ceremony of celebrations in late December 1954 marking the anniversary of the founding of the Popular Army of Vietnam, Ho Chi Minh suddenly appeared "like a Phoenix from its ashes" on a stage in simple, brown peasant garb amidst diplomats and soldiers in full dress. Everyone joined in and cheered.

Warnings by Canadian military observers that the United States should refrain from military interference in the area were not heeded. The following memorandum of 16 May 1955 from the Canadian delegation to the under-secretary of state for External Affairs is typical:

[Ngo Dinh] Diem should not be leader of South Vietnam . . . . He does not have the backing of the people. After all he is a Northerner and a Catholic . . . . His efforts to suppress the religious sects is very poor politics for without their support he cannot possibly succeed.[10]

As the government of South Vietnam was not a party to the Geneva agreements, it did not follow its terms, which included the holding of free elections in 1956. This encouraged North Vietnam to also ignore the Geneva settlements. By the late 1950s a campaign of rural insurgency was under way against the regime in the South aided from the North and the ICSC found itself ineffective.

According to the Geneva agreements, armaments in Vietnam were to remain at 1954 fixed levels. Monitoring of this provision reached a ludicrous state. From time to time the South Vietnamese would assemble the military observers to witness the destruction of obsolete arms which they subsequently replaced with new weapons. However, the North Vietnamese did not even attempt this. They simply did not allow adequate inspection.

Colonel Robert T. Bennett served with the ICC in Vietnam in 1961-1962 and, later, as a brigadier-general, was the senior military officer and acting commissioner there in 1971-72. He recalled going to inspect a train alleged to be carrying arms in North Vietnam. The inspection consisted of seeing a bill of lading in a language that he could not read. As well, he was not permitted to inspect the sealed railway cars. The enforcement of the status quo of arms as set out in the Geneva Accords had become a farce.[11]

The parties to the Geneva agreements were to supply the commissions and their teams with food, lodging and, most important, transportation. In order to supervise and control, the commissions became totally dependent on the Cambodian, Laotian, North and South Vietnamese governments for transport. Without adequate transportation or protection the teams were unable to function. Tape recorders and binoculars were eventually prohibited by North Vietnam, as was the taking of photographs there, without the liaison officers' prior consent. While many serious incidents remained unresolved, minor occurrences, such as a water buffalo wandering across the demilitarized zone, occupied the commission for Vietnam. Meanwhile, arms and soldiers were flowing into South Vietnam and incidents increased as the commission became more and more irrelevant.

Teams of military observers were usually dependent upon a liaison officer particularly in North Vietnam. Should the liaison officer present an excuse such as the collapse of a bridge or breakdown of a jeep, an investigation could not take place. As the host governments were in charge of vehicle transportation, they could control where a team went. On one occasion, while a convoy was proceeding to a prearranged investigation, a Canadian military observer was able to carry out an unscheduled inspection in North Vietnam by insisting he had to urinate near an antiaircraft site. The resulting investigation created great consternation among the Communists.

Translators were also a necessity, particularly in communicating with the Poles. The Polish delegation had Polish-English and Polish-French interpreters. Additional interpreters were required to communicate with the local populace. Consensus on the interpretation of language in written reports would also create problems.

Although the Indian army provided communications for the commission, fourteen Canadian Army cryptographers were assigned initially to Hanoi, Phnom Penh and Vientiane to keep its own messages to Canada secret. As the usefulness of the commission declined so did cipher requirements. The cryptographers departed from Laos in June 1958 and Cambodia in June 1960. On the average there remained five cryptographers in Saigon and one in Hanoi. In the early 1960s, there were again several in Vientiane as the commission there had resumed its work.[12]

The Canadian commissioner, appointed by the Department of External Affairs, was the senior Canadian official. Often next in importance was his senior military adviser who frequently became the senior official in the commissioner's absence. As the commissions became increasingly ineffective, the number of military observers was reduced and the quality of some of them declined. There were several cases of alcoholism and even some Canadian involvement in smuggling. Parties, rotations among sites and compulsory participation in sports programs were attempted to overcome a growing malaise and improve morale.[13]

Lieutenant-Colonel David Veitch, Royal Canadian Engineers, served from the summer of 1965 to the summer of 1966 as an international military observer in South Vietnam. He found himself with lots of time and little work. Hobbies, such as stamp collecting or photography, helped keep him occupied. The members of observer teams in Indochina were not members of that society and tended to be isolated in their own separate world.[14]

Dr. G.E. Chenard, the Canadian medical officer with the ICSC in 1962, noticed sharp differences between North and

Indochina

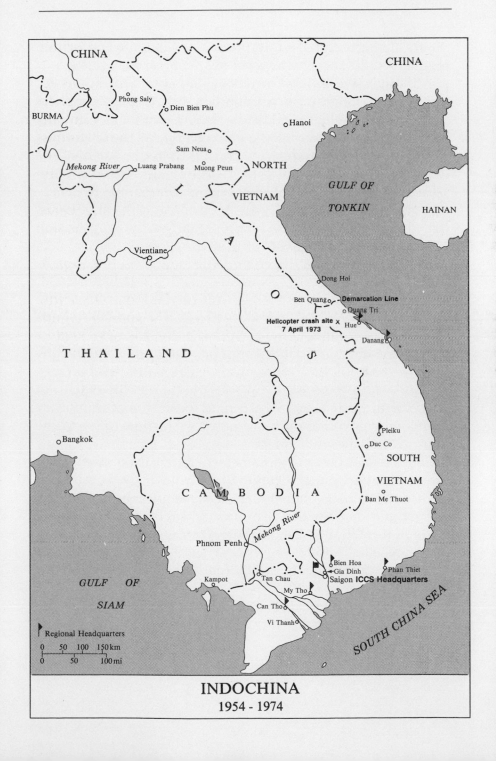

CHINA

Phong Saly
Dien Bien Phu

BURMA

Sam Neua

Mekong River Luang Prabang Muong Peun

Hanoi

CHINA

NORTH

VIETNAM

GULF OF

TONKIN

HAINAN

L
A
O
S

Vientiane

Dong Hoi

Ben Quang ■ Demarcation Line
Quang Tri
Hue
Helicopter crash site x
7 April 1973
Danang

T H A I L A N D

Pleiku
Duc Co

SOUTH

VIETNAM

Ban Me Thuot

Bangkok

C A M B O D I A

Mekong River

Phnom Penh

Bien Hoa
Gia Dinh
Saigon **ICCS Headquarters**

Phan Thiet

Kampot Tan Chau

My Tho

GULF OF

SIAM

Can Tho

Vi Thanh

SOUTH CHINA SEA

▶ Regional Headquarters

0 50 100 150 km
0   50   100 mi

INDOCHINA
1954 - 1974

South Vietnam. In Hanoi, the streets were clean, the people regimented and there was no overt poverty. In contrast Saigon's streets were dirty, with beggars, prostitutes and orphans in evidence. Chenard witnessed the beginning of the large-scale influx of American forces to assist the South Vietnamese in trying to combat a guerrilla war. The deleterious effects of American troops with considerable money and leave would become evident.[15] What was obvious to many Canadians who served in South Vietnam was rampant corruption and mismanagement. Members of the ICSC discovered that there was less bribery and stealing of their personal belongings in Communist-controlled regions.

For those such as Brigadier Donald E. Mounteer, now retired in Naniamo, BC, who was with the ICSC in 1955-1956, and again in 1963-1964, it was obvious that the influx of American goods and personnel would not prevent South Vietnam from falling to the North. The division of the South into many small and largely independent provinces kept it from uniting for the common struggle. South Vietnamese generals and others were amassing great wealth at the expense of the war effort. The innate weakness of the South Vietnamese government was evident at the time of the Communist offensive in January 1964. For a time it was even feared the Viet Cong (Vietnamese Communists) might capture the building in the Cholon district of Saigon which housed the Canadians' signal and cipher equipment. The war was gaining momentum. By 1965 the seven fixed teamsites north of the 17th parallel had been removed at the insistence of the North Vietnamese who stated that they could not guarantee the team's security in the face of American air attacks.

There were Canadian fatalities on 18 October 1965 when an aircraft chartered by the ICSC, en route to Hanoi from

Vientiane, went down over North Vietnam, likely as a result of ground fire. Among those killed were two Canadian military personnel, Sergeant J.S. Byrne and Corporal V.J. Perkin. The wreckage of the aircraft was never recovered. At the same time there were other fatal accidents among ICSC staff in the region. Brigadier-General G.J.H. Wattsford of Kingston, the senior military adviser in Laos, remembers it as a very sad time.

Life for members of the ICC in Saigon could be frustrating, interesting, monotonous or exhausting. The senior Canadian military adviser lived in a villa in a guarded, park-like compound. Other military members of the Canadian delegation were assigned hotel rooms in downtown Saigon.[16]

By 1972 the Canadian military delegation to the ICSC for Vietnam consisted of about twenty members. Their usefulness had long since passed. As a result of South Vietnam's exclusion of Indian personnel, ICSC headquarters for Vietnam was transferred back to Hanoi. Its last official business took place in March 1973. When it ended, it had four officers and two other ranks on its ICSC establishment.[17]

During the American-Vietnam conflict, the Communists alleged that the Canadians on the international commission were, in fact, spies for the Americans. Statements of that sort did tend to discredit our role on the ICC in the eyes of some Canadians. In spite of many obstacles, most Canadian observers gave dedicated and honourable service.

INTERNATIONAL COMMISSION OF CONTROL AND SUPERVISION

In January 1973 the Canadian government agreed to serve on the 1,160-member International Commission of Control and Supervision (ICCS) for South Vietnam for an initial period of sixty days, subject to renewal. The ICCS was composed of Canada, Hungary, Indonesia and Poland (CHIP). The main purpose of the force was to monitor a cease-fire in South Vietnam agreed to in the Paris peace accords. It was also to supervise the exchange of prisoners and ensure that no buildup of military equipment would occur. The Canadian delegation consisted of a military component of 240 servicemen and some fifty officials from the Department of External Affairs.

The ICCS was organized similarly to the ICSC. At the head were four ambassadors, one to lead each of the four delegations. Canada's ambassador, Michel Gauvin, became the first chairman. Had it not been for his initiative the ICCS would never have struggled so hard to organize itself in those first few weeks. The diplomats and the military supported each other and this mutual assistance gave the Canadians added strength.

With little prior notice, 150 soldiers were initially brought from all parts of Canada to Longue Pointe Depot, Montreal, where most of the preparation took place. The Department of National Defence code named this observer mission to Vietnam "Operation Gallant." The name reflects how the Canadians viewed their role. There were endless lectures and briefings by experts on all aspects of what could be expected. Those who had no pistol training were given a quick course. The chief of defence staff, General Jacques Dextraze, wanted the Canadians to wear sidearms although their safety was assured by the South Vietnamese. Once they were in Vietnam, however, it was decided that they would not carry them. Canadian flag patches were sewn on uniforms and the men were issued shorts, raincoats, first-aid kits, a pamphlet on Vietnam and a thick military-observer manual prior to departure. An advance party of two officers as well as the civilian and military heads of the Canadian delegation preceded the main body of soldiers.

When the first Canadian delegation left Dorval Airport in late January 1973 aboard a Canadian Forces 707, little did they realize what would lie ahead for them. After twenty-five and a half sleepless hours, they arrived at 3:30 on the morning of 29 January at Tan Son Nhut Air Base, Saigon, in eighty-degree heat. They were greeted by Michel Gauvin along with Major-General Duncan A. McAlpine, the senior military adviser and commander of the Canadian troops. The cease-fire had gone into effect on 27 January and the American troops were to withdraw within sixty days.

At the American air base the Canadians were assigned to 1300 Block, a group of sandbagged and wire-enclosed Stalag-type huts that were to be their main working and sleeping quarters. The Canadians quickly adapted to their new surroundings. Operations and logistics staff began to set up liaison, communications equipment, maintenance facilities, even banking arrangements. Much had been organized when the second wave of Canadians left Canada on 11 February.

ORGANIZATION

The old ICSC headquarters in Saigon became the new ICCS headquarters. Thanks to the drive of the Canadian ambassador, Michel Gauvin, the ICCS was pushed into operation.

The Canadians were the first to assume the rotating chairmanship of the commission. They also took the key post of director of personnel and logistics. Without the Canadians, the commission likely would never have ventured out of Saigon. The Canadians led the way in administration, communications, transportation, supply, investigations, prisoner exchanges and press information. They were also responsible for helping to organize regional headquarters and for sending out field teams. There were representatives from each of the four participating countries on these teams. Two Canadian officers usually represented their country on a local teamsite. According to the Paris agreement the teams had to be in position within fifteen to thirty days after the cease-fire and this requirement was met. The siting of these teams was specified in the protocol to the agreements.

There were seven regional headquarters in the various geographical areas of South Vietnam which, in turn, had twenty-six sub-regional teams. The Saigon area formed an additional region with three teams. There were further teams responsible for supervising the release and repatriation of captured and detained prisoners. Some were located at potential entry points for war materiel and a few sites were located at ports designated by the South Vietnamese as legitimate points of entry for armaments. Several other teams were available for special assignments to help meet the commission's mandate.

During February and March 1973, teams were deployed around South Vietnam. A few sites were even manned briefly in Communist-held territory. In March and April, greater efforts were directed where possible to investigating cease-fire violations as the departure of the Americans in March had led to an escalation of incidents.

The Canadians were the most keen and thorough members of the investigation teams. At first the Communist team members refused to go to investigate incidents primarily on the grounds of a lack of security. Once the Canadians were issued cameras and tape recorders some six weeks after their arrival, they were able to take photographs and record interviews where an incident occurred. Since non-refutable evidence could then be obtained, the Communist members then became more willing to go to an incident site, although they nervously stuck quite close to the Canadians.

The Canadians' enthusiasm turned to frustration as the Poles and Hungarians were unwilling to criticize the Communists. As an example, there was the case of a blown-up Bailey bridge near the village of Vi Thanh in the lower Mekong Delta. While it was obvious that the Viet Cong had destroyed the bridge, the Communist members of the investigation team attributed its collapse to the weight of heavy vehicles.[18]

EXPERIENCES

What probably remains with all those who served in Egypt, India-Pakistan, or Indochina, are the smells to which sensitive noses were not accustomed. For the unwary, eating or drinking anything not prepared according to North American hygienic standards would result in dysentery or "gyppo stomach." The intake of a suppressive drug, Paludrin, usually prevented malaria and inoculations stopped most of the Canadians from contacting other serious diseases (excluding VD).

Although minefields were believed to be a major threat to the peacekeepers, a few water buffalo gave the Canadians

several scares. The strange scent of these foreigners sometimes caused the buffalo to charge, and with no weapons
several of the Canadians had a frantic time trying to escape
through rice paddies flooded with water and human
excrement.

The tour of duty with the ICCS could not be described as
a real hardship. One former serviceman with the ICCS con-
fided to the author that had all the details of life with the
ICCS been disclosed there would have been a lot of divorces
back in Canada. Finding a Canadian member of the ICCS in
a remote area with two "maids" in his quarters, his commanding officer asked, "What do you think you are up to?"
To which the man replied, "Keeping the piece, sir."

Apart from the ICCS medal, a select number also received
the Golden Butterfly award. This was a small gold pin worn
discreetly behind the lapel. It could be worn by any Canadian
on the ICCS who had sex with at least ten Vietnamese women.

Every serviceman on the ICCS had his own personal memories. Former Warrant Officer Garry Handson of the School
of Intelligence kept a record of his experiences and selected
excerpts follow:

On the morning of 23 November 1972, the chief instructor handed
me a message inviting me to join a group of Canadian military and
External Affairs personnel tasked with the problem of helping to
create peace in South Vietnam . . . . To prepare I had to report to the
hospital for a medical checkup, have some needles, a dental checkup,
etc. The only things that sort of reminded me that this wasn't a
vacation was when they asked if I had made out a current will. Briefing
sessions also followed . . . .

An uneventful flight to Montreal after a sad farewell didn't ready
me for the hectic pace going on in the drill hall at Longue Pointe.
Additional kit had to be issued — short pants — 'you have to be
kidding,' briefings on the bad things in Vietnam: bad guys (VC), bad

girls (VD), bad buys, bad water, etc. Ouch! Somehow Borden missed giving me a needle — enough activity to keep us up until one a.m . . . . As soon as I saw the twinkle of Saigon City from far out at sea, I knew — I'm in Vietnam.

. . . . Region 1 was the northernmost region and approximately one-half of it under Communist control. The headquarters was at the old capital city of Hue. We flew from Saigon to Hue on 20 February. The trip was uneventful except for the magnificent view we had. Stretching out to the west and south lay the shimmering rice paddies of the delta. We could see the craggy mountains running into Laos and the green plateau areas of the central highlands . . . . A helicopter was waiting to take us north to Quang Tri to observe a prisoner exchange. Quang Tri is, or was, a city like Hue. All that is left are destroyed mounds and bomb craters that make the area appear like a grey-red moon surface . . . .

Region 2 is mostly mountains and the remainder coastal plain. Danang, basking in a late afternoon sun, appears as the military complex that it is. The area is dominated by the large airbase located on the flat dusty plain. The ICCS headquarters here, as in Hue, is in a French style hotel . . . . It was a ball ordering a Vietnamese supper in our pidgin dialect . . . . Our vegetables turned out to be boiled sea urchin (it tastes like pork fat) and our chicken legs turned out to be one-year old preserved chicken feet. The skin was supposed to be the delicacy.

Region 3 is by far the largest ICCS region. Team sites are spread along the coastal plain, through the rugged central highlands and onto the plateau areas. The regions' headquarters is at Pleiku. The cooling breezes of the mountain plateau were welcome after the humidity of the coastal plains and the Saigon area. We spent a pleasant afternoon meeting the representatives from the various delegations and discussing the truce problems of the area. After an evening proving that Canadians can out-sing and out-drink all Hungarians, Poles and US helicopter pilots, we had a deep sleep.

After breakfast we went along to investigate a complaint of an ambush around the Ban Me Thuot team site. The trip by helicopter took an hour to reach the investigation team. Then three jeeps continued the journey for an hour and a half until the rutted path of a

road petered into a foot path. Five Montagnard tribesmen were waiting to guide us. They were clad only in a loin cloth and armed either
with a spear or crossbow for hunting and a carbine for defence . . . .
After reaching the ambush site where four tribesmen and a boy had
been killed, our team started scouring the area. Our team was composed of Canadian and Indonesian ICCS members (the Hungarians
and Poles wouldn't go). When the tribesmen saw the interest and
care of the team, they became friendlier . . . . By the time we reached
the village we had become friends . . . .

After a plentiful meal we sat around smoking and drinking some
type of rice liquor. The chief announced that members of the tribe
would like us to be their brothers . . . . The ceremony was very simple. First both individuals say "You are my brother" then each brother
hammers a brass ring around the other's wrist. Final acceptance into
the tribe is when I ate a tribal delicacy with my new brother. Fortunately, this only consisted of deep fried sparrows with their feathers
on. Actually, I've heard of friends of mine who had to eat fresh
monkey brains during this ceremony . . . . Soon the flash of the South
China Sea heralds our arrival on the coast.

Region 4 . . . I was happy I wouldn't be sleeping here tonight
because the hotel is right beside a condiment factory. Pungent sea-
soning is produced there by draining the liquid from barrels containing six-month old rotten fish and you can imagine the smell!

The headquarters for Region 5 is at Bien Hoa . . . . The multinational headquarters is housed in a hotel-like structure behind a massive iron fence. The compound is off limits to outsiders and is guarded
by a South Vietnamese police detachment. The local regional commander said that they shoot at anything that moves at night. The
normal method of patrol that these 'brave' policeman use is to stand
at the entrance to an alley and let fly with whatever they carry as
weapons. It was quite a sight to see children, dogs, cats, chickens,
etc. come flying out the other end of the alley.

The Saigon/Gia Dinh Region came directly under the control of the
chief of staff at headquarters MCCD (Military Component Canadian
Delegation) in Saigon. Incidents did occur within the capital district
but they were few and minor when compared to the outlying
regions . . . .

On the 28th of February we flew in a helicopter from Saigon to the headquarters of Region 6 located in the city of My Tho situated by one of the tributaries of the Mekong River . . . . the action here is heavy because of the convoy activity on the Mekong . . . .

I've toured the more dangerous waterfront bars both in Canada and Europe. Nothing matches the river bars in the My Tho area. A more blood-thirsty looking bunch of pirates and wharf rats you couldn't imagine . . . . A couple of these river boatmen tried us on for size but after one of us threw several of them out of the bar room window and into the river below we had no further trouble . . . . This sergeant was a paratrooper and black belt in karate.

. . . . We chugged along during the misty early morning hours from My Tho airfield to Region 7 headquarters at Can Tho . . . . There it is spread below us, mile after mile of rice paddies and tin-topped clusters of hamlets and villages . . . . Region 7 has a high level of military activity due to it containing not only most of the rice producing areas but also Viet Cong training and supply facilities . . . .

The Canadian public can take pride in the dedication and hard work exhibited by the Canadian contingent . . . . On our motor pool we had a sign which read in part: "The time is now — the word is PEACE" — but nobody would listen to us nor were they interested.[19]

THE CANADIANS AND THE VIET CONG

A total of forty-seven sites (thirty-five manned) in South Vietnam were assigned to ICCS personnel to help supervise the truce. Many could only be reached by aircraft or by helicopter. Some had to be abandoned. The US army at first provided air transport. They were replaced by an American civilian firm (Air America) using the same helicopters as those supplied to the South Vietnamese army but with ICCS markings. The Provisional Revolutionary (Communist) Government, hereafter also referred to as the Viet Cong (VC), demanded and received ICCS pre-flight clearance for all flights into or over territory under their control. In spite of obtaining approval, most of the ICCS helicopters received ground fire; VC troops in the field treated all aircraft as hostile.

Of the thirty-five teamsites that were occupied, none was typical. One in Viet Cong controlled territory was Duc Co near the Cambodian border. Major J.O.W. Ross and his partners, Captain H.A. Vos and later Captain A.H.C. Smith, were assigned that teamsite. The purpose of that location was to check on the entry and replacement of Communist war materiel coming from the north along the Ho Chi Minh Trail. In the compound, each ICCS team was assigned a thatched hut with a dirt floor and beds and benches handmade from sawn boards. Bathroom facilities consisted of a daily basin of hot water to wash and shave in the morning, a fifty-gallon oil drum containing cold 'scummy' water and chlorinated water to drink. An outdoor privy was located on stilts as a precaution against snakes. It had no toilet seat but there were two places to put one's feet and squat — definitely not recommended for those with a poor sense of balance. Meals of canned field rations were heated by Viet Cong cooks. Communication was by radio, and power was supplied by an electric generator.

There were two major problems. Serious fighting proved to be dangerously close. A small war was waging fifteen miles northeast of the site so heavy bombers and fighter aircraft were traversing overhead. The compound was illuminated throughout the night by flares. At one point, wills were revised and final letters to loved ones drafted. Malaria, however, was an even larger threat. The Hungarian delegate was stricken after fifteen days. Three days later Major Ross, too, had to be evacuated. Other team members suffered from malaria as well. The site was eventually abandoned until health and safety conditions could be improved, which they never were.[20]

Despite previous flight clearance, on 7 April 1973, a shoulder-launched missile shot down an ICCS helicopter on a mission to set up a teamsite near the Laotian border.[21] The accompanying helicopter on this assignment managed to evade a ground-to-air missile by descending quickly to earth; nevertheless, it sustained damage from small-arms fire. Forty-two year old Captain Charles E. Laviolette, of Quebec City, was killed, along with two Hungarian officers, one Indonesian, two Viet Cong liaison officers and a three-man civilian crew.

An investigation of the incident revealed the cause was due to navigational error. The helicopter had been led astray by a newly-built North Vietnamese all-weather road into South Vietnam. The pilot had followed the actual road and not the map. The new road was not on the ICCS map.[22]

VIETNAM — FAREWELL

Originally Canada was to serve on the ICCS for sixty days, with longer participation to be considered. On 27 March, more than a week prior to the shooting down of the ICCS helicopter carrying Captain Laviolette, External Affairs Minister Mitchell Sharp warned in the House of Commons that unless there was a substantial improvement in the situation the Canadian contingent would be withdrawn by 30 June. The helicopter incident reinforced that decision. However, Mr. Sharp announced on 29 May that the Canadians would remain an extra month in order to give the parties time to find a replacement for the Canadian delegation. At the request of the United States, that withdrawal date was extended by one month. The last members of the Canadian delegation left Vietnam on 31 July 1973.

In late June, just east of Saigon, Canadian captains Ian Patten and Fletcher Thomson were abducted by the Viet Cong for seventeen days. Both men had been reconnoitering an area where they had safely been before. The VC's purpose was to assert their control of that territory. It was evident that the safety of the Canadians could not be assured. Thus the decision to withdraw the Canadian delegation from the ICCS was justified.

In the last six months of 1972, prior to the cease-fire, there were 80,000 casualties, while in the first half-year of the truce there were 76,000.[23] In August 1973, following Canada's tour in Vietnam, Major-General McAlpine described the truce as an illusion.

Only a small percentage of the total number of incidents were ever investigated. Most investigations originated on the part of the South Vietnamese government. There was obstruction, delaying tactics, even refusal to go and investigate by Communist members of the commission.

On the ICSC for Vietnam, the Poles supported the Communist position with Canada often taking the opposite side. On the ICCS, Hungary and Poland maintained the Communist position while Canada enunciated the Western point of view. Although supporting the Western position, the Indonesians tried not to offend anyone. Canadian participation in this commission had been conditional and for a brief period dependent upon the effective performance of the ICCS. When it became clear that the ICCS was ineffective, Canada withdrew.

A relatively unknown aspect to the ICCS operation was the presence of two Canadian destroyers, *Terra Nova* and *Kootenay*, on manoeuvres in the South China Sea to support a possible evacuation of Canadians from Vietnam. The presence of both ships would have facilitated a quick escape in case a sudden unfavourable turn of events occurred.[24]

In "Operation Gallant," a comprehensive report by the Department of National Defence about the ICCS operation, one of the summary conclusions was that, "Many [Canadian officers] found themselves unprepared for the unique nature of the adversary negotiations they were required to conduct with the Polish and Hungarian delegations to the ICCS." In spite of this criticism, the Canadian officers handled themselves quite well often using logic to out-debate their Communist counterparts. The Communist members had a propensity to try to maintain their position through long drawn-out speeches.

One moderately successful aspect of the ICCS presence was the release and exchange of over 32,000 prisoners of war, in which the Canadians were prominently involved. However, the release of civilian detainees was beset with difficulties. Only 1,700 had been released out of an estimated 5,700 when the last Canadians left in July 1973. The chief obstacle was the lack of Viet Cong cooperation.

During the Canadians' stay over a thousand investigations were ordered although there were 18,000 recorded incidents.[25] Many of the latter, however, were minor or were incidents from which it would have been difficult to draw any conclusions. The number of ordered investigations, however, reasonably reflected the capacity of the ICCS to carry out such inquiries. Lack of security guarantees or Viet Cong liaison officers curtailed the activities of the military teams.

The ICCS was caught up in events that were beyond its scope to control or influence. After the Canadians departed the ICCS continued to operate for almost two years, but, hobbled by restraints, it no longer played an effective role. The Americans withdrew their forces in March 1973 and the regime they had supported was left unprotected. A Communist victory in the south ensued on 30 April 1975 with formal reunification of Vietnam being declared on 2 July 1976.

CONCLUSION

A cease-fire agreement in South Vietnam helped result in a cease-fire in February 1973 in Laos and the formation of a new Laotian coalition government. In December 1975, the coalition government collapsed and the Communist People's Democratic Republic of Laos was established. As a result of its long border with South Vietnam, Cambodia also became more and more affected as the war intensified. A protracted civil war developed in Cambodia with the Khmer Rouge guerrillas eventually defeating the American-backed military regime and gaining control of Phnom Penh in April 1975.

While both the ICSC and ICCS facilitated the withdrawal of French and American military involvement in Indochina, these commission were unable to bring peace to this region. The ICCS was a face-saving means of achieving a dignified withdrawal while temporarily reducing the fighting. The inclusion of the term "control" in the titles of both commissions proved a misnomer as they were not given any powers of control. Their only terms of engagement were as observers to supervise the implementation of the agreements.

12

WEST NEW GUINEA

THE WESTERN HALF OF NEW GUINEA had been in Dutch possession since 1828. During the Second World War, Sukarno, an Indonesian nationalist, cooperated with the Japanese who had expelled the Dutch from the East Indies including New Guinea. After the war, Sukarno led the struggle against the Dutch, who sought to re-establish their rule. On 27 December 1949 the Netherlands transferred sovereignty of the Indonesian archipelago to the Republic of the United States of Indonesia. Not included in the transfer was the western half of New Guinea. The Netherlands felt West New Guinea should become independent or at least vote to decide its future. Sukarno, now the first president of Indonesia, already considered it an integral part of his territory.

In January 1962, impatient with a lack of progress in the negotiations, Sukarno attempted to strike at West New Guinea with torpedo boats which were repelled by Dutch naval forces.[1] While negotiations were under way with the UN, Indonesia parachuted troops into West New Guinea. Both sides quickly accepted a mediation plan for the formation of a United Nations Temporary Executive Authority (UNTEA) that would administer West New Guinea for eight months. The entire expense of this UN effort was to be borne equally by the Netherlands and Indonesia. Approval of the initiative of the secretary-general, U Thant, was given by the UN General Assembly on 21 September 1962. The agreement worked out also provided for a UN Security Force (UNSF) to assist the UN Temporary Executive Authority with as many troops as were deemed necessary. The force commenced operation on 3 October 1962 and finished its activities on 30 April 1963.

The UN Security Force, numbering over 1,500 men, was composed mainly of Pakistani soldiers and twenty-one military observers from various countries. Canada did not supply any observers but was asked for an air adviser and a float-equipped Otter with flying and maintenance crew. Canada recommended that there should also be a backup plane and this suggestion was accepted.

New Guinea is the second largest island in the world, exceeded in size only by Greenland. Located just south of the equator, it is made up of tropical rain forests and marshes. A complex mountain range runs along the centre of the island. The main island is surrounded by groups of smaller islands to the northwest. One of these islands is Biak, and this is where Canada's peacekeepers were based. The average temperature in New Guinea is about 81 degrees Fahrenheit, the average morning temperature being about 72 and the average noon temperature about 92. In 1962, West New Guinea had a population of about 700,000 Papuans many of whom lived in a stone-age culture and about 10,000 Europeans, many of whom had moved there when Indonesia obtained its independence.

Two Hercules heavy transport planes left Trenton, Ontario, with the dismantled Otters and crew and arrived at Biak on 3 September 1962. Unfortunately, the second Otter

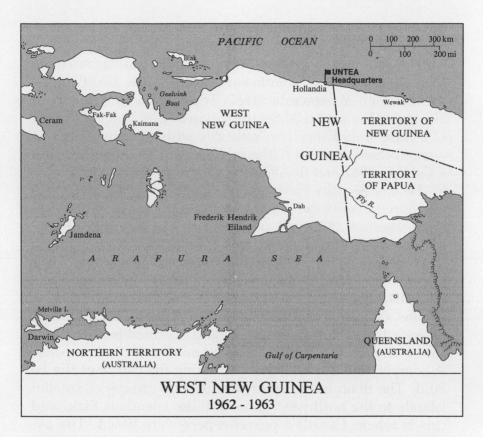

WEST NEW GUINEA
1962 - 1963

Map labels: PACIFIC OCEAN; Biak; UNTEA Headquarters; Hollandia; Geelvink Baai; Wewak; Ceram; Fak-Fak; Kaimana; WEST NEW GUINEA; NEW GUINEA; TERRITORY OF NEW GUINEA; TERRITORY OF PAPUA; Fly R.; Frederik Hendrik Eiland; Dah; Jamdena; A R A F U R A   S E A; Melville I.; Darwin; NORTHERN TERRITORY (AUSTRALIA); Gulf of Carpentaria; QUEENSLAND (AUSTRALIA)

could not be made serviceable due to a lack of some parts that could not be obtained until 16 October. Wing Commander R.G. Herbert, RCAF, who was to act as air adviser and an air staff officer to the UN Security Force, was based at the capital, Hollandia. He was of immense assistance to the Canadians in resolving some of the problems. The commander of the Canadian crews based at Biak was Flight Lieutenant A.E Richards. He was responsible to the commander of UNSF for his personnel and to the commander of the Air Transport Unit for air operations and local administration.[2]

211

Problems were to be referred to UNTEA headquarters at Hollandia.

The commanding officer of the entire air transport unit of UNSF was an American, who also headed the United States Air Force (USAF) there. The US contribution increased from one Dakota and crew on 3 September to an average of some sixty airmen manning up to four Douglas Dakota aircraft and six helicopters. While the American contingent considered itself a part of the USAF seconded to support UNSF, the RCAF detachment regarded itself as an integral part of UNSF. The commander of the RCAF detachment had to work through the American commander with respect to quarters, food and transport for his men.

Upon arrival, the twelve Canadians of 116 Air Transport Unit discovered their main problem was a lack of adequate food. Although food was available locally, they found it to be of poor quality. As a result each airman lost eight to ten pounds in the first month, until meals to which he was accustomed could be provided. At first officers lived in the KLM Hotel and the airmen in various Dutch barracks. Lavoratory and washroom facilities were dirty and inadequate. After October 1962 motel accommodation was provided for the airmen and houses for the officers. Messing was eventually provided by a USAF field kitchen located in part of an old hotel. Because they did not carry Canadian passports, the servicemen could not take brief vacations in Manila, and indecision about allowances they would receive added to the confusion and to the administrative problems. Relations with the native population posed no problems, in contrast to USAF airmen, who at one point were reported to have a VD rate of 25 percent.[3]

The lack of modern navigational aids, meteorological information and communications made air operations difficult.

Maps supplied by former Dutch pilots in the area proved invaluable. As only amphibious aircraft or sea transport could reach Fak-Fak, a regional centre southwest of Biak, this route particularly was assigned to the Canadians and their Otter aircraft. However, one of the Otters remained unserviceable for three months while awaiting a shipment of the proper brake discs. A good supply of parts proved to be a major difficulty in most peacekeeping operations.

There were no serious incidents. One minor accident occurred when a Pakistani solider mistakenly backed a truck, from which he was unloading supplies, into the float of one of the Otters during a stopover at Kaimana. After temporary repairs, the aircraft was able to return to Biak.

The political control of West New Guinea by the UN commenced on 1 October 1962 and ended on 1 May 1963.[4] As previously agreed in 1962, West New Guinea, or West Irian, was transferred to Indonesia and a plebiscite was held there in 1969 to decide its future. As a result of that plebiscite, it became a province of Indonesia.

PART
III

AFRICA

13

THE CONGO

Opération des Nations Unies au Congo

AFRICA, THE SECOND LARGEST CONTINENT, was formerly an appendage, politically and economically, of Western European powers. The emergence of new independent states on that continent reached a peak in 1960, when seventeen achieved independent status and became members of the United Nations. Among those new countries was the Congo. The problems of new African states, especially the Congo, were to involve Canadian military personnel.

BACKGROUND

The trouble that brought about UN intervention in the Congo came about as a result of poor preparation for independence by the colonial administration of Belgium. The Congo, about one-quarter the size of Canada, was ruled by a governor general in Leopoldville, the capital, and a minister for colonies in Brussels. The country was divided into six provinces. The Roman Catholic church, which controlled the educational system, had succeeded in producing only a small number of university graduates. This was a country where only a small minority had enough schooling to read or write. Large companies, up to 50 percent owned by the Belgian government, controlled the economy, notably the copper mines of Katanga province. A poor communications system — telephone, rail, road and air — was to prove a major obstacle to the job of the UN there. With over two hundred different tribes in the Congo, the country lacked cohesion.

In May 1960 the first elections were held in the Belgian Congo, a native administration led by Patrice Lumumba took office on 30 June and the colony became independent. Soon afterwards the 25,000-member native army/police "Force Publique" (later to change its name to Armée Nationale Congolaise, ANC) mutinied against its white officers, resulting in the breakdown of law and order. White men were killed and white women raped. To protect its nationals, Belgium began flying in troops. The new government of the Congo asked the UN for military "technical assistance" on 11 July. On that day the copper-rich province of Katanga seceded. On the 12th, the Congolese authorities asked for UN troops referring to aggression (by Belgian troops) that threatened world peace. By 19 July, there were ten thousand Belgian troops in the Congo.[1] They withdrew as UN troops took over. By the beginning of September the last Belgian troops had left.

The Congo became, for some, an example of the chaos that could develop should independence be given in Africa without adequate preparation. In the absence of law and order came anarchy and discord. For a century, maltreatment and exploitation at the hands of the Belgians had embittered a good number of Congolese, so that soon after independence this hatred expressed itself in atrocities against the former rulers.

Having obtained in advance the approval of the African nations and with the USSR anxious to please the neutralist states, the Security Council gave its unanimous approval on 14 July 1960 for a security force for the Congo. The force was placed under the command of General Carl von Horn of Sweden, then head of UNTSO.

If those who approved of the force believed it would consist of a small cadre to help the Congolese authorities restore order, they were mistaken. The force rose from 1,200 troops on 15 July to over 14,000 troops from twenty-four states a month later. It became the largest peacekeeping operation ever established by the UN as it eventually rose to a maximum of 20,000 soldiers. Thirty-five countries contributed military personnel but most of the soldiers came from ten African nations: Ethiopia, Ghana, Guinea, Liberia, Mali, Morocco, Nigeria, Sudan, Tunisia and the United Arab Republic (Egypt). Among the non-African states that contributed contingents were Canada, India, Indonesia, Ireland, Pakistan and Sweden.

THE CANADIAN RESPONSE TO THE CRISIS

In response to a question in the House of Commons on 14 July 1960, Prime Minister Diefenbaker replied that his government was responding favourably to the secretary-general's initial request to second two officers from UNTSO to the Congo force as well as for RCAF aircraft and personnel to ferry supplies, personnel and foodstuffs.[2] The degree of participation by Canada was soon increased as a result of public opinion. On 30 July[3] Diefenbaker announced that Canada would be making a substantial contribution to the Congo force and two days later parliamentary approval was given.[4] The Soviet Union initially objected to Canadian participation because of its membership in NATO but relented in the face of an argument pointing out the bilingualism of our troops.[5]

Originally, it was thought that the Canadian contribution in the Congo would be somewhat similar to UNEF I, which was primarily logistical support. The Canadians had also provided much of the early organizational assistance at UNEF headquarters. The size of the Canadian force was not to exceed five hundred. Colonel Albert Mendelsohn, who had served as an observer with the UN Military Observer Group in India and Pakistan and whose background was with the Royal Canadian Electrical and Mechanical Engineers, was chosen to lead an advance party. It arrived in Leopoldville on 1 August. Mendelsohn remained as commander of the Canadian forces in the Congo. When it became clear that the Canadian role was to be primarily signals, a separate headquarters was unnecessary and he was replaced at the end of October by Colonel Paul Smith, a signals officer. Henceforth signallers such as Colonel H.W.C. Stethem and Colonel D.G. Green headed the Canadian contingent.

Canadian forces in the Congo served in many capacities. There were a sizeable number of Canadians at ONUC headquarters and about a dozen military police. Signals, however, remained the primary role. There were also various Royal Canadian Air Force personnel performing a number of tasks. A few Canadian Army officers served at UN headquarters. Unfortunately, national jealousies sometimes hampered operations. Regular army officers headed the signal detachments in different parts of the Congo. The detachments were a part of 57 Signal Squadron, whose headquarters and the remainder of the unit were located at Leopoldville.

THE BEGINNING

In July 1960, headquarters for 57 Squadron, responsible for supplying communications and its own logistic support for the UN force in the Congo, was at Barriefield Camp, Kingston, Ontario. Personnel arrived from Gagetown, New Brunswick, Wainright, Alberta, and elsewhere. On 9 August the first party of signallers departed for the Congo from Trenton.[6] Some two hundred army personnel followed that month. Communications equipment, supplied by the Americans, was transported by the United States Air Force on behalf of the UN. Headquarters of the Canadian forces in the Congo and the headquarters of 57 Squadron were initially at the Athenée Royale boarding school for young boys in Leopoldville.

The main signal equipment was located in the school grounds. To function adequately the weak transmitter had to be at maximum power. This caused frequent breakdowns. As well, the average temperature of the transmitter room was 95 degrees Fahrenheit with the ventilator going.

The school had been used by the children of whites who had left the country prior to July 1960. The men were assigned cubicles with beds, toilets and sinks intended for boys under fifteen years of age. In the fall of 1961 the school was opened for Congolese children and the Canadians were encouraged to leave.[7] The Canadians then moved to the Leie Building, also in Leopoldville, and were crowded into apartments.

In spite of many difficulties, the Canadians first established communications between UN headquarters in Leopoldville and seven regional centres across the country. They also installed and operated the telephone system in the high-rise apartment building which housed ONUC headquarters.

THE RCAF CONTRIBUTION

The tasks of the RCAF were to help meet the United Nations' need for assistance with internal air movements in the Congo with air flights and from the outside world to Leopoldville. Beginning on 18 July, its initial involvement was in shipping food to the Congo using North Star planes. The aircraft transported a Canadian contribution of 20,000 pounds of powdered milk and 20,000 pounds of canned pork to help relieve the food shortage caused by the breakdown of order. This was followed with the August airlift, primarily by North Stars, of signallers and others for service with ONUC. As well, two C-119s of 436 Squadron at Downsview, Ontario, provided initial internal transport. From late September until the beginning of December, these two aircraft helped to transport vehicles, men and baggage within the Congo. The North Stars of 426 Squadron based at Trenton, Ontario, provided flights from Canada to Pisa and then on to the Congo beginning on 1 September. The RCAF was responsible for the rotation of Canadian personnel after their tour of duty had expired. Two key Canadian personnel included the chief air transport officer, Group Captain W.K. Carr, then Air Commodore C.G.W. Chapman.

Within the Congo, Carr and a non-Canadian staff of ten were initially responsible for administrating an air operation consisting of aircrews of eleven nationalities flying seventy-eight aircraft of thirteen different types. They were faced with language barriers, the inadequate training of some aircrews and shortages of supplies. Nevertheless, these obstacles were overcome and regular air communication was established between the major Congolese cities. Air transport tasks were varied including airlifting UN troops, supply flights and even evacuations from troubled areas. The air link was essential to keep ONUC bases supplied. RCAF air-control personnel manned air-control towers at airfields handling UN air operations. In August 1960 RCAF strength rose to fifty-eight men but had declined to fifteen by December. The RCAF Air Transport Command's contribution consisted of 392 flights to lift four million tons of freight and 11,746 UN passengers.[8]

EARLY PROBLEMS

There were cases of mistaken identity. Warrant Officer 2 F.E. Collins and two colleagues were mistaken for Belgian paratroopers while on an inspection tour of Stanleyville Airport.[9] Similarly, the switch from North Stars to the larger Yukons in November 1961 confused the Congolese who thought the new aircraft must belong to the Soviets.[10] After coming off the plane, the aircrew was surrounded by the Congolese and the aircraft impounded and searched. Both incidents fortunately ended without any serious injury apart from harried nerves. However, in November 1961, when Congolese soldiers murdered and dismembered thirteen UN personnel — crew and passengers of an Italian aircraft — the omnipresent risk faced by all airmen was re-emphasized. The Yukons continued in service until the termination of ONUC in June 1964. Thus ended the largest airlift of passengers and supplies by the RCAF since the Korean War.

The UN in the Congo was faced with many problems that prevented its efficient administration. As with peacekeeping forces in the Middle East, the Canadian forces in the Congo faced the problem of equipment procurement through the UN civilian agency. It was found to be more expedient to get the materiel from Canadian troops stationed in West Germany rather than to wait for the UN administration in New York to obtain what was needed through international tender.

To help the signallers with various chores at their headquarters, Congolese were hired. In an interview in the summer of 1986, Brigadier-General Mendelsohn recalled one laundry employee who had to be discharged because a witch doctor had cast a fatal spell upon him and other Congolese refused to work with him. It was later learned that the individual returned to his village and shortly afterwards died from natural causes.

The rapid expansion of the ONUC force initially resulted in all efforts being devoted to organizing ONUC rather than helping the host government. The almost total lack of telephonic and other forms of communication was a monumental task hampered by growing unrest and a number of incidents. One of these occurred on 18 August 1960 soon after the Canadians' arrival. Two signals detachments at Ndjili Airport, Leopoldville, were preparing to leave to reconnoiter sites for signals stations. While one group going to Coquilhatville under Captain J.P.A Therrien was on their aircraft, the other signallers going to Luluabourg led by Captain J.C.A.A. Taschereau were waiting for the second aircraft to be refuelled. The Canadian headquarters diary described the subsequent events:

Congolese soldiers approached this latter group and began to arrest them on the grounds that they were Belgian paratroopers. The Canadians were searched and made to lie on the ground where they were kicked and hit . . . . Captain J.C.A.A. Taschereau . . . was hit on the side of the head with a rifle butt and almost knocked unconscious . . . . After about five minutes they were forcibly placed in the back of a truck. The Coquilhatville group meanwhile were still in their aircraft and saw the incident taking place . . . . Congolese troops surrounded the plane, forcing it to shut down its engine, and told the passengers to get out . . . . They were not beaten but were mishandled as they too were made to get into the truck. Just as they got into the truck a Danish officer approached the truck and tried to delay the Congolese until reinforcements could be brought up. He succeeded in doing this for about another five minutes until sufficient Ghanaian troops could be mustered to control the Congolese . . . .[11]

This affair pointed out the fear and mistrust of the Congolese and the precarious situation of Canadian troops in the Congo.

On 22 August a further incident occurred at Stanleyville where Captain J.B. Pariseau, the officer in charge of the Canadian signals detachment there, and three other ranks were held and questioned for four hours after their arrival. The Congolese soldiers believed the Canadians were Belgian paratroopers. The commander of the Ethiopian brigade in Stanleyville came to their rescue and shortly afterwards they were released.[12]

Five days later, after Captain Pariseau had obtained approval for additional signallers to open communication, two Globemaster aircraft from Trenton landed at Stanleyville Airport with men and equipment. At the same time the Congolese were about to receive a visit from Premier Patrice

225

Lumumba. A Canadian officer and his three men who came on the first plane were escorted by the Ethiopians to the Hotel Wagenia, the local UN headquarters. Meanwhile at the airport, a rumour spread that Belgian paratroopers were hiding in the hotel. Their intention, some said, was to assassinate Lumumba. As a result, Congolese troops were sent to the Hotel Wagenia and arrested all the Canadians there. After some delay the second Globemaster landed. The American crew and two Canadian signallers on board were then attacked and beaten. Minutes later, Lumumba arrived but made no attempt to interfere. All of the prisoners and injured were subsequently released as a result of Ethiopian intervention.[13]

After the incident, Pariseau made contact with the Congolese commander, Commandant Captain Kabongo, invited him to dinner and explained that there were no hard feelings. Pariseau accepted the explanation of a "ghastly mistake" on the part of some unknown person[14] but warned that in the future his troops would fight and the Congolese would be answerable to the Canadian Army.[15]

Although the Stanleyville incident was not the last, from then on Canadian signallers settled down to fulfill their tasks. The incident at Stanleyville had been, in part, fabricated by local authorities to show their loyalty to Lumumba. At one point Lumumba had favoured the removal of the white contingents.

Why were Canadian troops with the UN in the Congo subjected to beatings and other forms of humiliating treatment by Congolese troops? A logical reason was mistaken identity. The Congolese troops believed English-speaking Canadians to be Flemings and the French-speaking Canadians to be Walloons. Canadian uniforms also were similar to those of the Belgian parachute troops. Some airborne crests and other badges led some of the Congolese troops to believe that the wearers were Belgians or perhaps mercenaries from Katanga. Other reasons for this mistreatment were lack of discipline, illiteracy and non-existent standards of behaviour on the part of the Congolese forces.

The Canadian signal unit reached an overall strength on average of 280.[16] The communications squadron was the heart of the unit and was based mainly in Leopoldville with detachments scattered throughout the interior. By the end of September there were small detachments of initially one officer and some nine men in Elizabethville, Coquilhatville, Luluabourg, Kamina, Stanleyville, Gemena and Matadi. Detachments were also stationed at Goma, Kindu, Albertville, Kongolo and Bukavu (see map). Detachments would close down and new ones would open up as the communication needs of the UN force changed due to the movement of their troops from one area to another. Accommodation in smaller centres was usually better than in Leopoldville.

POLITICAL PROBLEMS

The political situation in the Congo was quite chaotic. Belgian paratroopers had arrived to protect their nationals just after independence. This was followed by the secession of the copper-rich province of Katanga supported by mercenaries. Both actions heightened tension and suspicion among the Congolese towards whites. By August 1960 the newly elected Premier Lumumba, who had shown pro-Soviet leanings, was losing power and in September the pro-Western Colonel Joseph Mobutu established military rule. In October, it was Mobutu who seemed to be about to topple as evinced by demonstrations in favour of Lumumba, but this was only temporary. Mobutu, now a general and commander of the Congolese forces, was suspicious of the UN force, particularly the Ghanaian and Guinean troops and Indian staff officers, whom he felt were too overtly sympathetic to the Lumumbist factions.

For the next six months the Canadians experienced a number of incidents. For example, on 22 November small-arms fire and two stray cannon shells hit the Canadian officers' mess in Leopoldville when Congolese troops attacked the Ghanaian Embassy that had been ordered evacuated by Mobutu.[17] While Mobutu's fortunes were on the rise, Lumumba had become a political prisoner. Lumumba, revered by his supporters as an almost mythical figure, remained a threat. With the killing of Lumumba in early 1961, it was expected more trouble would develop. On 27 February two Canadian officers along with two other ranks were robbed by ANC paracommandos, relieved of their arms, beaten and forced to run barefoot more than half a mile over a dirt road. A new order that henceforth UN troops were to fire in self defence was enthusiastically welcomed by the Canadians.[18]

A further incident involving the Canadians occurred at Matadi on 4 March 1961 when a Canadian signal detachment was pinned down at the signals office during an exchange of fire between Sudanese soldiers of the UN guarding their post and Congolese troops. The fighting left a number of Sudanese killed and wounded. One of the Canadians, Captain Gerald Belanger, survived by temporarily taking shelter in a gully. Eventually the Canadians were flown back to Leopoldville. After this incident the signallers' role became stabilized. Several times in 1961 and 1962 UN forces were employed militarily against mercenary and secessionist forces

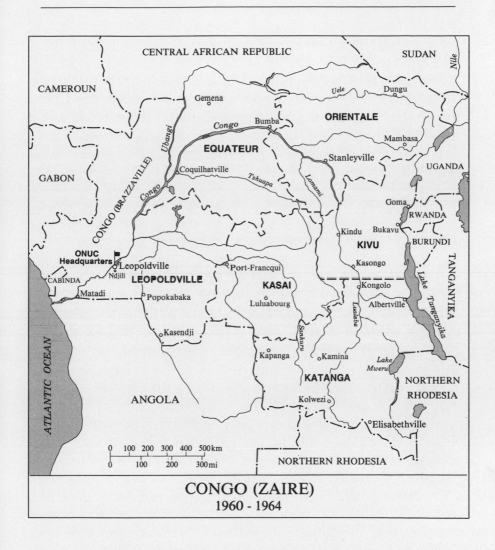

CONGO (ZAIRE)
1960 - 1964

in Katanga, but this did not directly affect most of the Canadians.[19]

By early 1963 National Defence was looking forward to a reduction in the number of signallers serving with the UN. In March 1963 the Canadian chief of the general staff informed 57 Signal Unit that as a result of the strain on Canada's military manpower, no further increases in manpower for ONUC could be authorized.[20]

LIVING CONDITIONS

Life for the Canadians at Leopoldville was not bad. A diet of local produce was supplemented by imported food. Canteen profits paid the cost of expensive items such as eggs selling for sixteen cents each and onions for $1.25 per pound.

With the rainy reason came an increase in humidity and the appearance of mosquitoes and snakes that could invade living quarters. The humidity combined with the heat proved tiring for some. This could be temporarily alleviated by a cool refreshing drink or a dip in the swimming pool. A movie provided by Canadian and United Nations welfare sources or bingo and card games offered diversion at night. Valuables had to be safeguarded as thieving was rife.

Accommodation varied depending on rank and date of tour of duty. For example, most Canadian forces personnel with ONUC headquarters lived in apartments in Leopoldville. Non-commissioned officers and privates would sleep up to ten per three-bedroom apartment. A hotel in Luluabourg was home for one detachment, while a mansion in Bukavu provided the quarters for a signal group stationed there.[21]

Another example was Kamina where three small villas housed the Canadians. Each man received a ration allowance for food. One member of the detachment was made responsible for the purchase of food that was cooked by a Congolese employee.

The normal tour of duty for Canadians in the Congo was six months. Certain officers, particulary those on UN headquarters staff, usually served for a year. Probably the most trying time for the Canadian signallers was during the fighting in Katanga when they handled a heavy volume of traffic. They worked long hours under great stress.[22]

RELATIONS WITH THE CONGOLESE

Thirty-three Canadian servicemen were injured in the Congo — twelve of these from severe beatings by the Congolese. What did most of the Canadians generally think of the Congolese? A good number of the Canadians considered them illiterate, very volatile, superstitious and easily influenced. One RCAF air-traffic controller recalled leaving his post at a busy airport to go to the washroom, placing his Congolese assistant in charge. He returned shortly after to find his assistant listening to a local radio station oblivious to the aircraft above him. Major Michael Kolesar of the Van Doos recollected a Canadian corporal who jokingly told one of the Congolese employees about to be inoculated that it would cause sterility only to watch the individual flee in terror never to return, not even to collect his back pay.

A number of Canadians returned with unfavourable comments about the competence of some Congolese. For example, Major-General Victor Lundula, the first commander-in-chief of the Congolese army, a former medical orderly, has been described by a former Canadian serviceman as "someone so lacking in ability that I wouldn't allow him to give an enema to my worst enemy." Behind the scenes there was a great deal of politicking and jousting for power and position among UN staff as well as among the Congolese.

CANADIANS DECORATED

Serving in the Congo was a challenge for many Canadian service personnel. The heat as well as the sights, sounds and particularly smells, for example at the market in Leopoldville, will remain unforgettable. During the course of their stay, a number of Canadians performed heroic rescues that merited bravery awards. Lieutenant J.T.F.A. Liston, an officer in the Royal 22e Régiment, was named a Member of the Most Excellent Order of the British Empire (MBE) for saving a wounded Congolese lying in a minefield. Lieutenant-Colonel P.A. Mayer, the UN liaison officer with the ANC, and Sergeant J.A. Lessard were both awarded the George Medal.

On 27 January 1964 at Kasendji, Lieutenant-Colonel Mayer rescued two nuns and three fathers. Eight sisters and one priest remained . . . . During talks . . . Colonel Mayer was hit on the back of the neck with a club and knocked unconscious. Members of the Jeunesse [a loosely, organized militant group responsible for the attacks on missionaries and others] removed his revolver, beret and web belt . . . . A frenzied Jeunesse thrust the pistol in Colonel Mayer's stomach and pulled the trigger. Fortunately, there was no round in the chamber. In the meantime three fathers and two sisters were able to board the helicopter. After arrangements had been made to free the remaining eight sisters, Colonel Mayer was allowed to leave amongst a wild and screaming mob . . . .[23]

During the follow-up rescue operations the next day a Van Doo, Sergeant J.A. Leonce Lessard of Quebec City, was second in command of the ground pickup groups:

Sgt. Lessard's helicopter landed where two nuns lay literally surrounded by some fifteen to twenty Jeunesse. One sick nun was on a stretcher while the other lay on the ground. . . . Despite a shower of arrows aimed at the helicopter, Lessard jumped to the ground and without assistance proceeded to put the stretcher aboard the helicopter. While he was thus engaged he was tackled from behind by four Jeunesse who tried to drag him down. As he fought off his assailants, Lessard pushed the stretcher aboard and then reached out for the second nun who lay nearby. Without the slightest regard for his attackers he pushed the nun into the safety of the helicopter, holding off the last two attackers until the helicopter had actually started to leave the ground. Only then did he free himself completely and jump aboard . . . .[24]

As well, Brigadier J.A. Dextraze, the UN chief of staff in the Congo, was made a Commander of the Order of the British Empire in recognition of his "superb leadership and control during the missionary rescue operations." His citation credits him with saving over thirty missionaries and students from death.[25]

Another officer with the United Nations Truce Supervision Organization who served the UN with distinction in the Congo was Lieutenant-Colonel J.A. Berthiaume of Saint-Hyacinthe, Quebec. For his outstanding contribution he was made an Officer of the British Empire (Military Division). The citation reads:

Lieutenant-Colonel Berthiaume . . . arrived in the Congo on 17th July 1960 . . . . By perseverance and long hours of work he arranged for the release of Congolese communications and transport equipment so vital to ONUC functions. During the latter part of August he was

233

appointed personal military assistant to the supreme commander, a position he filled with distinction. This officer's experience, initiative, linguistic ability and special aptitude for negotiating, even with the most difficult type of people, made his service invaluable . . . . On the night of 21/22 November 1960, he exposed himself to fire in an endeavour to stop the fighting then going on. In so doing he was himself taken into Congolese custody . . . . While in custody, he was instrumental in preventing the maltreatment of both ONUC and Congolese personnel and was able to negotiate for their subsequent release . . . . This officer's service to ONUC was outstanding.

According to Berthiaume, there was a great deal of confusion in the early stages of UN activities in the Congo. The operation was launched in a hurry with almost no information or planning. Improvisation was the order of the day. As well, there was a marked gap between civilian and military components of ONUC, particularly as to whether or not the Congolese army should be armed. The civilian component prevailed and the Congolese were armed much to Berthiaume's chagrin.

With the assistance of Majors Wayne King and Jack George, Berthiaume helped to disperse the different national contingents to the various provinces of the Congo. Initially, there were restrictions on the use of certain foreign aircraft, including Canadian, for the internal airlift. Lieutenant-Colonel Berthiaume managed with the connivance of some members of the RCAF to circumvent this restriction and airlift the Tunisian contingent to Kasai province and its capital Luluabourg. As well as troops, there was a need for transport vehicles and telecommunication equipment at the various outposts. Berthiaume decided to send a road convoy. An Esso map showed a road meandering from Leopoldville to Luluabourg and he estimated the trip would take two days. After five days and still no word of the convoy, he sent out a search aircraft. It found that the convoy had progressed a third of the way. The reason was that the map had failed to indicate that the roads were impassable when the water level was high. Thus, it was necessary to move the trucks by raft. The incident typified the problems of communication within the Congo.[26] It also helps explain why he was decorated.

CONTRIBUTIONS BY OTHER CANADIANS

As in Berthiaume's case, one cannot emphasize enough the importance of the bilingual capacity of the French-Canadian officers. French and English were the two working languages in what seemed at times a Tower of Babel at ONUC headquarters. With each contingent from the Royal Canadian Corps of Signals sent to various district locations were officers, many from the Royal 22e Régiment, who served a very important liaison link, often as advisers between district Congolese commanders, UN troops and ONUC headquarters.

An outstanding contribution was rendered by a good number of Canadian officers at ONUC headquarters, many of whom were members of the Van Doos. Lieutenant-Colonel Jean Berthiaume, Major Clement Bouffard and Lieutenant-Colonel J.G. Poulin earned the confidence and respect of the Congolese. They acted as trusted advisers and intermediaries. Without their help the loss of life of Congolese and UN troops would have been considerably higher. Captain Mario Côté, Major Réal Liboiron, Major Roger Monette and Major Louis Normandin as well as many others gave valiant service.

To cite a typical example of their work, Lieutenant-Colonel J.G. Poulin, who served during 1960-1961, wrote me about a meeting with Prime Minister Omahri of the northeast province of Kivu:

On a certain occasion, one Malayan battalion, having served its six-month stint, was to be relieved by another unit from the same country. The advance party arrived which greatly perturbed Mr. Omahri who suspected that the first unit was being reinforced by another one in order to keep him more firmly in check. I was dispatched to try to parley with him.

When I arrived in Kivu, I was properly invited to visit Mr. Omahri to have tea and what not, very much *à l'occidentale*. Gradually the subject gravitated toward what I knew to be a relief in the line as opposed to the reinforcement conviction he harboured. It was not easy to convince the man. Banking on the Congolese, not to say the central African attitude of quasi-veneration of sex, I told him that that poor Malaysian soldiers of the first unit, having been deprived of the joy of sex with wives or girl friends, etc., for six months should not be forced to remain in this forced state any longer . . . . The relief in line took place without further ado.

During the course of the preliminary conversations of that meeting, the prime minister, who feared the power of black magic, asked me if it was true that the Malaysian troops were capable of stopping a rifle bullet in flight. I retorted that I was sure they could not stop a bullet in flight, but then, I knew for a fact that they could divert one from its intended path. That, in itself, made the Malaysian soldiers more or less invulnerable in Omahri's eyes and he probably decided there and then, that the better policy would be to be on the side of the UN.[27]

Captain Mario Côté of Chicoutimi, a liaison officer, became involved in the removal of foreign military personnel by the UN from Katanga province from 28 August to 13 September 1961. Captain Côté balked at acting severely towards several Belgium military personnel in the Katangese security forces as was expected of him. Instead, he acted in a humanitarian manner, particularly towards their dependents. While in

Elizabethville he had to fight off a band of rampaging youths who were protesting measures by the UN to end their province's secession. After shooting broke out between UN and Katangese forces on 13 September, Côté managed to make his way to the airport and meet his replacement, a fellow Van Doo, Major J.A.O. Woodcock. Côté had followed the dictates of his conscience rather than those of his superiors in the UN force.[28] Officials at External Affairs believed he should have acted as instructed. Colleagues in the force there were more understanding. In January 1963 the secession of Katanga was brought to an end.

Mobutu learned to trust the Canadian officers. This trust was of inestimable value in arranging cease-fires between Congolese and UN forces, negotiating the release of prisoners as well as liaising between UN and Congolese authorities. Mobutu, who became president of the Democratic Republic of Zaire, visited Canada in May of 1964. At that time he thanked those Canadian officers who had contributed so much to the maintenance of the unity of his country.

CONCLUSION

ONUC commenced in July 1960 when the problems of the newly independent Congo were raised in the Security Council. Following independence, the Congo had been unable to maintain internal order and meet the separatist threat of the Province of Katanga. The decision of the Security Council to organize help for the newly independent government of the Congo reflected the influence of Dag Hammarskjöld. However, the secretary-general, while working on behalf of ONUC, lost his life in an airplane crash in 1961 and was succeeded by U Thant of Burma.

The Congo operation proved to be most costly as well as difficult. At its peak strength the force consisted of 20,000 men including over three hundred Canadian personnel. The total cost of ONUC was more than 400 million dollars.[29] The estimated cost to Canada was about eight million dollars.[30] The operation raised questions as to the role of the secretary-general and likely weakened his power. It also created financial problems for the UN and, by alienating the Communist bloc, threatened the financing of future peacekeeping operations. Mounting costs brought about the withdrawal of the UN peacekeepers. On the positive side, U Thant summed up the achievements of the force upon its withdrawal at the end of June 1964:

The presence of the United Nations force has been the decisive factor in preserving the territorial integrity of the country; it has been solely responsible for the cessation of the activities of the mercenaries in Katanga; and it has been a major factor in preventing widespread civil war in the Congo.[31]

This episode marked the first and only large-scale operation by the UN to restore order entirely within a sovereign state. In their hearts most Canadian contingent personnel would admit that their six-month tour of duty in the Congo was not a real hardship. However, among the signallers only 27 percent applied to stay for the full year.[32]

By the beginning of 1963 plans were being made to reduce the UN presence in the Congo. Canadian strength in February of that year numbered thirty-eight officers and 268 men from the army, and five officers and seven men from the air force. By the beginning of August 1963, army strength was down to 223 all ranks. One of the major problems facing UN operations in the Congo was financing. Since 1961 the viability of the United Nations had been threatened by the refusal of Soviet-bloc nations and France to contribute funds for peacekeeping. The issue was not resolved until early 1965 after the close of the Congo operation.[33] To sustain the UN forces in the Congo until the early summer of 1964, the United States made extra funds available.

Nearly two thousand Canadians served in the UN Congo force in the four years of its existence; most of them operated communications equipment, flew or serviced aircraft. The number of Canadians in the Congo was gradually reduced so that by 30 June 1964 only fifty-six were left and on that day the last draft boarded an RCAF Yukon and left the Congo.[34]

During the Congo peacekeeping operation, a total of over 93,000 men from thirty-five countries, the majority coming from nineteen Afro-Asian states, served in ONUC. One hundred and twenty-six UN soldiers were killed and at least as many others wounded. A further 109 died accidentally or from natural causes.[35] Among those were two Canadians who died as a result of illness.

A peacekeeping operation such as that in the Congo or Cyprus provided an opportunity for English- and French-speaking Canadians as well as air, army and naval arms to work together against a unifying exterior threat. It gave many Canadian servicemen an opportunity to see first-hand the result of national and tribal divisiveness. As a happy by-product, these operations did promote greater unity and cooperation within the Canadian forces. The experience also instilled a greater sense of national identity within the Canadians.

14

NIGERIA

ON 30 MAY 1967, THE EASTERN region of Nigeria declared itself the sovereign republic of Biafra. Civil war ensued. That war was fought over the world's media networks as well as on the battlefield. Pictures of starving civilians in Biafra brought pressure on Western governments to take some sort of action or at least to seem to be doing something to help.

Great Britain had a long history of involvement in Nigeria's history as a colony and continued to have close economic ties after its independence. Britain initially favoured a larger Commonwealth peacekeeping force and wanted Canada's contribution to equal its own. Participation of either Ghana or India was also favoured.

Continued fighting and other events had made this peace-keeping-force idea a dead issue by August 1968. At the initiative of the Nigerian federal government, an international team of observers was invited. Those contributing were Britain, Canada, Poland, Sweden, the Organization of African Unity and the United Nations secretary-general. This was not a United Nations sponsored mission. The task was to observe whether or not the Nigerian armed forces were following their own published code of conduct as well as to investigate charges that the military were guilty of genocide.

At the beginning of September 1968 the international team arrived in Nigeria, and it began its work on the 25th. The group worked well together. After its inspections, it would issue reports to the international press based on its observations. In brief, the observers found no evidence of genocide or that the Nigerian forces were generally disobeying their code of conduct. The Canadian team usually consisted of two officers. Among those who served during this observer mission were Major-General W.A. Milroy, Brigadier-General J.L. Drewry, Brigadier-General C.J.A. Hamilton, Lieutenant-Colonel E.B.M. Pennington, Major G.C. Bristowe and Major G.R. Harper.

A separate operation involved Canadians who flew emergency relief for the Red Cross. Some Hercules aircraft of Air Transport Command were to fly in relief supplies to Biafra but this plan never did become operational as a result of jurisdictional problems. Direct involvement by the Canadian Forces in this situation came to an end in early 1970 with the final report by the observer team.[1]

15

OTHER AFRICAN COUNTRIES

BELGIUM HAD ADMINISTERED THE TRUST territory of Ruanda-Urundi since 1916, first under the League of Nations then under the United Nations. To help meet the demands for political change in early 1960, a UN commission was created. Part of the UN commission to oversee the independence of the territory of Ruanda-Urundi consisted of two military advisers, a lieutenant-colonel in the Indian army and Major Michael Kolesar from Canada, who had been serving in the Congo. The commission's job during 1961 was to facilitate the transfer of the territory from Belgium to establish two separate independent states, Rwanda and Burundi. As a result of the commission's work, independence was received by both countries in 1962 and both were admitted to the UN.

Members of the Canadian forces have rendered assistance to a few English-speaking African countries. From 1961 to early 1972 the Canadian Armed Forces Training Team Ghana (CAFTTG), consisting of a maximum of thirty officers and men, helped instruct members of the Ghanaian armed forces. A total of about a hundred Canadian military advisers and instructors were involved in Tanzania from 1965 to 1970 with the Canadian Armed Forces Advisory and Training Team Tanzania (CAFATT)[1] and even in flying election observers into newly independent Zimbabwe (Rhodesia) in 1980. In addition, military personnel from other African countries have received specialized training in Canada. The Canadian servicemen involved in these programs were struck by the young Africans' hunger to better their lot as well as their great thirst for knowledge. Although these efforts were not strictly peacekeeping operations but a form of military aid, perhaps the personal contacts cultivated through training of people from different backgrounds have also helped to promote international understanding.

PART
IV

LATIN AMERICA

16

DOMINICAN REPUBLIC

CANADIANS HAVE GENERALLY IGNORED Latin America, yet it may prove to be one of the most turbulent regions of the world over the next twenty-five years. Only one Canadian has been involved in peacekeeping there. It is earnestly hoped that he will remain the only one.

The Dominican Republic occupies the eastern two-thirds of the Island of Hispaniola with Haiti the other third to the west. The political crisis that arose in 1965 in the Dominican Republic had its roots in the dictatorship established in 1930 by Rafael Trujillo. His cruel regime lasted until his assassination in 1961. Trujillo's heirs tried to hang on but were ousted as well and in 1963 a democratically elected social-reformist government took over under Juan Bosch. After seven months Bosch was overthrown by a conservative, do-nothing administration. Frustrations and pressures began to mount.

On 25 April 1965, heavy fighting broke out in the Dominican Republic between those in power and those wanting to take over the government. The United States, fearing a second Cuba, intervened militarily. The Security Council requested that the secretary-general report on the situation there and among those sent was Lieutenant-Colonel P.A. Mayer, then serving with the Canadian delegation to the UN. Mayer, the only Canadian who served in the Dominican Republic, replaced an Ecuadorian officer who had been there one month. As a miliary observer, negotiator and mediator from June 1965 to October 1966, Mayer helped establish cease-fire lines, maintained liaison with the military, and dealt with human-rights violations. The departure of the senior military advisor, Major-General I.J. Rikhye, to head UNEF I, left Mayer alone in that position. After his return to Canada, Mayer, who had received the George Medal for bravery in the Congo, gave advice in a report that is as true now as it was then: "I would offer this remark to any peacekeeper in the forces: that what a man does, what he stands for or what he is ready to fall for, that, in the long run, is what really matters."[1]

The Organization of American States had created an Inter-American Peace Force specifically for the Dominican Republic situation, consisting mainly of US troops assisted by contingents from other Latin American states. The election and subsequent installation of the newly elected government of President Joaquin Balaguer on 1 July 1966 helped to resolve the situation along with the withdrawal, by 21 September 1966, of the Inter-American Peace Force. As a result of these developments and the UN secretary-general's recommendation, the UN mission in the Dominican Republic was withdrawn on 22 October that year.

There have been in recent years newspaper reports and rumours that Canadian troops might be called upon to act as peacekeepers in Nicaragua. All such reports have been denied; public opinion appears to be against such a undertaking at this time. Whether the Canadian government will send peacekeepers to this part of the world in the future remains to be seen. It is hoped that this country's experiences with previous peacekeeping undertakings in other trouble spots will not be forgotten if such an operation is contemplated.

CONCLUSION

*Those who cannot remember the past
are condemned to repeat it.*

GEORGE SANTAYANA

THIS OFT-QUOTED STATEMENT IS AS relevant to the lessons to be learned from Canada's involvement in peacekeeping as it is to those gained from other periods of this country's history. For example, peace in the Middle East or elsewhere was only as assured as the willingness of both sides to want it. In Indochina limitations on arms as agreed to by the terms of the Geneva Conference proved ephemeral as there was no means to effectively monitor or assure compliance except through the good will of all the parties. Those negotiating arms limitations ought to remember how that agreement fell apart.

While military conflicts have significantly shaped this country so has peacekeeping, if not as profoundly. Canadian Forces have been keeping the peace much longer than they have fought overseas. Like their countrymen back home, the first Canadian UNEF troops who came off the plane in Egypt were filled with idealism. This idealism gradually soured.

251

Following the Canadian contingent's ejection from Egypt, the problems in the Congo, the failure to reach any accord in Cyprus, and the pullout of the ICCS from Vietnam, peace-keeping ceased to be held in such high repute. Instead, the emphasis has turned to collective security through NATO, NORAD and arms modernization.

Peacekeeping forces under the United Nations have become mere shadows of the original hope of a large UN standby army that could stop aggression or enforce peace. However, for Canada, it has served as a means to help offset the preeminence of this country's alliances with NATO and NORAD, and has helped maintain the dream of eventual collective security through the United Nations. Canadian participation in UN military activities has given the Canadian Forces a highly visible role and helped to justify expenditures in the post-Second World War years for a military that some in Canada found distasteful. Over almost forty years contributions made by Canadian men and women to peacekeeping have been both significant and beneficial.

Have peacekeeping operations been, on balance, a success or failure? My response is that the failures should not obscure the successes. The term "failure" ought to be qualified because without the presence of peacekeepers the consequences would have been much worse for the disputants and the world.

Since the establishment of UNEF I, Canada has participated in some manner in every UN peacekeeping operation. With the threat of nuclear warfare and the continuing arms race among the superpowers, the use of peacekeeping forces to contain disputes remains relevant.

The Canadian Forces have been in the forefront of efforts to keep the peace. In fact Canada has participated in more peacekeeping missions since Korea than any other country. More than seventy-five Canadians have been killed. From 1949 to 1987 over 50,000 Canadian military personnel have served on peacekeeping operations conducted under the auspices of the United Nations, excluding Korea. To put the number of peacekeepers in another light, the total manpower of the regular Canadian forces as of 1987 was 87,000. Thus the peacekeepers are only a minority within the Forces, albeit an influential group.

The Canadian Forces have been the world's leading contributor to peacekeeping tasks. In this role almost all Canadians take pride. Canadians tend to look on peacekeeping with a certain proprietary air and indeed they should. They have well earned that right. I have tried to make that clear. Through the efforts of its armed forces, this country has gained an outstanding international reputation. The Canadian Forces have gained experience and demonstrated their expertise particularly in logistics, communications, engineering and with air transport units. Their efficiency and their ability to improvise have been recognized by the armed forces of other countries with whom they served. Should the need arise again for Canada's help in peacekeeping, the reputation earned by the Canadian Forces will likely result in their being called on for assistance once more.

On Cyprus and in the other peacekeeping and observer missions, Canadian servicemen, whose training was mainly for war, found themselves acting as diplomats or negotiators. Amidst fear, hatred and violence, they exhibited and maintained a professionalism that is a credit to their uniform and to their country. For their contribution over almost forty years as peacekeepers and observers, Canada's servicemen deserve a Nobel Prize and, if that is not possible, at least some form of recognition by their country. Without their assistance, whatever has been achieved would not have been possible.

Unlike troops returning from the First and Second World Wars, who received enthusiastic official receptions upon their arrival home, Canadian Forces on peacekeeping duty do not receive such a welcome back. It is quite a letdown for those who have been wounded or have risked their lives not to be granted some public recognition. On Remembrance Day we remember those killed in both world wars and in Korea. Why do we not also honour those killed on peacekeeping duty?

In this country two different cultures have managed to live in peace along with peoples from all over the world. We ought not to be reluctant to share this success by sending some of our service personnel to help where national, racial or religious strife threatens world peace. It is not unnatural, therefore, that Canadian soldiers trained primarily for war should have made a most worthwhile contribution to world stability for about forty years through peacekeeping.

The use of Canada's military forces to help preserve peace in the world has resulted in success as well as failure. In the process its members have experienced both good and bad times with many unforgettable memories. Peacekeeping has become part of this country's history as has its involvement in military conflicts. Canadians should take pride in our efforts to help preserve peace in the world and redouble their efforts to work for it in the future.

On occasion in the Congo, Cyprus, Egypt, the Golan Heights, Indochina, Lebanon and Yemen, a good number of Canada's peacekeepers felt as if they were in the eye of a sudden raging hurricane of violence. Some were even engulfed and became fatalities. Fortunately, as in the relative calm of the centre of a hurricane, most survived, protected by their neutral status as peacekeepers. They would live to see another day and continue to soldier for Canada and for peace.

APPENDIX A

Canadian Forces Involvement in Peacekeeping Operations

NAME OF MISSION	CANADIAN PARTICIPATION	UN AUTHORIZATION
UN Military Observer Group in India and Pakistan (UNMOGIP)	1949-	April 1948
UN Truce Supervision Organization (UNTSO)	1954-	May 1948 (UNTSO is considered the first UN peacekeeping operation since it commenced activity in June 1948.)
International Commission(s) for Supervision and Control (ICSC)	Cambodia 1954-69 Laos 1954-74 Vietnam 1954-73	July 1954

NAME OF MISSION	CANADIAN PARTICIPATION	UN AUTHORIZATION
UN Emergency Force I (UNEF I)	1956-67	November 1956
UN Observation Group in Lebanon (UNOGIL)	June-December 1958	June 1958
Opération Nations Unies au Congo (ONUC)	1960-64	July 1960
UN Security Force in West New Guinea	1962-63	September 1962
UN Yemen Observation Mission (UNYOM)	1963-64	June 1963
UN Peacekeeping Force in Cyprus (UNFICYP)	1964-	March 1964
Mission of the Representative of the Secretary-General in the Dominican Republic (DOMREP)	1965-66	May 1965

NAME OF MISSION	CANADIAN PARTICIPATION	UN AUTHORIZATION
UN India-Pakistan Observation Mission (UNIPOM)	1965-66	September 1965
International Observer Team to Nigeria (OTN)	1968-69	September 1968
International Commission of Control and Supervision (ICCS)	January-July 1973	January 1973
UN Emergency Force II (UNEF II)	1973-79	October 1973
UN Disengagement Observer Force (UNDOF)	1974-	May 1974
UN Interim Force in Lebanon (UNIFIL)	March-October 1978	March 1978
Multinational Force and Observers (MFO)	March 1986-	August 1981

APPENDIX B

CANADIAN FORCES PARTICIPATION IN
PEACEKEEPING OPERATIONS

MISSION	AREA	PEAK MILITARY STRENGTH	PEAK STRENGTH CANADIAN FORCES
UNMOGIP	Kashmir	100	27
UNTSO	Egypt Israel Jordan Lebanon Syria	600	20
	current strength:	300	20
ICSC	Cambodia Laos Vietnam	400	150
UNEF I	Egypt	6,000	1,000
UNOGIL	Lebanon	591	77
ONUC	Congo	20,000	420
UNTEA	West New Guinea	1,600	13

Appendix B

MISSION	AREA	PEAK MILITARY STRENGTH	PEAK STRENGTH CANADIAN FORCES
UNYOM	Yemen	150	50
UNFICYP	Cyprus	6,500	1,100
	current strength:	2,388	515
DOMREP	Dominican Republic	2	1
UNIPOM	India-Pakistan	200	112
OTN	Nigeria	12	2
ICCS	South Vietnam	1,200	240
UNEF II	Egypt	7,000	1,145
UNDOF	Israel/Syria	1,335	
	current strength:	1,335	230
UNIFIL	Lebanon	7,000	120
	current strength:	5,700	0
MFO	Egypt/Israel	2,600	140

APPENDIX C

HONOURS AND AWARDS
CYPRUS

ONLY IN CYPRUS WERE LARGE numbers of Canadian troops involved over a long period of time. Events and circumstances account for the numerous awards there.

In the centennial year (1967) the Order of Canada was created. Five years later the Order was revised. In addition, in 1972, an Order of Military Merit was instituted for outstanding meritorious service in varying degrees of responsibility. Commander, Officer and Member comprise the three levels of the Order.

In 1972 the government also introduced three distinctive Canadian decorations for bravery. They replaced British non-combatant awards. The Cross of Valour is awarded for "acts of the most conspicuous courage in circumstances of extreme peril." The Star of Courage honours those who have performed "acts of conspicuous courage in circumstances of great peril." The Medal of Bravery recognizes "acts of bravery in hazardous circumstances."

ORDER OF MILITARY MERIT (COMMANDER)

COLONEL C.E. BEATTIE

Colonel Beattie conducted his duties in an outstanding and meritorious manner during the political coup on the island and the ensuing Turkish invasion in July 1974.

Colonel Beattie and the forces under his command in the Nicosia District, under hazardous and difficult conditions, maintained a cease-fire between Greek- and Turkish-Cypriots during a revolt by the Greek-Cypriot National Guard. Thereafter they expended every effort to confine hostilities during the ensuing invasion by Turkish forces by manning vulnerable positions between the opposing forces and by negotiating numerous local cease-fire agreements. Following the declaration of a cease-fire, by the United Nations Security Council, Colonel Beattie and the Canadian contingent restored a tenuous peace in the Nicosia area with extremely limited resources. Colonel Beattie used his personal influence in several instances to cease hostile action by the opposing forces. Throughout this period, his concern for the safety of his men was paramount, as was evidenced by the minimum casualties his contingent suffered despite their imposition between the protagonists under fighting conditions. His personal leadership and influence over the situation was outstanding.

Colonel Beattie made every effort during the period to ensure the safety of Canadian citizens, other foreign nationals and innocent Cypriots from danger. This humanitarian action, involving his personal intervention during a Turkish attack to ensure the safety of captured Greek-Cypriot civilians, has earned the Canadian Forces the highest worldwide commendation.

The danger to Colonel Beattie while he conducted his duties throughout this period from air attack, artillery, mortar, tank and small-arms fire was extreme.

Order of Military Merit (Officer)

LIEUTENANT-COLONEL D.S. MANUEL

As Commander Nicosia District, Lt.-Col. D.S. Manuel displayed the highest standard of leadership and military professionalism during the period 15-30 July 1974. Throughout this period Lt.-Col. Manuel personally handled tense and dangerous situations in such a manner as to avert escalation into fierce and bitter fighting with possible resulting casualties on both sides. His prompt action prevented a possible tragedy at the Ledra Palace Hotel when several hundred civilians were exposed to shooting from both sides. During the two weeks and under intense pressure, Lt.-Col. Manuel maintained a cool and professional approach to all problems, even when his men were incurring casualties. His conduct has proven an inspiration to all his men deployed under difficult and often dangerous circumstances.

Member of the Most Excellent Order of the British Empire (Military Division)

COMPANY SERGEANT-MAJOR (WO2) GEORGES OUELLET

As a member of the Canadian Contingent, United Nations Force in Cyprus, Warrant Officer 2 Ouellet served as reconnaissance patrol leader with the 1st Battalion, Royal 22e Régiment. On 10 April 1964, when Turkish-Cypriots in the Kyrenia Pass area advanced toward the Greek-Cypriot positions in the area of Kato Dhikomo they attacked with direct small-arms fire. Twelve unarmed Greek-Cypriot farmers scattered in the open fields on the Onisha cooperative farm. It was at this time that W.O.2 Ouellet arrived in the area with his patrol. He deployed his men and with complete disregard for his own safety, personally went to the rescue of the twelve farmers. During the next twenty minutes, under constant direct small-arms fire, he moved from one to the other, and safely brought them for protection into a farm building. Leaving two of his men with them, he then approached the Turkish-Cypriot positions, arranged for a temporary cease-fire and succeeded in evacuating the farmers to safety in a nearby Greek-Cypriot village. By his quick thinking and at the risk of his own life, he saved the lives of twelve Greek-Cypriots, gained the respect and admiration of his men and of the Greek- and Turkish-Cypriots, enhanced the prestige of the Canadian peacekeeping force and paved the way for an eventual stabilization of the cease-fire line in the area.

STAR OF COURAGE

CAPTAIN ALAIN ROBERT PIERRE JOSEPH FORAND

On 23 July 1974, during the war in Cyprus, a Canadian patrol conducting a group of combatants out of a UN controlled area came under fire. Several soldiers were killed or wounded and the Canadian officer leading the escort party was wounded. One of his men who began to give him first aid was also hit. At the bottom of a creek bed, the victims were exposed to continuing machine-gun fire. Coming on the scene, Captain Alain Forand arranged for covering fire and, with complete disregard for his own safety, he crawled forward over the exposed ground to aid the two casualties. Single-handedly, he managed to drag the wounded officer some distance up onto the bank of the creek where others helped carry him out of the danger area. Captain Forand then directed the rescue of the wounded soldier.

PRIVATE JOSEPH MICHAEL CLARISSE PLOUFFE

On 23 July 1974, during the war in Cyprus, a Canadian patrol conducting a group of combatants out of a UN controlled area came under fire. Some soldiers were killed, others were wounded, and the Canadian officer commanding the patrol was wounded. Private Plouffe, a member of the escort party, went at once to the aid of the fallen officer. Moments later he sustained a bullet wound in the face but despite this injury, he continued to render first aid completely disregarding the peril to his own life.

MEDAL OF BRAVERY

COLONEL GUY H. LESSARD

On 17 August 1974, Colonel Guy Lessard with another Canadian officer was attempting to gain the cooperation and withdrawal of two groups of the belligerents stationed at opposite ends of a street in Nicosia. While they were thus engaged, a truck driven by a Turkish-Cypriot civilian entered the area. The driver was forced from his vehicle and his life threatened. In this tense and hazardous situation, Colonel Lessard immediately placed himself in front of the man and shielded him until a military vehicle was brought up into which the man climbed and was removed from danger. Colonel Lessard's conduct in the face of the combatant soldiers was a prime factor in restoring calm.

Appendix C

CAPTAIN JOSEPH NORMAND BLAQUIÈRE

In July, 1974, when the conflict on Cyprus was most intense, Captain Blaquière was constantly at the scene of the heaviest firing, establishing the UN presence and attempting to restore peace. On July 15, when tank fire was falling in the Turkish enclave, he drew his UN jeep across the tank's line of fire and effectively prevented further destruction and possible loss of life. On July 23, he organized the evacuation of a number of combatant troops who had moved into the UN compound and thus prevented an exchange of fire which would undoubtedly have resulted in casualties among the Canadian contingent. In the course of the evacuation the group came under machine-gun fire and several of the combatants were killed and wounded. During this perilous action, Captain Blaquière sustained wounds.

PRIVATE JOSEPH MICHEL GINGRAS

On 20 July 1974, during the war in Cyprus, Private Gingras and Corporal Gratton were members of a reconnaissance patrol making their way through a narrow street in the old part of Nicosia when they came under sniper fire. One soldier was hit and fell to the ground. Disregarding their own safety, Private Gingras and Corporal Gratton went at once to the aid of their comrade and in the face of continuing rifle fire, they succeeded in carrying the wounded man some considerable distance to the safety of the platoon position.

CORPORAL JOSEPH ROLAND MICHEL WHELAN
PRIVATE JOSEPH MIKE BELLEY
PRIVATE JOSEPH GILLES PELLETIER

On 23 July 1974, during the war in Cyprus, a Canadian patrol, conducting a group of combatants out of a UN-controlled area, came under fire. Some soldiers were killed and others wounded and the Canadian officer leading the patrol sustained wounds. One of his men who began to give him first aid was also hit. At the bottom of a creek bed, the victims were exposed to continuing machine gun fire. Corporal Whelan and Privates Belley and Pelletier volunteered to join a rescue party. In these hazardous circumstances, they assisted in carrying the wounded officer out of the danger area. Privates Belley and Pelletier then returned, scrambled down to the creek bed, and carried the other wounded man to safety.

PRIVATE ERROL JOSEPH GAPP

On 1 February 1975, while caught in the crossfire between Greek and Turkish forces at the United Nations Post Mojave in Cyprus, Private Errol Gapp of the 1st Battalion Royal Canadian Regiment risked his life in order to administer treatment to casualties of the fighting and to negotiate for a ceasefire with the opposing factions. During the exchange of heavy machine-gun fire a Turkish private was seriously wounded and had to be evacuated. With complete disregard for his own safety, Private Gapp exposed himself to direct fire and was instrumental in removing the soldier from the scene. Later Private Gapp contributed to the safety of another Turkish soldier suffering from severe shock. The man was led to his section by Private Gapp who then returned to his own bunker where he resumed negotiations until relieved from his post.

Appendix C

Cyprus Service

Other peacekeeping missions involved individuals and minor units. In Cyprus, on the other hand, major units served in rotation:

1.	1 R22eR & Recce Sqn RCD	Mar 64 — Sep 64	
2.	1 Cdn Gds & Recce Sqn LdSH (RC)	Sep 64 — Mar 65	
3.	1 QOR & Recce Sqn RCD	Mar 65 — Sep 65	
4.	2 Cdn Gds & RCD Recce Sqn, W Bty 4 RCHA	Sep 65 — Apr 66	
5.	2 RHC & Recce Sqn 8 CH	Apr 66 — Oct 66	
6.	1 RCR & FGH Recce Sqn	Oct 66 — Apr 67	
7.	2 QOR & RCD Recce Sqn	Apr 67 — Oct 67	
8.	1 RHC & FGH Recce Sqn	Oct 67 — Apr 68	
9.	1 PPCLI	Apr 68 — Sep 68	
10.	3 R22eR	Sep 68 — Mar 69	
11.	2 R22eR	Apr 69 — Sep 69	
12.	2 RHC	Sep 69 — Mar 70	
13.	1 RCR	Mar 70 — Sep 70	
14.	3 PPCLI	Oct 70 — Mar 71	
15.	1 PPCLI	Mar 71 — Oct 71	
16.	2 R22eR	Oct 71 — Apr 72	
17.	LdSH (RC)	Apr 72 — Oct 72	
18.	2 PPCLI	Oct 72 — Mar 73	
19.	3 R22eR	Mar 73 — Oct 73	
20.	2 RCR	Oct 73 — Apr 74	
21.	1 Cdn AB Regt	Apr 74 — Oct 74	
22.	1 RCR	Dec 74 — May 75	
23.	2 R22eR	May 75 — Nov 75	
24.	3 R22eR	Nov 75 — Apr 76	
25.	2 PPCLI	Apr 76 — Nov 76	

26.	3'RCR	Nov	76 — Apr	77
27.	12e Régiment blindé du Canada (12th Armoured Régiment of Canada)	Apr	77 — Nov	77
28.	2 RCR	Nov	77 —Apr	78
29.	1 PPCLI	Apr	78 — Nov	78
30.	8th Canadian Hussars (Princess Louise's)	Nov	78 — Apr	79
31.	3 R22eR	Apr	79 — Nov	79
32.	LdSH (RC) augmented by 126 troops 3rd Regt RCHA	Nov	79 — Apr	80
33.	3 PPCLI	Apr	80 — Oct	80
34.	5e Régiment d'Artillerie légère du Canada (5th Regt. of Light Artillery) augmented 5e Régt de Génie (5th Regt of Engineers)	Oct	80 — Apr	81
35.	Cdn AB Regt	Apr	81 — Oct	81
36.	2 R22eR	Oct	81 — Apr	82
37.	RCHA	Apr	82 — Oct	82
38.	2 PPCLI	Oct	82 — Apr	83
39.	12e Régiment blindé du Canada	Apr	83 — Oct	83
40.	2 RCR and units of Force Mobile Command	Oct	83 — Apr	84
41.	1 PPCLI	Apr	84 — Oct	84
42.	1 RCR	Oct	84 — Mar	85
43.	3 R22eR	Mar	85 — Sep	85
44.	2 RCHA	Sep	85 — Mar	86

45. 3 RCR	Mar 86 — Sep 86	
46. Cdn AB Regt	Sep 86 — Mar 87	
47. 2 R22eR	Mar 87 — Aug 87	
48. 5e Régiment d'Artillerie du Canada	Aug 87 — Mar 88	

APPENDIX D

ROLL OF HONOUR

MIDDLE EAST

RANK	REGIMENT OR CORPS	INITIALS AND SURNAME	DATE OF DEATH
Spr.	RCE	R.H. Vezina	9 Mar 57
Lt.	RCAC	C.C. Van Straubenzee	10 May 57
Cpl.	RC Sigs	K.E. Pennell	15 Sep 57
Pte.	RCASC	B.O. Adams	20 Sep 57
Sgt.	RCE	I.L. Stark	27 Sep 57
Tpr.	RCAC	G.E. McDavid	29 Nov 57
Pte.	RCASC	I.A. Sawyer	22 Apr 58
Sig.	RC Sigs	N.E. Mason	15 May 58
Lt.-Col.	PPCLI	G.A. Flint	26 May 58
Cpl.	RCASC	J.T. Roberts	10 Jun 58
Cpl.	C Pro C	G.S. Porter	23 Apr 59
Maj.	RCOC	H. Morewood	26 Jul 59
Tpr.	RCAC	R.H. Allan	28 Nov 59
Pte.	RCASC	A.T. Hurst	4 Feb 60
Cpl.	RCAC	G.A. Gauthier	20 Feb 60
Tpr.	RCAC	R.J. Wiley	7 Sep 61
Cfn.	RCEME	D.S. Roster	19 Nov 61

Appendix D

RANK	REGIMENT OR CORPS	INITIALS AND SURNAME	DATE OF DEATH
Cpl.	RCEME	J.M. Albert	19 Nov 61
Cpl.	RC Sigs	E. Olivier	9 Dec 61
Spr.	RCE	G.G. Thompson	18 May 62
Cpl.	RCOC	E.G. Groom	3 Oct 63
W/C	RCAF	E.D. Harper	2 Nov 63
Sgt.	RCAF	J.K. Hermann	26 Dec 63
Pte.	CPC	R.L. Morin	29 May 64
Tpr.	RCAC	A.A. Bons	27 Nov 64
Cpl.	RCAC	P.R. Wallace	27 Nov 64
Pte.	RCASC	D.A.J. Lamothe	16 Mar 66
F/O	RCAF	R.V. Edwards	28 Apr 66
F/O	RCAF	J.M.L.P. Picard	30 Apr 66
Spr.	RCE	J. Lorienz	12 Jul 66
Sig.	RC Sigs	P.M. Crouse	19 Aug 66
Pte.	RCASC	E.J. Fickling	17 Oct 66
W.O.	RCAF	D.M. Henderson	21 Nov 73
Capt.	424 Sqn	K.B. Mirau	9 Aug 74
Capt.	RCAF	G.G. Foster	9 Aug 74
Capt.	424 Sqn	R.B. Wicks	9 Aug 74
M.W.O.	R22eR	G. Landry	9 Aug 74
A/M.W.O.	RCR	C.B. Korejwo	9 Aug 74
M/Cpl.	424 Sqn	R.C. Spencer	9 Aug 74
Cpl.	RCASC	M.W. Simpson	9 Aug 74
Cpl.	RC Sigs	M.H.T. Kennington	9 Aug 74
Cpl.	424 Sqn	B.K. Stringer	9 Aug 74
Cpl.	R22eR	J.P.C. Blais	24 Dec 74
Cpl.	RCEME	N. Edwards	24 Dec 74
Cpl.	RCHA	R.W. Miller	24 Dec 74
Pte.	RC Sigs	T.E. Abbot	14 Jun 75

RANK	REGIMENT OR CORPS	INITIALS AND SURNAME	DATE OF DEATH
Sgt.	CANMILCON	L.W. Daily	10 Nov 77
Sgt.	CANMILCON	J.F.B. Demers	5 Dec 77
Cpl.	CANMILCON	D.C. Ross	3 Mar 78
Pte.	CANMILCON	C.A. Dodge	2 Jul 79

CYPRUS

RANK	REGIMENT OR CORPS	INITIALS AND SURNAME	DATE OF DEATH
Lt.	C Int C	K.E. Edmonds	25 Dec 64
Tpr.	RCAC	J.H. Campbell	31 Jul 64
Rfm.	QOR	P.J. Hoare	14 Aug 65
Gdsm.	RCIC	J.J.P. Chartier	14 Mar 66
Pte.	RCIC	J.P.E. Bernard	9 Jul 66
Tpr.	RCAC	L.W. Nass	27 Sep 66
Cpl.	RCIC	O.J. Redmond	10 Mar 67
Cpl.	C Pro C	K.A. Salmon	24 Sep 67
Pte.	RHC	J.A. Lerue	9 Feb 70
Pte.	RCR	T.J. Hall	31 Jul 70
Cpl.	PPCLI	P.C. Isenor	25 Oct 70
M/Cpl.	PPCLI	J.R.M.J.P. Lessard	1 Dec 72
Cpl.	RCR	A. Roach	17 Feb 74
Sgt.	RCN	C.A.H. Wamback	30 Jun 74
Pte.	Cdn AB Regt	J.L.G. Perron	6 Aug 74
Pte.	Cdn AB Regt	J.J.C. Berger	10 Sep 74
Capt.	RCR	I.E. Patten	1 Apr 75
Pte.	RCR	S.J. Kohlman	11 Apr 75
Pte.	PPCLI	D.R. Krieger	17 Aug 76
Sgt.(R)	RCAMC	J.R.A. Dupont	24 Apr 77
M/Cpl.	PPCLI	J.D.G. McInnis	30 Mar 80

Appendix D

RANK	REGIMENT OR CORPS	INITIALS AND SURNAME	DATE OF DEATH
		INDIA/PAKISTAN	
A/B.Gen.	RCAC	H.H. Angle	17 Jul 50
		INDOCHINA	
Cpl.	RCIC	V.J. Perkin	18 Oct 65
Sgt.	RCIC	J.S. Byrne	18 Oct 65
Capt.	RCAC	C.E. Laviolette	7 Apr 73
		CONGO	
S/Sgt.	RCOC	J.P.C. Marquis	6 Feb 62
Sgt.	RC Sigs	R.H. Moore	6 Oct 60

ABBREVIATIONS

ATC   — Air Transport Command

ATU   — Air Transport Unit

HQ   — Headquarters

ICCS   — International Commission for Control and Supervision

ICSC   — International Commission(s) for Supervision and Control

MFO   — Multinational Force and Observers

ONUC   — Opération des Nations Unies au Congo

OP   — Observation Post

RCAF   — Royal Canadian Air Force

RCN   — Royal Canadian Navy

UNEF   — UN Emergency Force

UNFICYP   — UN Peacekeeping Force in Cyprus

UNIFIL   — UN Interim Force in Lebanon

UNIPOM   — UN India-Pakistan Observation Mission

UNMOGIP   — UN Military Observer Group in India and Pakistan

UNOGIL — UN Observation Group in Lebanon
UNTEA — UN Temporary Executive Authority
UNTSO — UN Truce Supervision Organization
UNYOM — UN Yemen Observation Mission

NOTES

CHAPTER 1

1. E.L.M. Burns, *Between Arab and Israeli* (Toronto, 1962), p. 161.
2. Carl von Horn, *Soldiering for Peace* (London, 1966), pp. 85, 93-94.
3. Odd Bull, *War and Peace in the Middle East* (London, 1973), p. 117.
4. I.J. Rikhye, Michael Harbottle and Bjorn Egge, *The Thin Blue Line* (New Haven, 1974), p. 311.
5. Letter to author, 7 April 1987.
6. Letter to author, 9 December 1986.
7. Letter to author, 27 January 1987.

CHAPTER 2

1. Hugh Thomas, *The Suez Affair* (London, 1966), pp. 123-126; Tareq Y Ismael, "Canada and the Middle East," *Behind the Headlines*, Vol. XXXII, No. 5, December 1973, p. 9; See also External Affairs, UNEF, Vol 1, File No. 50366-40.
2. Donald Neff, *Warriors at Suez* (New York, 1981), pp. 378, 382.
3. "United Nations, Suez," *Britannica Book of the Year, 1957*, p. 764; A.J. Barker, *Suez: The Seven Day War* (London, 1964), p. 97.
4. L.B. Pearson, *Mike, the Memoirs of Lester B. Pearson* (Toronto, 1973), Vol. 2, pp. 252-253.
5. For further explanation see Michael J. Tucker, "Making Peace and Keeping It," *Horizon Canada*, Vol. 35, pp. 827-828 and J.L. Granatstein's article "Canada: Peacekeeper" in *Peacekeeping: International Challenge and Canadian Response*, Canadian Institute of International Affairs, 1968, p. 118.
6. I.J. Rikhye, M. Harbottle and B. Egge, *The Thin Blue Line*, p. 52.
7. Burns, *Between Arab and Israeli*, p. 189.
8. S.G. Tait, "RCEME in the UNEF," *Canadian Army Journal*, Vol. XII, No. 1, (January 1958), pp. 134-135.

9. Blair Fraser, "How Tommy Burns Tries to Keep the Peace," *Maclean's*, 19 January 1957, p. 45.
10. Public Archives Canada (PAC), Record Group (RG) 24, Vol. 18,446, p. 3.
11. PAC, War Diary, (WD) 56 RCEME, RG24, 18, 494, 29 December 1956.
12. RG24, Vol. 18,446 and RG24, Vol. 18,494, 11 January 1957.
13. "Maggie's Last and Greatest Mission," *Crowsnest*, Vol. 9, No. 5 (March 1957), p. 8.
14. RG 24, Vol. 18,446, Appendix (newspaper clippings).
15. RG 24, Vol. 18,448.
16. RG 24, Vol. 18,448, Appendix.
17. RG 24, Vol. 18,449, 9 March 1957; External Affairs, UNEF, Vol. 16, File No. 50366-40.
18. RG 24, Vol. 18,449, 14 May 1957, pp. 6-7.
19. RG 24, Vol. 18,489, 7 March 1957.
20. RG 24, Vol. 18,449, 7 March 1957.
21. RG 24, Vol. 18,448, 8 March 1957.
22. W.F. Pratt, "The Signals' Job in the UNEF," *Canadian Army Journal*, Vol. XIV, No. 2 (Spring 1960), p. 132.
23. Army Headquarters (AHQ) Historical Report No. 78, p. 1.
24. 435 and 436 Sqn Diaries; E. McVeity, "UNEF's Air Support," *Roundel*, Vol. 10, No. 2 (March 1958), pp. 2-4; K.G. Roberts, "Ten Years of Service," *Sentinel* (September 1967), p. 11.
25. Larry Milberry, ed., *Sixty Years: RCAF and CF Air Command, 1924-1984* (Toronto, 1984), pp. 309-311.
26. J.D. Burge, "Somewhere East of Suez," *Roundel*, Vol. 12, No. 2 (March 1960), p. 4.
27. *Ibid.*, p. 8.
28. RG 24, 18,479, 1 March 1959, p. 1.
29. Letter to author, 24 March 1986.
30. Brereton Greenhous, *Dragoon: The Centennial History of the Royal Canadian Dragoons, 1883-1983* (Ottawa, 1983), p. 433; for the same story see External Affairs, UNEF, Vol. 15, File No. 50366-40, 7 May 1959, unpublished article by G.R. Tomalin, "The Strangest Police Force in the World," pp. 4-5.
31. Larry Worthington, *The Spur and the Sprocket* (Kitchener, 1968), p. 130.
32. External Affairs, UNEF, Vol. 15, File No. 50366-40; G.R. Tomalin, "The Strangest Police Force in the World," pp. 2-6.
33. RG 24, 18, 475, 28 February 1962; External Affairs, UNEF, Vol. 16, File No. 50366-40.
34. Philip Neatby, formerly commanding "A" Squadron, 8th Canadian Hussars (Princess Louise's) to author, October 1985.
35. Army Headquarters Historical Report No. 78, p. 8.
36. Notes of D.R. Mathews, Moose Jaw, Saskatchewan.
37. RG 24, 18,490, 4 February 1959.
38. Worthington, *The Spur and the Sprocket*, pp. 133-134.
39. *Sand Dune*, 25 December 1964; RG 24, Vol 18,474, 2 December 1960, p 1; RG 24, Vol. 18,465, 6 July 1963, p. 1.

CHAPTER 3

1. Summary of interview on 21 March 1968 with General I.J. Rikhye, late commander of UNEF in Egypt, D. Hist., 112.3HI.001 (D19).
2. In February 1958, Egypt and Syria formed a union and renamed the two countries the United Arab Republic. The union was dissolved in September 1961. However, Egypt continued the usage of UAR as its name even though Syria returned to its original name. In September 1971 Egypt adopted the title Arab Republic of Egypt, dropping United Arab Republic.
3. "Report on Operation Leaven," D. Hist., 112.302.005 (D1).
4. CFHQ Operations Log, 19 May 1967, 18352, serial 35, D. Hist., 112.302.005 (D2).
5. CFHQ Operations Log, 17 May 1967.
6. CFHQ Operations Log, serials 13 and 14, 18 May 1967, 16502 and serial 31.
7. *Canada Gazette*, 16 September 1967, 2355. See D. Hist., 112.301.006 (D11).
8. Indar Jit Rikhye, *The Sinai Blunder* (London, 1980), pp. 41-42, 49, 74-75, 77.
9. W.A.B. Douglas, "Canada and the Withdrawal of the United Nations Emergency Force," *Canadian Defence Quarterly*, Vol. 2, No. 3 (Winter 1972/73), p. 50; *Canada and the United Nations, 1945-1975* (Ottawa, 1977), p. 42.
10. 115 ATU Commander's Report, D. Hist., and transcript of interview of 30 October 1967, Col. D.H. Power with L/Cdr. W.A.B. Douglas on events preceding and during UNEF withdrawal, p.4, D. Hist., 112.3H1.001 (D18).
11. Rikhye, *The Sinai Blunder*, pp. 84,87; Tareq Y. Ismael, "Canada and the Middle East," *Behind the Headlines*, Vol. XXXII, No. 5 (December 1973), p. 16.
12. CFHQ Operations Log, serial 164, telephone call from John Hadwen, special assistant to Paul Martin, D. Hist., 112.302.005 (D2). See also serial 189.
13. D. Hist., 112.302.005 (D1).
14. "Interim Report on Withdrawal and Close-Out of CBU UNEF," dated 2 June 1967, prepared by Col. D.H. Power, D. Hist., 112.302.005 (D6).
15. Michael G. Belcher, "Exodus El Arish," *Airforce*, Vol. 7, No. 3 (September 1983), pp. 26-27.
16. Michael Harbottle, *The Blue Berets* (Harrisburg, Pa., 1972), pp. 25-26; Anthony Verrier, *International Peacekeeping: United Nations Forces in a Troubled World* (London, 1981), p. 37.
17. "Withdrawal of CDN contingent, UNEF — Lessons Learned," Paper V3451-7 (D. Ops.), 22 June 1967, D. Hist., 112.302.005 (D5).
18. "Interim Report on Withdrawal and Close Out of CBU UNEF," dated 2 June 1967, prepared by Col. D.H. Power, D. Hist., 112.302.005 (D6).

CHAPTER 4

1. von Horn, *Soldiering for Peace*, p. 295.
2. External Affairs, UNYOM, Vol. 1. File No. 11282-B-40; "Blue Flag Over Yemen," *Canadian Army Journal*, Vol. XVIII, No. 1 (1963), p. 37.

3. At the time the United Nations was in deep financial trouble as a result of the high costs of the Congo operation and the refusal of the Soviet Union and other states to pay their assessment for the Congo and UNEF I. There was also disagreement among the Security Council, the General Assembly and the secretary-general as to their roles in peacekeeping operations.
4. 134 Air Transport Unit Historical Summary, D. Hist., 709.
5. *Ibid.*
6. von Horn, *Soldiering for Peace*, pp. 354-360; for another opinion see David W. Wainhouse, ed., *International Peacekeeping at the Crossroads* (Baltimore, 1973), pp. 161-170.
7. 134 Air Transport Unit, Historical Summary.
8. 115 ATU, 4 September 1964, D. Hist., Historical Report.

CHAPTER 5

1. J. King Gordon, "The UN in Cyprus," *International·Journal*, Vol. XIX, No. 3 (Summer 1964), p. 340; Paul Martin, *A Very Public Life*, Vol. II (Toronto, 1985), pp. 545-548; J.H. Munro and Alex Inglis, eds., *Mike: The Memoirs of the Right Honourable Lester B. Pearson*, Vol. 3 (Toronto, 1975), p. 135.
2. Order-In-Council PC 1964-389.
3. "History of the Nicosia Zone," April 1964 to September 1965, D. Hist.; J.L. Wightman, "Cyprus Mission," *Crowsnest*, Vol. 16, No. 3-4 (March-April 1964), pp. 12-15.
4. C.C. Moskos, Jr., *Peace Soldiers* (Chicago, 1976), p. 53.
5. War Diaries, 1st Bn R22e and Recce Sqn RCD, March 1964.
6. Letter to author, 7 July 1986.
7. "History of the Nicosia Zone, April 1964 to September 1965," p. 3.
8. *Time*, 24 April 1964, Vol 83, No. 17, p. 12.
9. See Jacques Castonguay, *Les Bataillons et le Dépôt du Royal 22e Régiment: Vingt ans d'histoire, 1945-1965* (Quebec, 1974), pp. 231-243 and Brereton Greenhous, *Dragoon* (Ottawa, 1983), pp. 446-451.
10. Letter to author, 8 May 1986.
11. Letter to author, 14 April 1987.
12. K.C. Eyre, "The Future of UN Peacekeeping," *Canadian Defence Quarterly*, Vol. XII, No. 1 (Summer 1982), p. 35.
13. Letter to author, 9 April 1987.
14. Al Ditter, "Cyprus . . . 20 years and counting," *Sentinel*, Vol. 20, No. 6 (1984), p. 4.
15. Ian Nicol "Cyprus," *Sentinel*, Vol. 10, No. 8 (1974), pp. 15-19; Vol. 10, No. 9 (1974), pp. 16-21; Vol. XI, No. 1 (1975), pp. 22-24.
16. K.C. Eyre, "The Future of UN Peacekeeping," p. 32.
17. CBC Sound Archives, 740815, 740424-3, "Cyprus 1974."
18. "Briefing Notes: The UN Operations in Cyprus," pp. 3-4, D. Hist.
19. C.C. Moskos, Jr., *Peace Soldiers*, p. 92.
20. *The Citizen*, Ottawa, 27 January 1986, p. D5.

21. "History of Nicosia Zone, April 1964 to September 1965," p. 8.

CHAPTER 6

1. War Diary, CCUNEFME, Vol. I, November 1973, Annex p. 3, D. Hist.
2. "CDS Explains ME medical controversy," 12 December 1973, DND Library.
3. Canadian Forces Communications and Electronics Museum, Kingston.
4. Encyclopaedia Britannica, 1975 and 1976, "Middle Eastern Affairs," pp. 482-485, pp. 509-512; Henry Wiseman, *Peacekeeping*, p. 98; Anthony Verrier, *International Peacekeeping* (London, 1981), p. 110.
5. Letter to author, 11 July 1986.

CHAPTER 7

1. Letter to author, 20 May 1986.
2. Canadian Forces Communications and Electronics Museum, Kingston.
3. Greg Hogan, "Canlog Comes Through," *Sentinel*, Vol. 15, No. 5 (1979), p. 28.
4. Tom Coughlin, "UNDOF Samaritans," *Sentinel*, Vol. 19, No. 5 (1983), p. 37; J. Spaans, "UNDOF Relief Convoys to Lebanon," *Golan News*, No. 18, May-July 1982, p. 9; J. Spaans, "The Last UNDOF Convoy to Lebanon," *Golan News*, No. 19, July-August 1982, p. 3.
5. Bill Aikman, "On the Golan," *Sentinel*, Vol. 14, No. 5 (1978), pp. 16-18; Geof Haswell, "Camp Roofless," *Sentinel*, Vol. 10, No. 7 (1974), pp. 15-18; Al Ditter, "Supporting the UN," *Sentinel*, Vol. 20, No. 6 (1984), pp. 6-8.

CHAPTER 8

1. Interview with Lt.-Col. G.D. Wallace, RCOC, who served as an UN observer on the North Bekaa station.
2. See Christopher S. Calhoun, "Lebanon: That Was Then," *Proceedings: U.S. Naval Institute*, Volume III/9/991 (September 1985), pp. 74-80.
3. Henry Wiseman, ed., *Peacekeeping: Appraisals and Proposals*, p. 51; Anthony Verrier, *International Peacekeeping*, p. 127.
4. Letter to author, 18 April 1987.
5. Letter to author, 28 April 1987.
6. See "Canadians with UNIFIL," *Sentinel*, Vol. 14, No. 6 (1978), pp. 18-20.
7. Canadian Forces Communications and Electronics Museum, Kingston.

CHAPTER 9

1. [1985] *Annual Report of the Director General, Multinational Force and Observers*, Rome, 25 April 1986, p. 7.
2. *Ibid.*, p. 3; Bob Butt, "Flying Peacekeepers," *Sentinel*, Vol. 22, No. 5 (1986), p. 4.
3. M.R. Dabros, "The Multinational Force and Observers: A New Experience in Peacekeeping for Canada," *Canadian Defence Quarterly*, Vol. 16, No. 2, Autumn 1986, pp. 32-35.

CHAPTER 10

1. Sylvian Lourie, "The United Nations Military Observer Group in India and Pakistan," *International Organization*, IX, (Winter 1955), pp. 23-24.
2. D.S. Robertson, "United Nations Military Observer Group in India/Pakistan, 1968-69," *The Patrician*, Vol. XXII (1969), p. 65.
3. The Caribou destroyed at Srinagar was No. 5324. The Caribous that arrived at Lahore on 3 October were Nos. 5325 and 5327. They joined Caribou No. 5320 from UNMOGIP.
4. 117 ATU Historical Report, 1965, D. Hist.
5. See Robin McNeill, "Through the Valleys of Kashmir," *Sentinel*, Vol. 6, No. 2 (February 1970), pp. 18-20.
6. J.R. Liss, "Some UN Memories," *Sentinel*, Vol. 10, No. 4 (1974), pp. 24-25.
7. Interview with G.F.B. Ritchie by Jean B. Pariseau, 30 July 1970, D. Hist., 82/530.

CHAPTER 11

1. For Vietnam the main headquarters was in Hanoi with a sub-headquarters in Saigon. The latter became the main headquarters following the withdrawal of fixed teams from North Vietnam in the mid-1960s as a result of American air attacks.
2. See R.F. MacKay, "A Report on Vietnam," *Canadian Army Journal*, Vol. XVII, No. I (1963), pp. 28-33.
3. *Ibid.*, p. 30; "Notes on the International Commission, Vietnam, 1954-55" by W.J. Megill, D. Hist. 83/25
4. Interview with A.L. Maclean by author, 17 May 1986, Candel-Cambodian Reunion, Ottawa.
5. Poem by A.L. Maclean.
6. James Eayrs, *In Defence of Canada; Indochina: Roots of Complicity* (Toronto, 1983), p. 266.
7. Interview with Frederick Clifford by author, 23 May 1986.
8. R.B. Tackaberry, "Keeping the Peace," *Behind the Headlines*, Vol. XXVI, No. I (September 1966), p. 6.

9. Letter to author, 12 July 1986.
10. War Diary, ICSC Cambodia, 16 May 1955, p. 2, D. Hist.
11. Interviews by author with Robert T. Bennett, 28 April 1986, and Donald E. Mounteer, 6 May 1986.
12. J.S. Moir, *History of the Royal Canadian Corps of Signals* (Ottawa, 1962),pp. 308-311.
13. R.H. Mahar, "Viet Nam as seen by a Team Officer, 1962-63," D. Hist.
14. Interview with David Veitch by author, 17 June 1986.
15. Interview with Dr. G.E. Chenard by author, 7 May 1986.
16. R.Guy C. Smith, ed., *As You Were! Ex-Cadets Remember*, Vol. II, RMC Kingston, 1984, pp. 367-370.
17. D.A. Ross, *In the Interests of Peace: Canada and Vietnam, 1954-1973* (Toronto, 1984), p. 331; "ICSC and ICCS: Strength and Casualties," D. Hist., 79/715.
18. See Pat Dillon, "Viet Nam: Looking Back: Five Months in Vi Thanh," *Sentinel*, Vol. 14, No. I (1978), pp. 21-22.
19. Letter of Garry Handson to author, 7 March 1986.
20. Interview with J.O. W. Ross, 13 August 1986.
21. D.G. Loomis, "An Outline of Canadian Operations within the ICCS", Saigon, 26 July 1973, pp. 8-11.
22. David Cox, "The International Commission of Control and Supervision in Vietnam, 1973," *Peacekeeping: Appraisals and Proposals*, pp. 323, 329; Ross, *In the Interests of Peace: Canada and Vietnam, 1954-1973*, p. 361.
23. *Ibid.*, p. 316; *Globe and Mail*, 12 April 1973, p. 10.
24. Letter from Commander R.H. Kirby to W.A.B. Douglas, 9 April 1974, D. Hist., 74/415.
25. D.G. Loomis, "An Expedition to Vietnam: The Military Component of the Canadian Delegation 1973," *Canadian Defence Quarterly* (Spring 1974), pp. 37-39.

CHAPTER 12

1. Paul W. Van der Veur, "The United Nations in West Irian," *International Organization*, Vol. XVIII, No. 1 (Winter 1964), p. 54.
2. Unpublished paper by Flight Lieutenant Richards, C.O. 116 ATU, D. Hist. 180.003 (D50).
3. *Ibid.*
4. "United Nations Administration Leaves West Irian," *External Affairs Bulletin*, Vol. XV, No. 6 (June 1963), p. 240.

CHAPTER 13

1. See Alan P. Merriam, *Congo: Background of Conflict* (Evanston, Illinois 1961).
2. House of Commons *Debates*, 14 July 1960, 6273.
3. *Ibid.*, 30 July 1960, 7263.

4. *Ibid.*, 1 August 1960, 7348-49.
5. *Globe and Mail*, 9 August 1960, pp. 1, 6.
6. PAC, W.D. 57 Signal Squadron (later Unit), 1-9 August 1960.
7. PAC, RG 24, Vol. 18484, 28 October 1961.
8. R.B. Tackaberry, "Keeping the Peace," *Behind the Headlines*, Vol. XXVI, No. I (September 1966), p. 15; R.M.L. Bowdery, "A Year in the Congo," *Roundel*, Vol. 13, No. 7 (September 1961), pp. 2-4.
9. T.G. Coughlin, "Candid Congo," *Roundel*, Vol. 16, No. I (January-February 1964), p. 14.
10. *Ibid.*, p. 15.
11. "Canada Peace-Keeping Operations: The Congo, 1960-64," D. Hist., Report No. 8, pp. 39-40; WD, RG 24, Vol. 18482, folder 1, Annex 26, 27; External Affairs, UNOC, Vol. 3, File No. 6386-C-40, 19-20 August 1960.
12. RG 24, Vol. 18482, folder I, Annex 28, a memo by J.B. Pariseau, 22 August 1960; External Affairs, UNOC, Vol. 4, File No. 6386-C-40, 2 September 1960.
13. RG 24, Vol. 18482 folder 1; "Canada and Peacekeeping Operations, The Congo, 1960-64," D. Hist., Report No. 8; von Horn, *Soldiering for Peace*, pp. 188-189.
14. Peter Worthington, *Looking for Trouble: A Journalist's Life and Then Some* (Toronto, 1964), p. 125.
15. *Ibid.*, p. 126.
16. "57 Canadian Signal Unit in the Congo," January 1963, D. Hist., 144.9.009 (57).
17. J.S. Moir, *History of the Royal Canadian Corps of Signals, 1903-1961*, p. 319.
18. W.D., 57 Signal Unit, 27 Feb. 1961.
19. Michael Harbottle, *The Blue Berets*, p. 51.
20. Report No. 8, p. 63.
21. See A.E. King, "UN Commander Honours Canadian Signal Unit in Congo," *Canadian Army Journal*, Vol. XVII, No. 1 (1963), pp. 95-96.
22. H.W.C. Stethem, "Signal Squadron in the Congo," *Canadian Army Journal*, Vol. XVII, No. 2, 1963.
23. "Proceedings of Commanding Officer's Investigation," 28 January 1963, 57 Sigs/Comm 2000, D. Hist., 114.9.009 (D36); See also P.A Mayer's account in *Weekend Magazine*, 12 and 19 December 1964.
24. 57 Cdn Sig Unit File, D. Hist., 144.9.009 (D65).
25. *Ibid.*
26. Letter from Colonel Berthiaume to author, 11 August 1986.
27. Letter to author, 9 August 1986.
28. *London Free Press, Montreal Gazette*, and *Ottawa Journal* of 7 September 1961; sworn statement of October 1961 by Mario Côté given to author.
29. Wiseman, *Peacekeeping: Appraisals and Proposals*, pp. 35-36.
30. G.F.G. Stanley, *Canada's Soldiers* (Toronto, 1974), p. 421.
31. *Peace and Security: Canada's Participation* Department of External Affairs, Ottawa, n.d., p. 45.
32. H.W.C. Stethem, "Signal Squadron in the Congo," *Canadian Army Journal*, Vol. XVII, No. 2, p. 120.

33. W.H. Barton, "Who Will Pay for Peace? The UN Crisis," *Behind the Headlines*, Vol. XXIV (April 1965).
34. RG24, Vol. 18488, folder 16X, 30 June 1964.
35. Rikyhe, Harbottle and Egge, *The Thin Blue Line*, p. 71.

CHAPTER 14

1. See scrapbook and diaries of W.A. Milroy and External Affairs, Nigeria, Vols. 1-4, File No. 21-14-6, 1 April 1968 — 31 December 1968.

CHAPTER 15

1. H.E.C. Price, "Tanzania Tale," *Sentinel*, Vol. 2, No. 2 (March 1966), pp. 24-27; Murray Johnston, *Canada's Craftsmen* (Ottawa, 1984), pp. 159-161.

CHAPTER 16

1. "A Canadian Officer's Account of Peacekeeping in the Dominican Republic," 24 July 1967, D. Hist., 112.3M2.001 (D2).

BIBLIOGRAPHY

THE PURPOSE OF THIS BIBLIOGRAPHY is to provide interested readers with a guide for further study. For a more detailed bibliography of secondary sources up to 1966, readers are advised to consult *A Selected Bibliography on Peace-Keeping* by Gordon S. Smith, Ottawa: Queen's Printer, 1966. The relevant sections of the annual reports of the Department of National Defence and the *Yearbook of the United Nations* offer concise accounts of peacekeeping. The *International Journal*, published by the Canadian Institute of International Affairs, contains a large number of articles relating to international events.

PRIMARY SOURCES

A major source of written information for peacekeeping operations is the Manuscript Section, Public Archives of Canada and the Directorate of History, Department of National Defence. War diaries at both locations present a daily account of events. In addition, the diaries often have thick appendices with incoming and outgoing messages. Copies of Canadian and United Nations newspapers for the larger operations also appear in the diaries. Going through the diaries will yield interesting gems such as the war diarist to Robert Stokely, Directorate of History, 28 May 1967: ". . . We have to get out in a hurry . . . . Things are rough." (RG24, Vol. 18,471). The papers of E.L.M. Burns, J.G. Diefenbaker, Paul Martin and L.B. Pearson may be consulted at the Public Archives.

The Department of External Affairs has a large number of files relating to peacekeeping operations. These files can be located by consulting their alphabetically arranged file index referred to as the "KWOC" (Key Word Out of Context) listing. Headings such as Congo UN Operations, Laos, Lebanon, UNEF, UNTSO, Vietnam, Yemen and others will indicate file numbers with information of varying usefulness. At the time of writing some of these files were being transferred to the Public Archives. As well, the UN Archives has a considerable amount of material relating to its peacekeeping operations. Among their volumes are files relating to Canada and Canadian military units. Copies of all letters quoted in the text are held by the author.

288

Bibliography

PUBLISHED DOCUMENTS IN OFFICIAL DEPOSITORIES

Eayrs, James, ed. *The Commonwealth and Suez: A Documentary Survey*. London: Oxford University Press, 1964.

Higgins, Rosalyn, ed. *United Nations Peacekeeping, 1946-1967, Documents and Commentary*. Vol. I — The Middle East, Vol. II — Asia, Vol. III — Africa, Vol. IV 1946-1979 — Europe. London: Oxford University Press, 1969, 1970, 1980, 1981.

Siekmann, Robert, ed. *Basic Documents on United Nations and Related Peacekeeping Forces*. The Hague: TMC Asser Institut, 1985.

SECONDARY SOURCES

BOOKS

Abi-Saab, Georges. *The United Nations Operation in the Congo, 1960-1964*. Oxford: University Press, 1978.

Alcock, Norman and Arnold Simoni. *The Peacemakers Association of Nations: A new concept for national security*. Huntsville, Ontario: Canadian Peace Research Institute, 1983.

Ballaloud, Jacques. *L'ONU et les opérations de maintien de la paix*. Paris: A. Pedone, 1971.

Barker, A.J. *Suez: The Seven Day War*. London: Faber and Faber Ltd., 1964.

Bloomfield, L.P. *International Military Forces: The Question of Peacekeeping in an Armed and Disarming World*. Boston: Little Brown and Co., 1964.

Bowett, D.W. *United Nations Forces*. London: Stevens & Sons, 1964.

Boyd, J.M. *United Nations Peace-Keeping Operations: A Military and Political Appraisal*. New York: Praeger Publishers, 1972.

Brecher, Michael. *The Struggle for Kashmir*. Toronto: Ryerson Press, 1953.

Brewin, Andrew. *Stand on Guard: The Search for a Canadian Defence Policy*. McClelland and Stewart, 1965.

Bridle, Paul. *Canada and the International Commission in Indochina, 1954-1972*.Toronto: Canadian Institute of International Affairs, 1973.

Bull, Odd. *War and Peace in the Middle East: The Experiences and Views of a U.N. Observer*. London: Leo Cooper, 1976.

Burns, E.L.M. *Between Arab and Israeli*. Toronto: Clarke, Irwin and Company, 1962.

Byers, R.B. and Michael Slack, eds. *Canada and Peacekeeping: Prospects for the Future*. Toronto: York Strategic Studies, 1984.

Canada. Dept. of National Defence. Directorate of Strategic and Air Defence Operational Research. *A Selected Bibliography of Peacekeeping*. Revised. Gordon S. Smith, Compiler. Ottawa: Queen's Printer, 1966.

Comay, M.S. *U.N. Peacekeeping in the Israel-Arab Conflict, 1948-1975; an Israel Critique*, Jerusalem: Hebrew University, 1976.

Cooke. O.A. *The Canadian Military Experience, 1867-1983: A Bibliography*. Second Edition, Ottawa: Department of National Defence, 1984.

Cordier, A.W. and Wilder Foote, eds. *The Quest for Peace*. New York: Columbia University Press, 1965.

Cox, David and Mary Taylor, eds. *A Guide to Canadian Policies on Arms Control, Disarmament, Defence and Conflict Resolution, 1985-86*. Ottawa: The Canadian Institute for International Peace and Security, 1986.

Creighton, Donald. *The Forked Road: Canada, 1939-1957*. The Canadian Centenary Series. Toronto: McClelland and Stewart, 1976.

Davis, John H. *The Evasive Peace: A Study of the Zionist-Arab Problem*. Second Edition. Cleveland, Ohio: Dillon/Liederbach, 1976.

Douville, Steven, Michael Pearson and Bradley Feasey. *Conflict Resolution and Negotiation Studies in International Relations: A Bibliography*. Ottawa: The Norman Patterson School of International Affairs, Carleton University, 1986.

Eayrs, James. *In Defence of Canada. Indochina: Roots of Complicity*. Toronto: University Press, 1983.

Elliot, S.R. *Scarlet to Green: A History of Intelligence in the Canadian Army, 1903-1963*. Toronto: Canadian Intelligence and Security Association, 1981.

External Affairs. *Canada and the United Nations, 1945-1975*. Ottawa: Supply and Services, 1977.

Fabian, Larry L. *Soldiers without Enemies: Preparing the United Nations for Peacekeeping*. Washington D.C.: The Brookings Institution, 1971.

Foley, Charles and W. I. Scobie. *The Struggle for Cyprus*. Stanford: Hoover Institution Press, 1975.

Fraser, Blair. *The Search for Identity: Canada, 1945-1967*. Toronto: Doubleday, 1967.

Frydenberg, Per, ed. *Peace-Keeping: Experience and Evaluation*. Oslo: Norwegian Institute of International Affairs, 1964.

Goodspeed, D.J., ed. *The Armed Forces of Canada, 1867-1967: A Century of Achievement*. Ottawa: Queen's Printer, 1967.

Gordon, J. King. *The United Nations in the Congo: A Quest for Peace*. New York: Carnegie Endowment for International Peace, 1962.

Granatstein, J.L. *A Man of Influence: Norman A. Robertson and Canadian Statecraft, 1929-1968*. Toronto: Deneau Publishers, 1981.

Granatstein, J.L. *Canada, 1957-1967: The Years of Uncertainty and Innovation*. The Canadian Centenary Series. Toronto: McClelland and Stewart, 1986.

Gordon, J. King, ed. *Canada's Role as a Middle Power*. Toronto: Canadian Institute of International Affairs, 1966.

Greenhous, Brereton. *Dragoon: The Centennial History of the Royal Canadian Dragoons 1883-1983*. Ottawa: Guild of the Royal Canadian Dragoons, 1983.

Hanning, Hugh, ed. *Peacekeeping and Confidence-Building Measures in the Third World*. Report No. 20. New York: International Peace Academy, 1983.

Harbottle, Michael. *The Blue Berets: The Story of the United Nations Peacekeeping Forces*. Harrisburg, Pa: Stackpole Books, 1972.

Hitchens, Christopher. *Cyprus*. London: Quartet Books, 1984.

Holmes, John W. *The Shaping of Peace: Canada and the Search for World Order, 1943-1957*. 2 Vols. Toronto: University of Toronto Press, 1979, 1982.

Bibliography

Horn, Carl von. *Soldering for Peace*. London: Cassell, 1966.

Ignatieff, George. *The Making of a Peacemonger*. Toronto: University of Toronto Press, 1985.

International Peace-Keeping in the Eighties: Global Outlook and Canadian Priorities. Carleton University, Ottawa: Norman Patterson School of International Affairs, 1982.

James, Alan. *The Role of Force in International Order and United Nations Peace-Keeping*. Ditchley Paper No. 20. Ditchley Park: Ditchley Foundation, 1969.

Johnston, Murray. *Canada's Craftsmen: The Story of the Corps of Royal Canadian Electrical and Mechanical Engineers and of the Land Ordnance Branch*. Ottawa: Lore Association, 1984.

Joint Canada/Norway Workshop on UN Peacekeeping. *Dialogue on Peacekeeping*. Kingston: n.p. 11-14 June, 1979.

Karaosmanoglu, Ali L. *Les Actions Militaires Coercitives et Non Coercitives Des Nations Unies*. Geneve: Librarie Droz, 1970.

Lefever, E.W. *Crisis in the Congo: A United Nations Force in Action*. Washington, D.C.: The Brookings Institution, 1965.

Levant, Victor. *Quiet Complicity: Canadian Involvement in the Vietnam War*. Toronto: Between the Lines, 1986.

MacDonald, J.D., ed. *The Canadian Airborne Regiment, Cyprus, 1974*. Nicosia: printed by Zavallis Press, 1974.

Marshall, S.L.A. *Sinai Victory*. New York: William Morrow and Company, 1958.

Martin, Paul. *A Very Public Life*. Vol. II. Toronto: Deneau Publishers, 1985.

Merriam, Alan P. *Congo: Background of Conflict*. Evanston, Illinois: Northwestern University Press, 1961.

Mitchell, Duff. *RCHA — Right of the Line: An Anecdotal History of the Royal Canadian Horse Artillery from 1871*. Ottawa: RCHA History Committee, 1986.

Neff, Donald. *Warriors at Suez*. New York: Simon and Schuster, 1981.

Nicholson, G.W.L. *Seventy Years of Service: A History of the Royal Canadian Army Medical Corps*. Ottawa: Borealis, 1977.

Pearson, L.B. *Mike: The Memoirs of the Rt. Hon. Lester B. Pearson*. 3 Vols. Toronto: University of Toronto Press, 1972-75.

Peacekeeper's Handbook. New York: International Peace Academy, 1978.

Peters, Joan. *From Time Immemorial: The Origins of the Arab-Jewish Conflict Over Palestine*. New York: Harper and Row, 1985.

Pierson, S.G. *What does a UN Soldier Do?* New York: Dodd, Mead and Co., 1965.

Pineau, Christian. *1956/Suez*. Paris: Editions Robert Laffont, 1976.

Raman, K. Vendata. *The Ways of the Peacemaker: A Study of United Nations intermediary assistance in the peaceful settlement of dipsutes*. New York: United Nations Institute for Training and Research, 1975.

Rannie, W.F., ed. *To the Thunderer His Arms: The Royal Canadian Ordnance Corps*. Lincoln, Ont.: W.F. Rannie, 1984.

Rikhye, I.J. Michael Harbottle and Bjorn Egge. *The Thin Blue Line*. New Haven: Yale University Press, 1974.

Rikhye, I.J. *The Sinai Blunder*. London: Frank Cass, 1980.

Robertson, Terence. *Crisis: The Inside Story of the Suez Conspiracy*. London: Hutchinson, 1964.

Rosner, Gabriella. *The United Nations Emergency Force*. New York: Columbia University Press, 1963.

Ross, A. Douglas. *In the Interests of Peace: Canada and Vietnam, 1954-1973*. Toronto: University Press, 1984.

Sharma, P.M. *Politics of Peace: UN General Assembly*. New Delhi: Abhinay Publications, 1978.

Sharp, Mitchell. *Viet-Nam: Canada's Approach to Participation in the International Commission of Control and Supervision*. Ottawa: Information Canada, 1973.

Sigler, J.H., ed. *International Peacekeeping in the Eighties: Global Outlook and Canadian Priorities*. Ottawa: The Norman Patterson School of International Affairs, Carleton University, 1982.

Souvannaphouma, Prince. *L'Agonie du Laos*. Vientiane: Plon, 1976.

Stanley, George F.G. *Canada's Soldiers: the Military History of an Unmilitary People*. Toronto: Macmillan, 1974.

Swettenham, John. *McNaughton*. Vol. 3. Toronto: Ryerson Press, 1969.

Tabory, Mala. *The Multinational Force and Observers in the Sinai: Organization, Structure and Function*. Boulder, Colorado: Westview Press, 1986.

Tackaberry, R.B. *Keeping the Peace: A Canadian Military Viewpoint on Peace-Keeping Operations*. Behind the Headlines, Vol. XXVI. Toronto: Canadian Institute of International Affairs, 1966.

Taylor, Alastair, David Cox and J.L. Granatstein. *Peacekeeping: International Challenge and Canadian Response*. Contemporary Affairs, No. 39. Toronto: Canadian Institute of International Affairs, 1968.

Taylor, Charles, *Snow Job: Canada, the United States and Vietnam, 1954 to 1973*. Toronto: Anansi, 1974.

Thakur, Ramesh. *Peacekeeping in Vietnam: Canada, India, Poland and the International Commission*. Edmonton: University of Alberta Press, 1984.

Thomas, Hugh. *The Suez Affair*. London: Weidenfeld and Nicolson, 1966.

United Nations. *The Blue Helmets: A Review of United Nations Peace-Keeping*. New York: United Nations Department of Public Information, 1985.

Urquhart, Brian. *Hammarskjold*. New York: Alfred A. Knopf, 1972.

Vanezis, P.N. *Cyprus: The Unfinished Agony*. London: Abeland-Schuman Ltd., 1977.

Verrier, Anthony. *International Peacekeeping: United Nations Forces in a Troubled World*. London: Penguin Books, 1981.

Wainhouse, D.W. *International Peace Observation*. Baltimore: John Hopkins Press, 1966.

Wainhouse, D.W. *International Peacekeeping at the Crossroads*. Baltimore: John Hopkins Press, 1973.

Waskow, A.I. *Toward a Peacekeeping Academy: A Proposal for a First Step Toward a United Nations Transnational Peacekeeping Force*. The Hague: World Association of World Federalists, 1967.

Wiseman, Henry, ed. *Peacekeeping: Appraisals and Proposals*. New York: Pergamon Press for the International Peace Academy, 1983.

Bibliography

Worthington, Peter. *Looking for Trouble: A Journalist's Life and Then Some*. Toronto: Key Porter Books, 1984.

World Veterans Federation Report. *The Functioning of Ad Hoc United Nations Emergency Forces*. Helsinki: World Veterans Federation, 1963.

ARTICLES

Aikman, Bill. "UNEF 2," *Sentinel*, Vol. 14, No. 5, 1978, pp. 4-8.

Aikman, Bill. "Canadians in the Middle East," *Sentinel*, Vol. 14, No. 5, 1978, pp. 9-13.

Anderson, A.W. "The Regiment in Cyprus," *The Maroon Beret*, Vol. I, No. 4, January 1975, pp. 1-15.

Anglin, Barbara. "Life in Israel," *Sentinel*, Vol. 7, No. 7, September 1971, pp. 15-19.

Beattie, Clayton E. "Preparations for Peacekeeping at the National and International Level," *Canadian Defence Quarterly*, Vol. 8, No. 2, Autumn 1978, pp. 26-29.

Bond, J.C. "Creating a Modern Army," *Sentinel*, Vol. 3, No. 2, March 1967, pp. 12-15.

Bonneau, John. "The Hussars Go Home," *Sentinel*, Vol. 2, No. 4, May 1966, pp. 20-21.

Bowdery, R.M.L. "With the RCAF in Yemen," *Roundel*, Vol. 15, No. 10, December 1964, pp. 6-10.

Bridle, Paul. "Canada and the International Commissions in Indochina, 1954-1972," *Behind the Headlines*, Vol. XXXII, No. 4, October 1973.

Burns, E.L.M. "The Withdrawal of UNEF and the Future of Peacekeeping," *International Journal*, Vol. XXXII, No. I, Winter 1967-68, pp. 1-17.

Butt, Bob. "Desert deployment," "Flying peacekeepers," "Spare-time pastimes," *Sentinel*, Vol. 22, No. 5, 1986, pp. 2-7.

Coughlin, T.G. "Our Men in the Desert," *Roundel*, Vol. 14, No. 8, October 1962, pp. 2-7.

Coughlin, T.G. "The UN and the RCAF," *Roundel*, Vol. 16, No. 10, December 1964, pp. 2-8.

Currie, G.H. "They Helped Build an Air Force," *Sentinel*, Vol. 3, No. 4, April 1967, pp. 10-13.

Dabros, M.R. "The Multinational Force and Observers: A New Experience in Peacekeeping for Canada," *Canadian Defence Quarterly*, Vol. 16, No. 2, Autumn 1986, pp. 32-35.

Delbridge, Claire. "Public Attitudes in Canada Towards the United Nations," *United Nations Association in Canada*, December 1985, pp. 1-6.

Dent, Len. "Canadian Forces Peacekeepers in the Golan Heights," *Canadian Military Journal*, Vol. LV, Spring 1986, pp. 26-29.

Dobell, William M. "Cyprus: the politics of confrontation," *International Perspectives*, November/December 1974, pp. 3-9.

Dunne, Tim. "Farewell to the Sinai: The End of UNEF 2," *Sentinel*, Vol. 16, No. 1, 1980, pp. 14-15.

Dunne, Tim, "Operation Finnegan," *Sentinel*, Vol. 16, No. 1, 1980, pp.16-17.

293

Eyre, K.C. "The Future of U.N. Interpository Peacekeeping Under the 1956 Pearson-Hammorskjold Formula: Conclusions Drawn from Personal Experiences in Cyprus, in the Tragic Summer of 1974," *Canadian Defence Quarterly*, Vol. 12, No. 1, Summer 1982, pp. 31-34, 35-36.

Fisher, Douglas. "The Unending Operation," *Legion*, Vol. 55, No. 7, December 1980, pp. 8-9.

Fitzpatrick, C.L. "Viet-Nam: They Came Back Proud," *Sentinel*, Vol 9, No. 7, 1973, pp. 11-19.

Goskell, Timur. "UNIFIL: Honour in Lebanon," *The Army Quarterly and Defence Journal*, Vol. 113, No. 4, October 1983, pp. 391-411.

Hamilton, C.J.A. "Nigeria: January to June, 1969," *The Patrician*, Vol. XXII, 1969, pp. 11-17.

Haswell, Geof. "Viet Nam: A Close Look at Teamsites," *Sentinel*, Vol. 10, No. I, 1974, pp. 6-10.

Haswell, Geof. "Camp Roofless," *Sentinel*, Vol. 10, No. 7, 1974, pp. 15-18.

Haswell, Geof. "Camp Roofless on the Golan Heights," *Legion*, September 1974, pp. 16-17.

Heine, William. "The need for peacekeeping guidelines," *International Perspectives*, January/February 1976, pp. 34-38.

Homonylo, Christina. "Peacekeeping," *United Nations Association in Canada*, October 1984, pp. 1-6.

Hoogenraad, Maureen. "Lester B. Pearson and the Nobel Peace Prize," *The Archivist*, Vol. 13, No. 6, Nov-Dec 1986, pp. 4-5.

Jackson, Robert J. "Tragedy out of intransigence," *International Perspectives*, November/December 1974, pp. 9-13.

Johnston, Murray, Jack Ross, Mike Dion and Pat Dillon. "Viet Nam Looking Back," *Sentinel*, Vol. 14, No. 1, 1978, pp. 18-22.

King, A.E. "UN Commander Honours Canadian Signal Unit in Congo," *Canadian Army Journal*, Vol. XVII, No. 1, 1963, pp. 92-96.

Kotani Hidejiro. "Peace-Keeping: Problems for Smaller Countries," *International Journal*, XIX, Summer 1964, pp. 308-325.

Lackonick, G., R. Bonner and G. Burtoft. "The Canadian Contingent United Nations Interim Forces in Lebanon," *Canadian Forces Communications and Electronics Newsletter*, 1981/82, pp. 44-76.

Legault, Albert. "Cyprus: Mediterranean strategic triangle," *International Perspectives*, November/December 1974, pp. 16-18.

Leslie, E.M.D. "The success and failure of UNFICYP," *International Perspectives*, November/December 1974, pp. 13-16.

Loomis, D.G. "An Expedition to Vietnam: The Military Component of the Canadian Delegation (MCCD), 1973," *Canadian Defence Quarterly*, Vol. 3, No. 4, Spring 1974, pp. 35-39.

MacKay, R.F. "A Report on Vietnam," *Canadian Army Journal*. Vol. XVII, No. 1, 1963, pp. 28-33.

Bibliography

MacPherson, J.R. "A Canadian Initiative and its Results: Active Peacekeeping after Thirty Years," *Canadian Defence Quarterly*, Vol. 16, No. 1, Summer 1986, pp. 42-48.

McIntosh, Dave. "Canada's Peacekeeping Role: A Passing Fancy," *Legion*, Vol. 56, No. 8, January 1982, pp. 13-14, 45.

Manor, F.S. "Case against peacekeeping," *International Perspectives*, July/August 1977, pp. 28-32.

Nichol, Ian. "Cyprus," *Sentinel*, Vol. 10, No. 8, 1974-75, pp. 15-20; Vol. 10, No. 9, pp. 16-21; Vol. 11, No. 1, pp. 22-24.

Price, H.E.C. "Tanzania Tale," *Sentinel*, Vol. 2, No. 2, March 1966, pp. 24-27.

Russell, W.N. "Airlift Danaca," *Sentinel*, Vol. 10, No. 4, 1974, pp. 18-20.

Stanley, G.F.G. "Dien Bien Phu in Retrospect," *International Journal*, Vol. 10, No. 1, Winter 1954-55, pp. 38-50.

Stanley, G.F.G. "Failure at Suez," *International Journal*, Vol. 12, No. 2, Spring 1957, pp. 90-96.

Stetham, Nicholas. "My War With the Army," *Maclean's*, March 1975, pp. 54-60.

Tedlie, A.J., J.M. Delamere and D.N.D. Deane-Freeman. "The Canadians in Indo-China," *Snowy Owl*, Christmas 1955, pp. 15-22.

Thant, U. "The Withdrawal of UNEF: Report of the Secretary-General," *UN Monthly Chronicle*, Vol. IV, No. 7, July 1967, pp. 135-170.

Tucker, Michael J. "E.L.M. Burns: soldier and peacekeeper," *International Perspectives*, November/December 1985, pp. 6-8.

Turner, L.R. "Cyprus Soldier," *Sentinel*, Vol. 3, No. 4, April 1967, pp. 28-29.

Utas, M.W. "Truce Watchers in Kashmir," *Sentinel*, Vol. 3, No. 6, June 1967, pp. 2-5.

Waern, Jonas. "Diary of a U.N. Peacekeeper," *Saturday Review*, Vol. 50, November 18, 1967, pp. 19-21, 55-56.

Wallace, H.C. "Connecting Link," *Sentinel*, Vol. 3, No. 4, April 1967, pp. 30-31.

Wilson, W.A. "Professional Peacemakers have their Limitations," *Legion*, Vol. 53, No. 9, February 1979, pp. 12-13, 22.

Wiseman, Henry. "Lebanon: The Latest Example of UN Peacekeeping Action," *International Perspectives*, January/February 1979, pp. 3-7.

Wiseman, Henry. "Has New Life Been Breathed Into U.N. Peacekeeping?," *Canadian Defence Quarterly*, Vol. 5, No. I, Summer 1975, pp. 22-28.

Yarymowich, B. "Tradesmen for Peace," *Canadian Army Journal*, Vol. XIV, No. 4, Fall 1960, pp. 134-139.

Yost, W.J. "Canada's U.N. Ready Force: Time for a Change," *Canadian Defence Quarterly*, Vol. XI, No. 3, Winter 1981/82, pp. 43-45.

MANUSCRIPT THESES

Harvey, P.C. "The Operational Effectiveness of United Nations Peace-Keeping Forces, with particular reference to the United Nations Emergency Force II, October 1973-September 1975," MA thesis, Keele University, 1977.

Murray, J.D. "Canada's Military Commitment to International Peace-Keeping," MA thesis, York University, 1975.

Stegenga, J.A. "The United Nations Force in Cyprus," PhD thesis, University of California at Los Angeles, 1966, published by Ohio State University Press as a Mershon Program Publication, 1968.

Wiseman, Henry. "Theoretical approaches and policy examination of Canada's role in peacekeeping," PhD thesis, Queen's University, 1971.

INDEX

I. GENERAL INDEX

Abu Suweir, 44, 48-9
Alexandria, 60, 117
Allan, Tpr. R.H., 61
Amy, Col. E.A.C., 87
Andrew, Arthur, 91
Angle, Brig. H.H., 166-7, 274
Aqaba, Gulf of, 51, 66, 71
Assad, Hafiz al-, 66
Aswan High Dam, 39
Australia, 160, 167
Austria, 115-6, 123, 137-140, 143

Bailey, Maj. William, 25-6, 28, 30
Balaguer, Joaquin, 248
Banks, Maj. Donald, 119-20
Bar-Lev Line, 113-4
Beattie, Brig.-Gen. C.E., 100-1, 263-4
Beirut, 34-8, 95, 133, 144, 146-150, 157
Belanger, Capt. Gerald, 228
Belcher, F/L Michael, 70
Belgium, 167, 217-218, 227, 236, 242
Belley, Pte. J.M., 102, 267-8
Bennett, Capt. G.R., 35, 190
Bennett, Brig.-Gen. R.T., 190
Berger, Pte. Claude, 103, 274
Bergevin, Lt.-Col. P.A., 167
Bernatchez, Maj.-Gen. J.P.E., 90
Berthiaume, Lt.-Col. J.A., 233-5
Bertrand, Lt.-Col. Paul, 24
Biafra, 240-1

Blaquière, Capt. Normand, 101, 267
Bloom, Capt. H.S., 32, 36
Bosch, Juan, 247
Bouffard, Maj. Clement, 235
Boulanger, Lt.-Col. Georges, 25, 37, 143
Brazil, 41, 71
Bristowe, Maj. G.C., 241
Britain, 27, 39-41, 85-6, 89, 108, 147-8, 160, 179, 189, 240
Buckberry, Pte. Robert, 62
Bull, Maj.-Gen. Odd, 148
Burge, F/O J.G., 54
Burns, Lt.-Gen. E.L.M., 23, 40-1, 43, 48
Byrne, Sgt. J.S., 195, 275

Cairo, 36, 47, 115-7, 128-9, 138
Cambodia, 179-80, 182-184, 208
Campbell, Cpl. J.E., 129
Camps: Blue Beret, 100-1; El Gala, 117, 127, 132-3; Maple Leaf, 94; Pearson, 153; Rafah, 49-52, 54, 56, 60, 70-2; Shams, 115-6, 120-1, 126-7, 129; Troodos, 91; Ziouani, 138, 142, 145
Canadian Armed Forces Advisory and Training Team Tanzania, 242
Canadian Armed Forces Training Team Ghana, 242
Carey, WO2 E.P., 92
Carr, G/C W.K., 222
Chapman, A/C C.G.W., 222

Index

Chenard, Capt. G.E., 192
Chile, 167
Clifford, Brig. Frederick, 185
Collins, WO2 F.E., 223
Colombia, 41, 63, 160
Côté, Capt. Mario, 235-7
Cyprus, 11, 21, 36, 85-112, 115, 117, 139, 146, 262-8

Delta Force, 92
Denmark, 41, 43, 63, 89, 167
DeWolfe, Maj. Wayne, 144
Dextraze, Gen. J.A., 121, 196, 223
Diefenbaker, J.G., 20, 219
Dominican Republic, 247-9
Drewry, Brig.-Gen. J.L., 241
Drummond, Lt. B.W., 152-3

Egypt, 21, 26-28, 39-40, 43, 64, 66-71, 73-4, 76, 84-5, 113, 121, 129-132, 134, 136, 147, 158, 160, 219
El Arish, 47, 50, 52, 54-6, 67, 70, 78, 81
El Ballah, 48-9
El Gorah, 160
Elms, Capt. G.R., 35
El Qantara, 27, 41, 49, 51
Ethiopia, 219, 226

Famagusta, 88, 97
Fatah, al-, 65, 138
Fawzi, Gen. Mahmoud, 66
Ferguson, F/O C.G., 56
Fiji, 160
Finland, 41, 63, 89, 93, 115-6, 123, 129-130, 138, 167
Fitzsimmons, W/C J.W., 68
Flint, Lt.-Col. G.A., 24, 272
Forand, Capt. Alain, 102, 265-6
Forbes, M/Cpl. M.B., 154
France, 35, 37, 39-41, 146-7, 152, 160, 179, 181, 239

Gapp, Pte. E.J., 268
Gauthier, Col. J.H.J., 167

Gauvin, Michel, 196-7
Gaza Strip, 50-1, 55, 58, 72, 160
Gee, Capt. W.F., 102
George, Maj. J.H., 234
Ghana, 116, 123, 129, 219, 228, 240, 242
Gilbert, Capt. Charles, 144
Gingras, Pte. J.M., 267
Golan Heights, 25-6, 71, 113, 137, 143-5
Green, Col. D.G., 220
Grehan Pte. E.P., 154
Grenier, Lt. Jacques, 90
Guinea, 219, 228
Gyani, Lt.-Gen. P.S., 82, 90

Hamilton, Brig.-Gen. C.J.A., 241
Hammarskjöld, Dag, 40, 237-8
Handson, WO G.W., 200-3
Hanoi, 192, 194-5
Harper, W/C E.D., 56, 273
Harper, Maj. G.R., 241
Harries, Maj. David, 100
Helman, Maj. Barry, 26
Herbert, W/C R.G., 212
Hermann, Sgt. J.K., 56, 273
Hilchey, Sgt. Douglas, 107
Hills L/Cpl. A.M., 59
Ho Chi Minh, 179, 189
Holmes, Brig.-Gen. D.E., 126-7
Howie, Pte. Robert, 143
Hungary, 196, 199, 206-7
Hussein, King, 66, 148
Hyslop, Maj. Malcolm, 169

India, 41, 63, 71, 131, 166-172, 175-178, 179-80, 196, 219, 240
Indonesia, 41, 63, 116, 123, 129, 196, 209-210, 213, 219
Inter-American Peace Force, 248
International Commission for Supervision and Control for Cambodia (ICSC Cambodia), 179-80, 182-184
International Commission for Supervision and Control for Laos (ICSC Laos), 179-80, 182, 185-188

298

Index

International Commission for Supervision
and Control for Vietnam (ICSC Vietnam), 179-80, 182, 189-195
International Commissions for Supervision and Control for Indochina (ICSC for Indochina), 179-80, 208, 257, 260
International Commission of Control and Supervision (ICCS) for Vietnam (1973), 196-208, 259, 261
International Observer Team to Nigeria (OTN), 240-1, 261
International Peace Academy, 13
Iran, 35, 137-8, 143
Iraq, 35, 71, 147-8
Ireland, 89, 116, 123, 219
Ismailia, 28, 51, 124, 127-8, 138, 143, 151
Israel, 21, 24, 37, 40, 64-6, 113-4, 129-132, 136-9, 144, 151, 157-8, 160
Italy, 37, 160, 167, 223

Jean, Cpl. J.L.R., 129
Jennex, M/Cpl. R.W., 129
Jordan, 21, 25, 27, 65-6, 147-8
Juteau, Capt. L.M., 129-131

Kashmir, 166-177
Katanga, 218, 227, 230-1, 236-8
Kelly, F/L Peter, 83
Kendricks, Pte. K.S., 154
Kerr, Maj. Irving, 26, 28
King, Maj. H. Wain, 234
Kissinger, Henry, 132, 137
Kolesar, Maj. Michael, 231, 242
Koller, Lt. Wilfried. See Lt. "Willy" Smith
Kyrenia, 92-3, 95-8, 107, 109, 264

Laos, 179-80, 185-189, 208
LaRose, Maj.-Gen. J.P.R., 133
Laviolette, Capt. C.E., 205, 275
Lebanon, 21, 33-4, 36, 146-157
Leopoldville, 217, 221-2, 224, 227-230
Lessard, Maj.-Gen. G.H.J., 266
Lessard, Sgt. J.A.L., 232
Lett, Sherwood, 182

Liberia, 219
Liboiron, Maj. Réal, 235
Libya, 114
Liston, Lt. J.T.F.A., 232
Lumumba, Patrice, 218, 225-8

McAlpine, Maj.-Gen. D.A., 197, 206
McCorkell, Maj. E.B., 185
McCormack, Capt. S.A., 117
Macdonald, Maj.-Gen. B.F., 169
McIntyre, Pte. T.W., 154
Mackenzie, Maj. L.W., 135
Maclean, Maj. A.L., 182
McNaughton, Gen. A.G.L., 166
MacNeil, Maj. W.R., 26, 33
Makarios, Archbishop, 86, 97, 105
Mali, 219
Manuel, Lt.-Col. D.S., 100, 264
Martin, Paul, 87
Mathews, MWO D.R., 60, 121
Mayer, Lt.-Col. P.A., 232, 248
Megill, Maj.-Gen. W.J., 182
Meir, Golda, 114
Mendelsohn, Brig.-Gen. Albert, 220, 224
Metaxis, Capt. Pericles, 34
Miller, Air Chief Marshal F.R., 77
Milroy, Maj.-Gen. W.A., 241
Mission of the Representative of the Secretary-General in the Dominican Republic (DOMREP), 247-9, 258, 261
Mitchell, Maj. G.D., 148
Mitchell, Lt.-Col. Robert, 110
Mobutu, Joseph, 227-8, 237
Monette, Maj. Roger, 235
Morocco, 219
Morton, Maj.-Gen. R.E.A., 182, 185
Mounteer, Brig. D.E., 194
Mulherin, Lt.-Col. H.W., 110
Multinational Force and Observers (MFO), 158-161, 259, 261

Nasser, Gamal Abdel, 27, 39-40, 65-9, 76, 114
Nepal, 118, 152, 154, 156-7

Netherlands, 160, 209-210, 213
New Zealand, 160, 167
Ngo Dinh Diem, 190
Nicholson, Brig.-Gen. D.S., 115
Nicosia, 90-101, 108, 111, 263-4, 266-7
Nigeria, 219, 240-1
Nobel Prize, 63, 253
Norman, WO G.W., 106
Normandin, Maj. Louis, 235
Norway, 41, 63, 167

Opération des Nations Unies au Congo
    (ONUC), 217-239, 258, 260
Organization of African Unity, 240
Organization of American States (OAS),
    248
Ouellet, CSM Georges, 92, 264-5

Pakistan, 166-178, 210, 219
Palestine, 21
Palestine Liberation Organization, 33, 37,
    65, 113, 151-3, 156
Palestinians, 37, 61, 65
Panama, 116, 124
Pariseau, Capt. J.B., 225-6
Patten, Capt. Ian, 107, 206, 274
Pavlovic, Col. Branko, 78
Peacekeeping, casualties, 253, 272-5; cost,
    14; definition, 13; numbers, 253, 260-1
Pearson, L.B., 40, 63, 68
Pelletier, Pte. J.G., 102, 267-8
Pennington, Lt.-Col. E.B.M., 241
Perkin, Cpl. V.J., 195, 275
Perron, Pte. Gilbert, 103, 274
Peru, 116, 137, 143
Petrick, Capt. P.R.W., 186-188
Plouffe, Sgt. J.M.C., 101-2, 266
Poland, 115-6, 119, 123, 126, 137, 143, 179-
    80, 196, 199, 206-7, 240
Porter, Maj. D.G., 138-140
Port Said, 41-47, 49-50, 117
Pospisil, Lt.-Col. P.P., 167
Poulin, Col. J.G., 235
Power, Col. D.H., 69, 72

Prest, Capt. Richard, 140
Provan, Maj. C.G., 189

Qaddafi, Muammar al-, 114
Qneitra, 138, 140, 143

Richards, Lt. A.E., 212
Rikhye, Maj.-Gen. I.J., 66-7, 69, 72, 248
Ritchie, Lt.-Col. G.F.B., 177
Ross, Maj. J.O.W., 204
Ruanda-Urundi, 242

Sadat, Anwar, 114
Saigon, 194-5, 197-8, 201-2
Samis, Maj. Clayton, 98
Saudi Arabia, 76-79, 82, 84
Senegal, 116-124
Sharm el Sheikh, 52, 55, 67-8, 160
Sharp, Mitchell, 205
Sharpe, Maj. E.R., 77
Sihanouk, Norodom, 183-4
Simpson, Col. G.D., 135
Simpson, F/O R.J.V., 67
Sinai, 27-30, 36, 40, 52, 71, 117, 134
Smith, Capt. A.H.C., 204
Smith, Col. P.D., 220
Smith, Lt. "Willy," 140
Snow, Maj.-Gen. T.E. D'O., 182
Soviet Union, 37, 39, 86, 114, 118-9, 134,
    147, 158, 179, 189, 219, 239
Sparks, L/Cpl. Wayne, 95
Spinelli, Pier P., 82-3
Stethem, Col. H.W.C., 220
Sudan, 219, 228
Suez, 38-30, 128-9
Suez Canal, 21, 25-26, 28, 39, 40, 48-51,
    113-4, 128-132, 134
Suez Crisis, 39, 147
Sukarno, 209
Sweden, 41, 63, 71, 89, 115-6, 123, 129,
    167, 219, 240
Syria, 21, 24-28, 33, 64-6, 71, 114, 133, 137-
    140, 143-4, 147, 150

Index

Tait, Maj. S.G., 45
Tanzania, 242-3
Taschereau, Capt. J.C.A.A., 224-5
Tasker, F/L M.S., 176
Tedlie, Brig. A.J., 90, 94
Thant, U, 66-8, 76, 87, 210, 238
Therrien, Capt. J.P.A., 224
Thomson, Capt. Fletcher, 206
Tiran, Strait of, 66
Tomalin, Capt. G.R., 58
Tremblay, Maj. J.P.R., 92
Trujillo, Rafael, 247
Tunisia, 219
Turkey, 85-7, 97-105, 110
Tweedie, Pte. J.B., 11

Umbach, S/L A.I., 78
UN Disengagement Observer Force (UN-DOF), 36, 115, 117, 133, 137-145, 259, 261
UN Emergency Force (UNEF I), 25, 63, 39-74, 117-8, 135-6, 258, 260
UN Emergency Force (UNEF II), 113-133, 151, 158, 259, 261
UN Force in Cyprus (UNFICYP), 85-112, 258, 261
UN India-Pakistan Observation Mission (UNIPOM), 169-176, 259, 261
UN Interim Force in Lebanon (UNIFIL), 36, 150-7, 259, 261
UN Military Observer Group in India and Pakistan (UNMOGIP), 166-169, 176-178, 257, 260
UN Observation Group in Lebanon (UN-OGIL), 38, 147-150, 258, 260
UN Temporary Executive Authority (UN-TEA), 209-213, 258, 260

UN Truce Supervision Organization (UNTSO), 21-38, 40, 71, 113, 128, 148, 153, 219, 257, 260
UN Yemen Observation Mission (UN-YOM), 75-84, 258, 260
United Arab Republic (UAR). See Egypt
United States, 37, 39, 118-9, 148, 150, 158, 160, 181, 194, 198, 205, 208, 239, 247-8
Uruguay, 160, 167
US Sinai Field Mission, 132, 158, 160
USSR. See Soviet Union

Veitch, Lt.-Col. David, 192
Vezina, Maj. J.P., 121
Vezina, Spr. R.H., 50, 272
Viet Cong, 194, 199, 203, 207
Viet Minh, 179, 181, 184
Vietnam, 36, 179-80, 189-195, 196-208
von Horn, Maj.-Gen. C., 77, 81, 219
Vos, Capt. H.A., 204

Waddell, Pte. C.D., 129
Wattsford, Brig.-Gen. G.J.H., 195
West New Guinea (West Irian), 209-213
Wetherup, Capt. Gordon, 91
Whelan, Cpl. J.R.M., 102, 267-8
Williams, Capt. Blaine, 151-2
Woodcock, Lt.-Col. J.A.O., 92, 237

Yom Kippur War, 114
Yost, W.J. Col., 143
Yugoslavia, 66-7, 71, 78, 80, 83

Zimbabwe, 243

Index

II. MILITARY INDEX

AIR FORCE

102 KU, 167
114 ATU, 52, 54
115 ATU, 54-6, 78, 83
116 ATU, 116, 124, 133, 212
117 ATU, 170, 172-176
134 ATU, 76, 78, 83
403 Sqn, 160
408 Sqn, 160
426 Sqn, 52, 222
427 Sqn, 160
430 Sqn, 160
435 Sqn, 52, 54
436 Sqn, 54, 222
USAF, 212-3, 221

ARMY

Canadian Airborne Regiment, 98, 102, 106, 117, 269-71
Canadian Guards, 110, 269-70
Canadian Provost Corps, 58
Lord Strathcona's Horse, 95, 102, 269-70
Princess Patricia's Canadian Light Infantry, 24, 28, 118, 269-70
Queen's Own Rifles of Canada, 42-3, 269
Royal Canadian Army Service Corps, 46, 49-50, 88

Royal Canadian Corps of Signals, 46, 186, 192, 235
Royal Canadian Dragoons, 57, 59, 87-8, 91-2, 269
Royal Canadian Electrical and Mechanical Engineers, 46, 50, 192, 220
Royal Canadian Horse Artillery, 110, 269-70
Royal Canadian Regiment, 11, 106, 268
Royal 22e Régiment, 87, 88, 91-3, 107, 235, 264, 269-72
1st Canadian Signal Regiment, 118, 151, 157
56 Infantry Workshop, 46, 60
56 Reconnaissance Squadron, 48
56 Signal Squadron, 46, 60
56 Transport Company, 46, 51
57 Signal Squadron, 221
57 Signal Unit, 230
73 Service Battalion, 117, 134
73 Signal Squadron, 117, 151
73 Signal Troop, 151

NAVY

Bonaventure, HMCS, 87-8, 91
Kootenay, HMCS, 206
Magnificent, HMCS, 46-7
Terra Nova, HMCS, 206